Key Issues in
Education Policy

Education Studies: Key Issues Series

In the last fifteen years or so Education Studies has developed rapidly as a distinctive subject in its own right. Beginning initially at undergraduate level, this expansion is now also taking place at masters level and is characterised by an increasingly analytical approach to the study of education. As education studies programmes have developed there has emerged a number of discrete study areas that require indepth texts to support student learning.

Introduction to Education Studies; Second Edition is the core text in this series and gives students an important grounding in the study of education. It provides an overview of the subject and introduces the reader to fundamental theories and debates in the field. The series, 'Key Issues in Education Studies,' has evolved from this core text and, using the same critical approach, each volume outlines a significant area of study within the education studies field. All of the books have been written by experts in their area and provide the detail and depth required by students as they progress further in the subject.

Taken as a whole, this series provides a comprehensive set of texts for the student of education. Whilst of particular value to students of Education Studies, the series will also be instructive for those studying related areas such as Childhood Studies and Special Needs, as well as being of interest to students on initial teacher training courses and practitioners working in education.

We hope that this series provides you, the reader, with plentiful opportunities to explore further this exciting and significant area of study and we wish you well in your endeavours.

Steve Bartlett and Diana Burton
Series Editors

Education Studies: Key Issues Series

Steve Bartlett and Diana Burton: *Introduction to Education Studies; Second Edition* (2007)

Stephen Ward and Christine Eden: *Key Issues in Education Policy* (2009)

Diana Burton and Steve Bartlett: *Key Issues for Education Researchers* (2009)

Alan Hodkinson and Philip Vickerman: *Key Issues in Special Educational Needs and Inclusion* (2009)

Key Issues in
Education Policy

Stephen Ward and Christine Eden

Los Angeles | London | New Delhi
Singapore | Washington DC

First published 2009

SAGE Publications Ltd
1 Oliver's Yard
55 City Road
London EC1Y 1SP

SAGE Publications Inc.
2455 Teller Road
Thousand Oaks, California 91320

SAGE Publications India Pvt Ltd
B 1/I 1 Mohan Cooperative Industrial Area
Mathura Road
New Delhi 110 044

SAGE Publications Asia-Pacific Pte Ltd
33 Pekin Street #02-01
Far East Square
Singapore 048763

Library of Congress Control Number: 2009920984

British Library Cataloguing in Publication data

A catalogue record for this book is available from the British Library

ISBN 978-1-84787-465-8
ISBN 978-1-84787-466-5 (pbk)

Typeset by C&M Digitals (P) Ltd, Chennai, India
Printed in Great Britain TJ International Ltd, Padstow, Cornwall
Printed on paper from sustainable resources

Mixed Sources
Product group from well-managed
forests and other controlled sources
www.fsc.org Cert no. SGS-COC-2482
© 1996 Forest Stewardship Council
FSC

This book is dedicated to Heather and to Colin, with apologies for the lost week ends.

Contents

List of abbreviations

ALTARF	All London Teachers against Racism and Fascism
AST	Advanced Skills Teacher
BME	black and minority ethnic (people)
CACE	Central Advisory Council for Education
CATE	Council for the Accreditation of Teacher Education
CCT	compulsory competitive tendering
CfBT	Centre for British Teachers
CNAA	Council for National Academic Awards
CRE	Commission for Racial Equality
CTC	city technology college
CWDC	Children's Workforce Development Council
DCSF	Department for Children, Schools and Families
DES	Department of Education and Science
DfEE	Department for Education and Employment
DfES	Department for Education and Skills
DIUS	Department for Innovation, Universities and Skills
EAL	English as an additional language
ECM	Every Child Matters
EFSS	Extended Full-Service School
EHRC	Equality and Human Rights Commission
EIC	Excellence in Cities
EYFC	Early Years Foundation Curriculum
EYPS	Early Years Professional Status
FSES	full-service extended school partnership
FSM	free school meals
FSP	Foundation Stage Profile
G&T	gifted and talented
GCE	General Certificate of Education
GCSE	General Certificate of Secondary Education
GIST	Girls into Science and Technology
GM	genetically modified
GRTP	Graduate and Registered Teacher Programmes (now the GTP)
GTP	Graduate Teacher Programme
HEFCE	Higher Education Funding Council for England
HESA	Higher Education Statistical Agency
HMI	Her Majesty's Inspectorate
HMSO	Her Majesty's Stationery Office
IB	International Baccalaureate
IDACI	Income Deprivation Affecting Children Index
ILEA	Inner London Education Authority

IMF   International Monetary Fund
ISC   Independent Schools Council
IRR   Institute of Race Relations
ITT   Initial Teacher Training
KS   Key Stage
LA   local authority
LEA   local education authority
LMS   Local Management of Schools
MSC   Manpower Services Commission
MTL   Masters in Teaching and Learning
NAO   National Audit Office
NCC   National Curriculum Council
NEET   (young people) not in employment, education or training
NESS   National Evaluation of Sure Start
NFER   National Foundation for Educational Research
NGO   non-government organisations
NHS   National Health Service
NLS   National Literacy Strategy
NNS   National Numeracy Strategy
NUT   National Union of Teachers
Ofqual Office of the Qualifications and Examinations Regulator
Ofsted Office for Standards in Schools
OPSI   Office for Public Sector Information
PFI   Private Finance Initiative
PGCE   Postgraduate Certificate of Education
PNS   Primary National Survey
QAA   Quality Assurance Agency
QCA   Qualifications and Curriculum Authority
QTS   Qualified Teacher Status
SACRE   Standing Advisory Council on Religious Education
SAT   Standard Assessment Test (formerly Task)
SCAA   Schools Curriculum and Assessment Authority
SCITT   School-Centred Initial Teacher Training
SEAC   School Examination and Assessment Council
SEN   special educational needs
SSLP   Sure Start Local Programmes
TDA   Training and Development Agency for Schools
TES   Times Educational Supplement
TGAT   Task Group on Assessment and Testing
THE   Times Higher Education
TTA   Teacher Training Agency
TVEI   Technical Vocational Education Initiative
UCET   Universities Council for the Education of Teachers
VA   voluntary aided (schools)
VC   voluntary controlled (schools)
WISE   Women into Science and Engineering

About the authors

Christine Eden is Assistant Dean of the School of Education at Bath Spa University. She uses her background in sociology to explore education systems and access to educational opportunities. In recent years she has undertaken evaluation research into the interface between education and the needs of the labour market. Her research interest is in educational inequalities with a particular focus on gender.
Tel: 01225 875481
E-mail: c.eden@bathspa.ac.uk

Stephen Ward is Professor of Education and Dean of the School of Education at Bath Spa University. He was formerly the subject leader for Education Studies. A founder member of the British Education Studies Association, he was Chair in 2006–7. He has published books on the primary curriculum, primary music teaching and Education Studies. His research interests are education policy, university knowledge and teacher training.
Tel: 01225 875549
E-mail: s.ward@bathspa.ac.uk

1

Introduction: education and the state

Parent to child after his first day at school: *How did you like school today?*
Child: *OK, but I'm not going any more.*
Parent: *Oh, yes you are!*

We tend to take for granted the fact that children go to school. Some take to it immediately; others are less easily persuaded of the benefits of spending six hours a day away from home. Schooling is perhaps the most important way in which the state intervenes in the life of the family and the individual. Education does not have to depend on the state: it can happen in independent schools, at home, between friends and for individuals working alone, but since the end of the nineteenth century the state has made education its business. In this book we look at the ways in which the state in Britain has provided opportunities for all to be educated while, at the same time, affecting people's lives with control and regulation. This chapter introduces ideas about the state and the politics of education which are then discussed as a series of topics in the following chapters. It gives a list of the key education legislation, then a brief overview of recent policy, together with a brief description of the issues in each chapter. Finally there are some suggestions about policy critique in Education Studies.

The Role of the State

Education is politics. It is the means by which a nation defines itself and sustains its cultural existence, transmitting beliefs, ideas and knowledge from generation to generation. Of course, parents can do this by passing on knowledge and skills to their children. But parents can only transmit the knowledge and experiences which *they* hold. Brighouse (2006) points out that, if the child is to flourish as an individual, there needs to be intervention and 'discontinuity' between experiences in the home and the child's education. In this intervention the state and the family or community can come into conflict. In the 1970s, the religious Amish Community in Wisconsin wanted to keep their adolescent children away from the secular influences of state schooling and challenged compulsory education to the age of 16. The state ruled against the Amish parents on the grounds that it would limit the young people's human rights: their right to education. This is a particular case, but it illustrates the way the state takes control of the lives of individuals through education policy. Radical educationists reject the intervention of the state in education (Freire, 1972) and some educate their children at home (Hicks, 2004; Apple, 2006).

The Nation State

It is worth reflecting on what governments are about and what they do. Nation states have not always existed. The Roman Empire at the beginning of the first millennium was a powerful state which spread itself across the known world through imperial domination. However, the Middle Ages saw the fragmentation of political power in Europe with small dukedoms and serfdoms. It was the sixteenth-century Renaissance that brought the unification of nation states with the definition of national borders and the organisation of state-controlled armies. 'Modernity' in the eighteenth-century Enlightenment brought strong nation states which controlled people's lives through laws, law enforcement and taxation. The nineteenth century began with the Napoleonic Wars which heightened the need for powerful states. In Britain the First World War (1914–18) required a large trained army to fight overseas; the Second World War (1939–45) required the whole population to be on a war footing, and this marked the height of the nation state, unified in the single purpose of defeating Nazi Germany (Bottery, 2000). State education systems, which began in Europe in the nineteenth century, became a feature of the nation state and the means of establishing nationalism and a commitment by the whole of society to the state.

We need to make a distinction between a 'nation' and a 'state'. A nation is a collection of people who identify themselves as a social community with language and culture; they might live in a particular geographical location, but for historical reasons they might be scattered across different countries, like Jewish or African peoples, in a 'diaspora'. A state is a political organisation that claims power or sovereignty over people; it exercises its powers through a legal system, a civil service, a police force and an army, and assumes the right to ensure that its children are educated. Ideally its power comes through the agreement of the people in a democracy: the majority of the people vote for a government which holds the power of the state, they are loyal to the state and it becomes 'legitimate'. A Marxist view is that the state protects the interests of powerful producers and holders of capital. Weber (1994) points out that the state claims a monopoly on the use of force; it is a bureaucracy designed to support the production of capital and wealth, but also to offset its negative effects:

... (i) to support the process of capital accumulation (*e.g.* by providing transport systems, business subsidies etc.); and (ii) to legitimate this role by maintaining electoral support and endeavouring to enhance the value of labour (for example, through education and training policies) and to ameliorate the social costs of private accumulation (for example, through welfare policies, environmental protection policies etc.). (Offie, 1984, cited in Codd et al., 1997: 254)

In a nation state the power of the state and its people come together. However, the democratic state is not necessarily geographically fixed. It might also use its powers in other countries as a colonial state; as we see in Chapter 9, Britain was a colonial power in a number of countries, particularly India and in Africa. The colonies have gone, but the British state still assumes power over the countries in the United Kingdom: England, Wales, Scotland and Northern Ireland, each of which has its own historically defined cultures and language. And not everyone is happy with it: nationalist movements in the constituent countries – the Scottish National Party (SNP) and Plaid Cymru in Wales – see themselves as separate 'nations' and would prefer not to be controlled by the British state in Westminster. While a majority in a democracy can create an elected government, there will be tensions and differences of view, and one area of difference is education policy. For example, we will see that in Wales there are differences in the National Curriculum and inspection arrangements. In 1998 in Britain there was some 'devolution' of power from the Westminster government with the setting up of the Scottish Parliament, the Welsh Assembly and the Irish Assembly.

Over the centuries, states have become stronger and better organised through taxation, with the strongest states being the former Soviet Communist nations. But the latter part of the twentieth century saw a decline of the power of the nation states through globalisation and the strengthening of multinational commercial corporations in the global economy (Green, 1997). Here we have seen education become the instrument of commercial success through the marketisation of schooling and the development of education as consumerism to feed the requirements of the global marketplace. While the strong state is a feature of the Enlightenment and modernity, postmodernity sees the 'hollowing out' and weakening of the nation state. Attempts to control education more strongly through a National Curriculum and through definitions and control of childhood are the vestiges of modernity. Prout (2004) suggests that governments try to keep control of education because they can no longer control economic activity in global markets.

The term 'statutory' comes from 'state', meaning that it is a law made by the state to apply to everyone in the state. So the National Curriculum is statutory because it is created by state legislation: the 1988 Education Act. In the UK the state has overall control through the government in Westminster, but it shares that power with local communities. As well as the devolution to the constituent nations of the kingdom, power is also delegated to local councils each of which has an administrative organisation, the local authority (LA). Councils are chosen through local elections and they may be controlled by different parties from the national government. Councils can make by-laws and regulations, but they do not have the same status as statutory legislation.

Education has been one of the services controlled by local councils; differences in education policy are a source of conflict between councils and government and we will see changes in the balance of power between the government and the local authorities.

〰️ Reader tasks

- How much should parents have a say in the education of their children?
- Are there any grounds for children deciding on their schooling?

The centralised government control of education in the 1988 Education Act has led to a proliferation of quangos (quasi non-government organisations) designed to monitor and control different aspects of education. They began in 1988 with the National Curriculum Council (NCC) and the School Examination and Assessment Council (SEAC), which were later merged into the Qualifications and Curriculum Authority (QCA). Examinations and testing in England are controlled by the Office of the Qualifications and Examinations Regulator (Ofqual). The regulation of teacher training was through the Teacher Training Agency (TTA), later the Training and Development Agency for Schools (TDA). From 2006 the Children's Workforce Development Council (CWDC) regulated developments in the wider children's services. Local authorities, schools and all childcare settings are inspected by the Office for Standards in Education (Ofsted). All are powerful bureaucracies employing large numbers of officials, some with little background in education.

UK Politics and Education

There are different political views about the role of the state. The Labour Party was formed at the beginning of the twentieth century to represent working people. It is known as a 'left-wing' political party: the term comes from the French Revolution when the radical reformers sat on the left-hand side in political assemblies. The Labour Party sees the state as creating social justice, making more equal distribution of resources and taxing the wealthy. Conservatives are a right-wing party that believes in conserving the status quo. Its members believe that unequal distribution of wealth is inevitable, and necessary to promote competition and achievement. Conservative governments are committed to low taxation, leaving as much as possible for individuals to spend as they wish. Traditionally, the difference is that, where Labour is committed to equality, Conservatives are committed to individual 'freedom'. Labour believes in 'big government', high taxation and a strong welfare state to improve people's lives; Conservatives believe in 'small government', low taxation and a minimal role for the state. The third party in British politics, the Liberal Democrats, comes between Labour and Conservative, favouring social justice and a welfare state, but with minimum state intervention in the lives of individuals.

Traditional education policies saw Conservatives retaining traditional values with the maintenance of elitist, selective grammar schools, while Labour tried to bring equality through comprehensive schools. Conservatives support independent fee-paying schools for the wealthy and minimum spending on state education. Labour policy has been to increase the resources for state education, with some left-wing members of the party arguing for the abolition of independent schools. However, this is a simple description of the basic traditional policies of the parties. In the forthcoming chapters we see that recent years have seen changes of policy and the refining of the traditional values, with the two major parties moving towards the 'centre ground' of educational politics.

 Reader tasks

- Margaret Thatcher's policy was to reduce the role of government in people's lives. Do you agree with her?
- Think about your own political views. Which party will you vote for in the next election, and why?

Key Education Legislation

Until 1870 schooling was provided either privately or, for the poor, by Church foundations. The Forster Education Act of 1870 introduced elementary schools for children aged 5–10 with Board Schools in areas not served by church schools and the state paying the fees for poor children. The 1880 Education Act made schooling compulsory for 5–10 year olds. The period from 1870 saw strong state intervention as the government sought to make schools and teachers accountable for the new investment of state money in the new compulsory schooling system. Under the Revised Code of 1862 grants were distributed to schools on the basis of pupils' success in tests of reading, writing and arithmetic conducted by Her Majesty's Inspectors (HMI) and teachers were rewarded on the 'payment by results' system.

The Balfour Education Act of 1902 abolished the School Boards and handed control of education to the local education authorities (LEAs). This created an education system which became known as 'a state system, locally administered'. It took central government out of direct involvement with the delivery and monitoring of education, leaving the curriculum and teaching to the professions in combination with advisers and officers in the local education authorities. For most of the rest of the twentieth century, until 1988, state involvement was mainly to dictate to LEAs the outline requirements of provision, including the statutory leaving age. The 1918 'Fisher' Education Act raised the school leaving age to 14 and introduced nursery education and medical inspections for children.

The next significant legislation came in 1944 at the end of the Second World War and provided free secondary education to all children from 11 to 15. Secondary education was in a tripartite system with selective grammar and technical schools for those who passed 11-plus examination, and secondary modern schools for those who failed. The government's priority was about types of school and access to education. There was no prescription for teaching or the curriculum. The one exception was that Religious Education should compulsory, reflecting the continuing commitment of governments to the Christian Church.

In 1965 the Labour government attempted to demolish the selective secondary system with universal comprehensive schools. This was not done through legislation, but by sending Circular 10/65 to the LEAs requesting change. The fact that some Conservative-controlled authorities simply ignored the request is a symptom of the power of the local councils and the weakness of central government's regulation of education during the twentieth century. In 1972 the school leaving age was raised to 16 and the 1981 Education Act made requirements for children with special educational needs.

It was only with the 1988 Education Act that the Conservative government began to remove control of education from the local authorities with the National Curriculum and national testing. The Act also introduced the local management of schools, designed to introduce free-market competition. There followed an avalanche of government directives and legislation, filling the chasm of the previous 86 years. The 1992 Education Act set up the arrangements for the Ofsted inspection of all schools every four years. In the same year the Further and Higher Education Act took polytechnics out of local authority control and made them into universities. The 1993 Education Act required local authorities and schools to comply with a code of practice for pupils with special needs. The 1994 Education Act set up the Teacher Training Agency to regulate and control teacher training.

While the Conservative governments of Margaret Thatcher and John Major had revolutionised education during the 1990s, Tony Blair's New Labour government from 1997 was even more eager to legislate with plans to drive up standards. New Labour policy was for the state to eradicate deficit and disadvantage in society; giving children and families skills and knowledge through schooling was seen as the solution. The policy was linked to New Labour's ambitious plans to remove child poverty by 2020. New Labour operated not just through the legislation with education acts, but through 'initiatives' and directives. Within three months of taking office a White Paper, *Excellence in Schools* (DfEE, 1997) announced that education would be 'at the heart of government' and contained the commitment to improve standards, as well as to introduce nursery places for all four year olds. The following year saw the introduction of the National Literacy Strategy, followed by the Numeracy Strategy, to control primary schools' practice of teaching. The same year 1998 also brought the National Childcare Strategy to make coordinated provision for young children across the education, health and social services.

The year 2000 brought revisions to the curriculum to include Citizenship as a subject and the two-part AS and A level examinations system. The 2002 Education Act introduced city academies. The 2004 Higher Education Act introduced variable top-up fees for university students. The 2005 Education Act amended the regulations for school inspection, giving the Welsh Assembly the powers to amend the framework for inspection in Wales. The 2006 Education and Inspections Act developed more choice for parents and pupils and set out statutory admissions procedures.

New Labour recognised the importance of early years education and care. In 2001 the *Sure Start* Programme was designed to give from birth education, health and childcare, targeted at children and families in socially deprived areas. Children's centres gave professional support for the whole child and family members, including advice on parenting. The Early Years Professional Status (EYPS) qualification in 2007 injected graduates with early years knowledge and practice into private nurseries and early years settings. The Laming Inquiry into the death of Victoria Climbié (HMSO, 2003) and the subsequent storm of publicity about child abuse and neglect stimulated the *Every Child Matters* initiative (DfES, 2003). It brought attention, not just to the education of children, but to their broader health, economic and social 'well-being'. *The Children Act* (DfES, 2004) required local authorities to make coordinated education, health and social services for children. In 2007 *The Children's Plan* (DCSF, 2007) set out an ambitious vision for the education and well-being of children and young people. The division in 2007 of the DfES into the Department for Innovation, Universities and Skills (DIUS) and the Department for Children, Schools and Families (DCSF) was a sign that the government intended to move closer to the lives of children and their families.

〰 Reader task

Look on the websites of the three main political parties in the UK and decide what you think about them and their education policies:

Labour: http://www.labour.org.uk/schools (accessed 3 July 2008)
Conservative: http://www.conservatives.com/ (accessed 3 July 2008)
Liberal Democrats: http://www.libdems.org.uk/ (accessed 3 July 2008)

Consult the important education websites to get an overview of the latest initiatives in education policy:

Department for Children, Schools and Families (DCSF):   http://www.dcsf.gov.uk/ (accessed 3 July 2008)
Sure Start: http://www.surestart.gov.uk/ (accessed 3 July 2008)
Every Child Matters: http://www.everychildmatters.gov.uk/
The Children's Plan: http://www.dcsf.gov.uk/publications/childrens plan/downloads/The_Childrens_Plan.pdf (accessed 3 July 2008)

Current Issues in Education Policy

This final section introduces the contentious issues addressed in each chapter of the book. One of the political controversies about state education has been the level of funding. An OECD (2008) report shows that across the world governments are spending more and more on education. From 1997, ten years of Labour government coincided with a period of strong economic growth; 'big government' ambitions could be realised with substantial resources injected into education. In 1997 spending on education was some £30 bn, rising in 2008 to £61 bn. It funded higher salaries for teachers, more support staff, better resources and school buildings with a programme to rebuild all secondary schools by 2016. However, state spending is not the only story. Margaret Thatcher's approach through the 1988 Education Act was to introduce free-market competition to education, making schooling a 'commodity' which is bought and sold. In Chapter 2 the political and economic theory underlying this is explained: parental choice of schools drives up standards, in the same way that private schools and the whole of private industry works.

The issue of equality and social justice runs through political debates about education. The view of the Conservative Party was that the education system should promote the highest attainment and allow individuals the freedom to excel through high quality grammar schools or independent schools. The traditional Labour Party view was that a government should promote equality in society by educating the poor and by eliminating educational advantage through wealth and social class. Chapter 3 analyses the debates about selective schools and the comprehensive system, explaining the details of changing government policies in school systems. In Chapter 4 we see New Labour abandoning the universal comprehensive school as the means to social equality with the introduction of specialist schools and of academies as state-funded independent schools. New Labour seemed to have left behind its commitment to universal state provision, espousing the traditional Conservative values of privatisation and individual excellence.

Marketisation in 1988 and the increased financial investment from 1997 brought a return to the accountability mechanisms of the nineteenth century with control of the curriculum and teachers' professional practice, high-stakes assessment, performance-related pay for teachers and, of course, Ofsted inspection. Chapter 5 describes the political manoeuvring behind the emergence of the National Curriculum and shows both Labour and Conservative governments' vision of education as preparing pupils for work in industry and the economy. International comparisons of children's achievements and worries about Britain's role as a competitor in the global knowledge economy created government policy. While Conservatives controlled the curriculum, from 1997 New Labour intervened even more strongly, using the national teaching strategies to regulate teachers' practice and methods. OECD (2008) describes Britain's as the most tested school population in the developed world and criticises the government for the ways in which testing detracts from children's learning. Chapter 6 discusses the effects which such controls have had on the teaching profession and gives a critique of 'high-stakes' national assessment.

The government's challenge to the autonomy of professionals and academics has been strongest in taking the teacher training curriculum from the universities to create a highly regulated national system. Chapter 7 shows how Conservative and Labour governments have controlled teacher training through a set of requirements, standards and a high level of inspection. One of the issues for the teaching profession is the extent to which it should simply be trained as a 'workforce' to deliver the National Curriculum. The chapter concludes by showing the way that academics have created Education Studies as a university subject to enable future professionals to be educated in critical and creative ideas about education and schooling.

While Chapter 3 examines inequalities created by the school system, Chapters 8, 9 and 10 look at the way education policies address the inequalities inherent in society: gender, race and social class. Chapter 8 traces policy responses to the disadvantaged position of women and girls in the education system and the underachievement of boys. The National Curriculum has benefited girls in providing an equal curriculum, and they have succeeded in levels of educational achievement, but women are still disadvantaged in the job market. The social inequality borne of racism in society and schools is discussed in Chapter 9, showing how the education system has adapted to the changes of ethnicity in the population with postwar immigration. Labour governments have attempted to address inequality and racism, but New Labour's commitment to diversity in the education system has strengthened faith schools. The chapter concludes by examining whether faith schools contribute to a cohesive society, or make it more divisive.

The New Labour government of 1997 attempted to use the education system to bring about a range of political ambitions: to skill the nation for the global knowledge economy and to bring social justice and equality to society through economic 'well-being'. Its underlying belief that education drives change, both in the economy and in society, became the rationale for the strongest state action in education and other social services. Labour policy has been to reduce class inequality and eliminate poverty in society, with the target of eradicating child poverty by 2020. Every Child Matters (DfES, 2003) and the Children's Plan (DCSF, 2007) attempted to make education much more than schooling in the curriculum: education policy became part of a wider approach to poverty and social inequality. The final Chapter 10 is an important one in that it summarises and evaluates recent New Labour policies and the relationships between class, poverty and education. We argue that, with a deficit model of working-class families and the culture of childrearing, the state now tries to control, not only the detailed content of schooling, but the way children are brought up and spend their leisure time. The sociologist Basil Bernstein (1971) suggested that 'education cannot compensate for society'; the New Labour government thought it could, making education policy a part of the solution to social inequality.

Each chapter can be read in its own right as an introduction to government policy on a topic. This makes for some overlap between chapters, and we have signalled links and connections with 'see Chapter ...'. The book does not attempt to cover every aspect of government policy, in particular there is not space to address further and higher education. But the issues are the ones that we find of interest when teaching Education Studies students.

Education Studies and Policy Critique

The Quality Assurance Agency (QAA) defines the content and quality of university degrees in the UK with a list of the requirements which it calls a 'benchmark' for each subject. In Education Studies (QAA, 2007) students should engage in 'a critique of education policy and processes'. A 'critique' of education policy doesn't mean simply criticism (Ward, 2008): it is easy for discussions of education policy simply to be complaints about politicians and the government. Instead, 'critique' means to know about policy: its history and the political assumptions that underlie it. It means being able to consider alternatives that have been proposed by different authors and commentators, perhaps from other countries.

A critique should ask questions:

- What is the role of the state in education?
- What are the political assumptions underlying policy?
- What historical factors have determined the policy?
- Which thinkers and ideas have affected decision-makers?
- Who has the power to make policy decisions: government, local authorities, parents?
- Who benefits and who loses from policy and changes in policy?
- How does education policy relate to other aspects of government policy, such as health, the economy, social policy and foreign policy?
- How are policies interpreted and contested?

A critique also involves having your own ideas and values about the many political and contestable ideas in education. We present a good deal of facts in the book, but you will notice the underlying values and opinions in the ways we have interpreted them. We hope that you will find our ideas both provocative and convincing. But you might draw different conclusions based on your values and you should be able to make a case to justify your point of view.

Conclusion

Education is *about* change and is *for* change. But keeping up with change in government policy from week to week in the early twenty-first century is bewildering, and a book on education policy is bound to be out of date before it is published. At the time of writing (late 2008) the assumptions about market forces, capitalism and the global economy were rocked by the 'credit crunch' and the threats to the global economy, which required last-minute rewriting of Chapter 2. We went to press before the publication of the government's 'root and branch' review of primary education in 2009 mentioned in the Children's Plan. By the time you are reading the book, there may well be a different government in power and the Children's Plan shredded. We ask your forgiveness for not being completely up to date, but hope that the book will have offered you the principles to understand government policy so that, when the latest initiative comes along, you will have your own informed critique.

Recommended reading

For a general introduction to most of the topics in the book, see:

Bartlett, S. and Burton, D. (2007) *Introduction to Education Studies*, 2nd edn. London: Sage.

There are a number of general sources for education policy which are worth consulting regularly to keep up to date. The DCSF website is updated daily with the latest government documents:

DCSF (2008) Recent publications. London: DCSF. Online at: http://www.dcsf.gov.uk/publications/ (accessed 31 July 2008).

The *TES* and the *THE* are weekly publications which keep you up to date with the latest political news and events

The Times Education Supplement: http://www.tes.co.uk (accessed 31 July 2008).
Times Higher Education: http://www.timeshighereducation.co.uk/ (accessed 31 July 2008).

See also newspapers:

The Guardian (on Tuesdays): http://www.guardian.co.uk (accessed 31 July 2008).
The Independent: http://www.independent.co.uk (accessed 31 July 2008).

Other sources:

Ball, S.J. (2008) *The Education Debate*. Bristol: Policy Press. Gives an up-to-date critique of the development of education policy.

Bottery, M. (2000) *Education Policy and Ethics*. London: Continuum. Gives a good theoretical analysis of policy.

Whitty, G. (2008) 'Twenty years of progress? English education policy 1988 to the present', *Educational Management and Leadership*, 36: 165–84.

References

Apple, M. (2006) 'Away with all teachers: the cultural politics of home learning', in D. Kassem, E. Mufti and J. Robinson (eds), *Education Studies: Issues and Critical Perspectives*. Buckingham: Open University.

Bernstein, B. (1971) 'Education cannot compensate for society', in B. Cosin et al. (eds), *School and Society*. London: Routledge & Kegan Paul.

Bottery, M. (2000) *Education Policy and Ethics*. London: Continuum.

Brighouse, H. (2006) *On Education*. Abingdon: Routledge.

Codd, J., Gordon, L. and Harker, R. (1997) 'Education and the role of the state: devolution and control post-Picot', in A.H. Halsey, H. Lauder, P. Brown and A. Stuart Wells (eds), *Education: Culture, Economy, Society*. Oxford: Oxford University Press.

DCSF (2007) *The Children's Plan: Building Brighter Futures*. London: DCSF. Online at: http://www.dcsf.gov.uk/publications/childrensplan/downloads/The_Childrens_Plan.pdf (accessed 20 July 2008).

DfEE (1997) *Excellence in Schools: A White Paper*. London: The Stationery Office.

DfES (2003) *Every Child Matters*. London: The Stationery Office.

DfES (2004) *The Children Act*. London: Office for Public Sector Information. Online at: http://www.opsi.gov.uk/acts/acts2004/ukpga_20040031_en_3#pt2-pb1-l1g10 (accessed 31 July 2008).

Freire, P. (1972) *Pedagogy of the Oppressed*. Harmondsworth: Penguin.

Green, A. (1997) *Education, Globalisation and the Nation State*. London: Macmillan.

Hicks, D. (2004) 'Radical education', in S. Ward (ed.), *Education Studies: A Student's Guide*. London: Routledge.

HMSO (2003) *The Victoria Climbié Inquiry: Report of an Inquiry by Lord Laming*. Online at: http://www.victoria-climbie-inquiry.org.uk/finreport.

OECD (2008) *Education at a Glance: OECD Indicators*. Paris: OECD.

Prout, A. (2004) *The Future of Childhood*. London: RoutledgeFalmer.

QAA (2007) *Benchmark for Education*. Cheltenham: QAA. Online at: http://www.qaa.ac.uk/academicinfrastructure/benchmark/honours/Education07.asp (accessed 4 August 2008).

Rose, J. (2006) *Independent Review of the Teaching of Reading*. London: DfES. Online at: http://www.standards.dfes.gov.uk/phonics/report.pdf (accessed 4 August 2008).

Ward, S. (2008) *A Student's Guide to Education Studies*, 2nd edn. Abingdon: Routledge.

Weber, M. (1994) 'The profession and vocation of politics', in P. Lassman (ed.), *Political Writings*. Cambridge: Cambridge University Press.

2

Education in the marketplace

Introduction

The period since the 1988 Education Act has seen a surge of educational change, reform, legislation and government intervention with the government getting its hands on the curriculum, assessment, inspection, childcare and teachers' practice. One feature links all the action by both Conservative and Labour governments: the marketisation of education. This chapter explains what it means for the government to put education into the marketplace and the political thinking behind it. To understand government policy it is necessary to know a little about the economic ideas which politicians hold and the political theory behind those ideas. As we trace the history of the development of education policy we show that what is happening in schools depends on what is happening not just to the economy in Britain, but to economies across the world.

Liberal economics

State education in Britain began in the nineteenth century when the nation was at its height economically. It dominated large areas of the world through the empire and its colonies, particularly in Africa, India and the Caribbean, and had enormous influence in Canada, Australia and other parts of the world. Britain could be said to have invented the Industrial Revolution and had an exceedingly effective economy (Porter, 2000), drawing its raw materials cheaply from the colonies and inventing high-technology machinery to process the materials into saleable goods. But while Britain had the most productive economy in the world with the richest people, the exploitation of the poor in wretched factory conditions prompted authors such as Charles Dickens to write about the scandals which they saw. It is important for us now to grasp why these conditions prevailed: how a society which had such wealth could tolerate such differentials between rich and poor. The answer is 'liberal economics'.

Economists explain that Britain's success in the nineteenth century as an industrial economy was because it was operating in the perfect conditions of economic 'liberalism', or freedom from state control of industry and production, know as 'laissez-faire'. First, there is low, or no, taxation: the money you make is yours. If your factory makes a large profit, it can be used to build another factory. Workers keep all their earnings and use them to buy as much food, clothing and other products as they want. The more products they buy, the more factories are needed to produce goods and more wealth. The theory of low taxation means that the rich can get very rich and that the profits they make will 'filter down' to the workers who will ultimately benefit from more production and more goods to buy. The second feature of liberal economics is freedom from government regulation on employment: an employer could pay workers, including children, as little as possible, given the availability of labour. This makes for profitability: the less you pay the workers, the more profit you can make to invest in the next factory, and then to more production and profits. Low wages lead to more production and a bigger economy. Being able to employ anybody, however young, at any time, and being able to sack them at any time, is 'economically' good. The third feature is 'free market competition', and this is the great trick of the capitalist economy. A free market for goods means that competition ensures that prices are kept low. So cheaper production means more goods, and cheaper prices mean that people can buy more and so more can be sold – a virtuous circle.

The nineteenth century did not see an entirely liberal economy in Britain; there was some taxation and there was some control of employees' conditions with a series of 'Factories Acts'. However, these were limited interventions and left employers largely free to exploit workers. For example, the Factory Act of 1833 stated that children and women could only work between 6.00 a.m. and 6.00 p.m. in the summer and the working week was limited to 60 hours – five 12-hour days. The Act of 1844 made some health legislation: it required that factory owners must wash factories with lime every 14 months. It was only the Factory Act of 1878 that stipulated that no child under ten years of age should be employed.

Another feature of the nineteenth-century economy was patronage and philanthropy. The wealthy would donate their surplus monies to foundations and good causes in exchange for recognition of their name. Giving to the poor and providing for the relief of poverty was common. But these were voluntary donations – acts of charitable conscience. Liberal economics provides wealth in the hands of a small number of individuals who may choose to be charitable. The state played only a limited role and was relatively weak compared with the power of the property-owning wealthy. There was little state provision for housing, health, welfare or education. One of the major agents of philanthropic care was the Church of England. And it was the Church which, through its foundations and donations from the rich, was able to provide education for the poor. But sustained education was mainly for the rich in independent fee-paying (or public) schools.

The Beginnings of State Education

In the nineteenth century the economy grew, but so did the concerns about social differentials and poverty. Publication in 1948 of Karl Marx's *Kapital* raised worries of social unrest and revolution. Marx argued that workers produced more than they were paid under the free-market capitalism and that the owner-ship of production – property, factories and machinery – should come into the hands of the proletariat – the workers. It was time, then, for the government to act to head off social breakdown and possible revolution and to take away some of the economic freedoms which capitalist industry had enjoyed. This meant stronger legislation on factories and included the introduction of state educa-tion with the 1870 Education Act which introduced elementary schooling for all to age 12. The Act set up School Boards which had the power to open board schools where the fees of poor children were paid. The Act was a part of the gathering momentum of state involvement in society and part of the move against free markets. It meant, of course, rises in taxation to pay for it.

In 1870 Britain was slow to embark upon state-funded education, behind Germany and France, for example. Schooling for the poor had been in the hands of the Church foundations which wanted to retain their control over education and resisted the onset of state education. Ball (2008) goes further and suggests that there was a cultural factor: that education was perceived as something to be retained within the family with resistance to the state:

> Its provision by deeply antagonistic, powerful denominational groups ensured that state interference was resisted until regulation became a matter of urgent social control and economic improvement that philanthropy was failing to meet adequately. (Ball, 2008: 59)

The board schools had 'filled the gaps' left by the Church and the state left education very much in its hands. The legacy of the large number of faith schools today is a symptom of nineteenth-century society's reluctance to cre-ate the universal state education system which had emerged in France and Germany.

When a government provides education, it wants to make the service 'accountable' to ensure that the taxpayer is getting 'value for money'. The first attempt at education policy was simple: children were taught a basic curricu-lum of reading, writing and arithmetic and given moral and religious instruc-tion (see Chapter 5). To ensure that children were taught the curriculum Her Majesty's Inspectors (HMI) tested them to determine the level of teachers' pay: the so-called 'payment-by-results scheme'. State education began with a high level of government intervention: a form of national curriculum and an inspectorial system to ensure teachers' accountability to the state. But after only thirty years the 1902 Balfour Education Act abolished the School Boards and gave the control of schooling to the local education authorities. The abo-lition of payment-by-results handed control of schooling and the curriculum to the teaching profession. It was an implicit statement of faith in teachers and, for the greater part of the century, left England with no national curriculum and no structure for monitoring education. The 1902 Act saw the beginnings of the welfare state in which professionals were in control.

The Twentieth-century Welfare State

During the twentieth century free-market liberalism receded and the economic theories of J.M. Keynes became dominant. Rather than free markets and competition, Keynes argued that the economy would be more successful if the state levied more taxes and provided social services in the form of housing, health and education. This was slow to progress in the first half of the century and it was the Second World War (1939–45) which brought about real change. The end of the war saw British society and its economy, like those of all the other European nations, in a poor state. Britain had lost a high proportion of its population through military action. The bombing of its cities had seriously damaged its industrial base and it is estimated that the war had cost Britain 25 per cent of its total resources (Judt, 2005). What is more, Britain had needed to borrow from America to support its military production for the war, and the end of the war meant paying it back.

The positive effects of the war were twofold. On the one hand it became obvious that society needed to be repaired and reconstructed; to do that, meant government taking a stronger role in providing social services, including education. Even before the end of the war, the 1944 Butler Education Act brought compulsory secondary education for all to age 15 (see Chapter 3). The other effect of the war was that the state had become powerful in the mobilisation of the total population (Bottery, 2000). The First World War had been damaging, but it was fought abroad by the military. The Second World War came home with the bombing of civil populations and required the complete commitment of the whole of society in the war effort under the control of the state. This contrasts with the non-interventionist, laissez-faire theory of free-market capitalism. Keynes's economic vision of a society with strong state control and fairer distribution of resources came with the general election immediately after the war when the Labour Party had its first victory.

From the end of the war state provision and state control became the direction of social and economic policy. Labour's centrepiece was the first National Health Service (NHS), but there was general expansion of social services and education with the building of new schools. However, this was against the backdrop of a war-damaged economy still struggling to repay America for the war loans. Food rationing continued after the war until 1954, the ultimate form of government control, and a very long way from the nineteenth-century free market, where the effects of poverty were met by charity and patronage. After the war, poverty and the welfare of people became the state's responsibility. Britain became a 'welfare state' with state education at its heart.

While the 1945 Labour government laid the principles of state intervention, it was continued by successive Conservative governments which sustained the

NHS and the expansion of education with more school building and the raising of the school leaving age to 16. After the war political interest in education lay mainly in debates about social class, types of schools and access to schooling. Conservatives argued for selective grammar schools to preserve high standards for an elite, usually middle-class, group. Labour wanted to see equal access for all, regardless of social class, and from 1965 tried to introduce secondary comprehensive schools open to all pupils regardless of income or ability (see Chapter 3). During this postwar debate about access and social class, central government took little or no interest in the curriculum, in teaching or in the running of schools (see Chapters 5 and 6). The administration and monitoring of education was left to the local authorities and a small number of HMI. It is as though the political parties were so concerned with social class and equality that they disregarded other aspects of education. The tacit agreement not to interfere with schools Lawton (1992) calls the 'post-war consensus' on education. There were no debates, and indeed no policies held by either party, on the nature of schooling and the school curriculum.

> Economics, again, are important in understanding the 'hands-off' approach. It is partly that, once Britain had started to recover from the stringencies of the war, the economy grew strongly. There were still cheap resources, including oil, from the former colonies, and industry was operating well to produce manufactured goods and new technologies: refrigerators, washing machines, even motor cars. As Harold Macmillan, the Prime Minister said at a Conservative Party rally in 1957, 'most of our people have never had it so good'. And this became a strapline for complacency about everything, including the education system. Education could be left to the local authorities and teachers. Politicians simply did not make a strong connection between the economy and the education system. However, the benign indifference wasn't to last for long as storm clouds gathered over Britain's share of the global economy.

Education and the Global Economy

The oil crisis of the 1970s brought the political neglect of education to an end. Conflict in the Middle East and the loss of Britain's colonial control there led to increasing oil prices which hit production in all European economies. Because of the shortage of oil, industry had to slow down and the economy fell into recession. At the same time, there were concerns about rising crime, lower moral standards and the breakdown of traditional moral codes. Politicians looked around for the culprits and decided that one of the offenders was the education service. For the first time politicians began to ask questions about what the education system was doing for the economy. It began with Jim Callaghan (1976), the Labour Prime Minister, who criticised primary teachers and accused schools of failing to equip young people for industry.

This was one of the first attempts to create 'moral panic' about education, with schools portrayed as the cause of the nation's economic and social ills. By the 1980s the effects of the global economy were being realised. The so-called Asian 'tiger' economies of Japan, South Korea and Taiwan were producing better industrial goods more cheaply and sucking away customers from Britain. Politicians also noted that their education systems appeared to benefit from teaching basic skills through traditional methods (see Chapter 6).

During the 1970s and 1980s British industry changed and multinational companies began to dominate. The Ford Motor Company is American, but invests in manufacturing plants and selling cars in Britain and providing jobs. However, if workers in Britain are not sufficiently skilled, or they demand higher wages, Ford will take its manufacturing elsewhere, to Spain or Singapore. This is the principle of globalisation and global markets: companies will invest and employ people where they can make the most profits; the cheapest and best workers get the jobs anywhere in the world. The successful Dyson vacuum cleaner company began in its factory in Malmesbury in England, but in 2002 moved production to Malaysia where labour costs are cheaper. With globalisation, markets became more competitive and employment became less certain.

It was in this context of economic fragility that governments began to see education as a key feature of the economy, and it was judged to be lacking. Making the curriculum suited to industrial production was seen as one of the means of enabling Britain to compete in the global economy and it made politicians begin to view education in a different light. Politicians began to treat education as the principal means of training industry for competition in the world, and it had to become more vocationally oriented. While the debate had been started by Jim Callaghan, it was the succeeding Conservative governments which moved from debate to action.

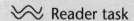 Reader task

Do you agree with Jim Callaghan that schooling should be designed to promote the economy?

The New Right: Neo-liberalism and the Marketisation of Education

The 1979 General Election saw the Conservative government elected under Margaret Thatcher. The first woman leader of any political party in the UK, she was determined to make changes to the economic and social structure of the country and had a hard-headed view of what had gone before in economic policy. She criticised Keynesian economics and social policy for creating a 'nanny state' in which people cease to be independent, functioning human beings. Her plan was to reduce taxation, 'roll back the state' and allow people to have greater personal control over their lives. This was the birth of so-called 'New Right' politics, derived from nineteenth-century liberalism and so known as 'neo(new)liberalism'. It is also known as 'Thatcherism'. Its ideas are based on the social philosopher Friedrich Hayek who argued in his book *The Road to Serfdom* (1991) that the welfare state disables people's creative energy and that individual freedom, while it appears to be self-serving and greedy, actually brings public good. For education, neo-liberal economics means introducing the kind of competition which makes private businesses successful. Neo-liberals want a 'free market' in education: education becomes a commodity which is bought and sold; schools are the providers and parents and children the consumers or 'customers'. The economic theorist who also influenced Margaret Thatcher was the American Milton Friedman (1990), who argued that the free market and consumer choice should be the overriding feature of both politics and economics. The first feature of market theory is that individuals are responsible for their actions and should 'invest in themselves' (human capital theory) and the role of schools is to equip them for the economy. Schools and professionals came into the firing line and teachers, their values, ideas and methods were systematically attacked by successive governments (see Chapter 6). England was heading for a 'post-welfare' society and a post-welfare education system. This was part of a global phenomenon, as Tomlinson puts it:

> Governments around the world, who were turning their welfare states into post-welfare societies, were discovering human capital theory, with individuals told to invest in themselves in a lifelong process of learning and re-skilling in order to get or retain any kind of job. Teachers were being gradually stripped of their professionalism and policed by new inspection regimes. Schools, teachers and local education authorities were increasingly held responsible not only for failing individuals, but also for failing to make the national economy competitive in global markets. (Tomlinson, 2001: 2)

Marketisation, though, has an additional dimension. It is not just that the education system should enable the nation to compete in global markets. Education itself needed an 'internal market' – competition between schools. The trouble with education, the new right politicians argued, was that schooling was controlled by the people who 'produce' it rather than by the people who 'consume it'. This is known as 'provider capture'. The provider tells you what you want and that's what you get. In a free market, people buy the goods they want, not the ones that manufacturers want to produce. During the twentieth century, from 1902 onwards, society and the government had handed the education system over to the professions: the teachers and the local authorities. Teachers taught what they wanted to teach in the ways they preferred and if it didn't suit the children, the parents, society or the economy, no matter. And local authorities, instead of taking responsibility for schools and dealing with the problem, were collaborating with teachers and were part of the problem. They regulated admissions to schools, preventing parental choice. No one was choosing what was produced, so teachers and schools became slack and complacent. Schools had to be made to compete with each other, and threatened with closure and loss of teachers' jobs if they didn't succeed.

An early attempt to bring the market into education suggested by Thatcher's first Secretary of State for Education, Sir Keith Joseph, was the 'voucher scheme'. Parents would be given an annual voucher to the value of one year's education for each child. The voucher could be used to spend in any state school, or it could be used to count towards the fee of an independent school and parents could 'top up' the additional amount. This would, of course, have been very beneficial to the parents who sent their children to fee-paying independent schools; it would have been a subsidy for them and would have enabled more people to use the private sector. However, in an interview with Stephen Ball, Joseph acknowledged that 'for largely political reasons it wouldn't be practical' (Ball, 2008: 128). The voucher scheme made sense to academic neo-liberal Joseph whose ideal system of education was private schooling: schools are the providers; parents pay the fees and they are the customers. The belief was that this is why independent schools are so successful, gaining good examination results. Of course, there are other factors affecting the performance of independent schools such as parental income to provide resources and high levels of parental aspiration. But the ideal for Thatcher and Joseph was a society in which everyone would pay fees for schooling with no government involvement; the market would guarantee quality and relevance to consumer needs. But the neo-liberal ideal wasn't going to happen, and a compromise with the politics of the time was needed. The country was not going to vote for the abolition of state schooling and it was only after Thatcher's third election win in 1987 – and ten years after Callaghan's first warning speech – that neo-liberal politics met education with the Education 'Reform' Act of 1988. By this time, the theorising Keith Joseph had been replaced as Secretary of State by Kenneth Baker, a more practical and politically astute operator who saw that markets in education would have to be within the state system.

The 1988 Act is well known for introducing a National Curriculum and standardised national testing (see Chapter 5). But its central and underlying purpose was not simply to ensure that children all learned the same curriculum. It was to create the conditions for a free market in education: parents were to be given choice of school in the state system and schools would be forced to compete with each other for those parents' choice. The theory was that, just as competition in production drives down prices and drives up quality, so quality in education would be 'driven up' in the same way. The most important feature of the Act was not the National Curriculum which attracted so much attention from teachers and the public; it was the much less obvious 'local management of schools' (LMS). This took financial control away from the local authorities by delegating the spending budget directly to schools. Schools were to use the money as they wished: to appoint teaching staff or non-teaching assistants, to purchase more computers or to repair the roof. Such decisions were now to be taken by the head teacher and the governing body of the school, not by local authority officials. The National Curriculum had an immediate impact on schools, but LMS was a bigger change, making schools into business corporations competing for pupils.

The neo-liberal ideal is that those selling their wares in a market are side by side and the shopper can easily compare prices and quality. So you can look at the clothes in Marks & Spencer and then go next door into Next and perhaps a dozen others before you decide to buy. The Internet makes this kind of price comparison even easier. But choosing a school is more difficult: schools are not likely to be next door to each other and the goods are not on display. The 1988 Act began the process of opening up the education service to inspection by its customers. The reason for setting up the machinery of a National Curriculum, national testing, school league tables and Ofsted inspection was to allow customers to make their choices. Parents could select on the basis of the schools' test results, positions in league tables and quality of Ofsted reports. And the Internet has made comparison easier with the ability to view Ofsted reports and test results online. There were always attempts to compare schools informally in conversations between parents. Now they have the factual data to make those comparisons. However, selecting a school online is still not as simple as choosing holidays or car insurance. Not all schools have places, not all schools are within reach of everyone who might like to go there. So it is more correct to refer to the education market as a *quasi-market*: it is similar to, or analogous to, a fruit and vegetable market, but it is not a *proper market*.

At first sight the 1988 Act appears to be contradictory (Bash and Coulby, 1991). On the one hand, the government had taken central control of the curriculum and national testing, but had *de*-centralised spending and management. In fact, the devolution of funding was designed not so much to empower schools, but to reduce the power of the local authorities which had run education. It was the Conservative government's political intention to limit the power of left-wing Labour-controlled local authorities, particularly the Inner London Education Authority (ILEA). So while the 1988 Act appears to devolve power from government to schools, it actually increased the power of central government. The noose tightened around the education service with legislation in 1992 to introduce the Office for Standards in Education (Ofsted) with powers to inspect every school in the state system every four years. The Ofsted (2005) Framework for Inspection gives the most detailed list of every possible dimension of a school's work and it can be seen as part of a general trend in society towards increased accountability and surveillance. It is difficult to convey the magnitude and complexity of the systems which were put in place for education by the legislation of the late 1980s and early 1990s. They generated prodigious amounts of consultative documents and a variety of government agencies. What was going on was not evident to teachers at the time. They thought they were dealing with a National Curriculum and testing. They were really facing a social and economic revolution in education.

While the National Curriculum was the most public element, the introduction of LMS, competition between schools and national testing to create the marketisation of education was the major reason for the Act and these could be seen as contradictory. If the idea is for 'customers' to choose their school, they ought to be able to choose their curriculum. So why have a uniform curriculum for all? This apparent contradiction was perceived by some of the right-wing architects of the policy. Chitty (2004) notes from an interview with one of Thatcher's advisers, Stuart Sexton, that he saw the National Curriculum as 'a quite separate and unnecessary piece of legislation serving mainly to divert attention from the free market objectives ...' (p. 53). So why was Thatcher, a neo-liberal politician who talked of 'rolling back government', introducing legislation designed to regulate education so strongly? The answer is that these were the very regulations needed to create the conditions for a market. Gray (1998) explains that free-market economics cannot actually happen without government intervention:

> ... free markets are a product of artifice, design and political coercion. *Laissez-faire* must be centrally planned: regulated markets just happen. The free market is not, as New Right thinkers have imagined or claimed, a gift of social evolution. It is an end-product of social engineering and unyielding political will. (p. 17)

Although the neo-liberal ideal is that markets operate on their own and that governments and legislation damage them, Gray's point is that free markets won't exist without strong governments creating the right conditions. Government regulation is needed make sure that one supermarket, like Tesco, doesn't take over all the others, leaving no competition. In the same way, the government legislation and controls were needed to set up the education market and take control away from the professions. So there was really no contradiction in the paraphernalia of education legislation in 1988 and the early 1990s. The free market needed customers to be able to choose between schools by comparing their performance on the same curriculum, by the results of standardised tests and by the evidence from Ofsted inspections. If all schools teach the same curriculum, it is easier to make comparisons between them. It needed a government with the 'political will' of Margaret Thatcher to do it.

〰 Reader task

Competition between schools is intended to improve standards of children's education. Do you agree with this, or can you think of other ways of raising the quality of schooling?

New Labour and the Modernisers

The Conservatives had enjoyed four terms of office until 1997 when Tony Blair swept Labour to power in a landslide election victory. Teachers looked forward to a return to the consensual days when they would be able to control education and the marketisation of schooling would end. They were soon disappointed, for this was 'New Labour'. Blair soon showed that his three priorities, 'Education, Education and Education', meant more of the same politics of education as under the Conservatives. He claimed that he had not been elected to return to 'old Labour' methods of high taxation and leaving education to the professionals. He meant to modernise the party and, for education, 'modernisation' meant continuing marketisation and keeping the pressure on schools to deliver education fit for a modern industrial society. This does not mean that the politics of New Labour were identical with the Conservative New Right. New Labour did not see market forces as a philosophical doctrine as the neo-liberal Conservatives did. For Blair, market forces were simply a pragmatic and effective way of operating to get the best from the system. So the political philosophy was different, but the effect was much the same.

New Labour's modernisation went even further than the Conservatives had done. Blair took up the Conservatives' theme of high quality in education with the new government's first Green Paper on Education entitled *Excellence for All* (DfEE, 1997a). In a green paper a government sets out its thinking for discussion. The term 'excellence' is significant here because it signals the idea of being outstanding, above the others and exclusive. For old Labour, the politics of education had been about achieving equality in a universal system of comprehensive schools. Equality would be achieved by schools all being the same (see Chapter 3). New Labour's emphasis on 'excellence' signalled an end to that equality through uniformity. 'Excellence' was much closer to the Conservative ideal of high standards through selection. Of course, *Excellence for All* is an oxymoron, a self-contradiction: by definition, not everyone can be outstanding. And in the subsequent White Paper (DfEE, 1997b), in which the government makes its formal proposals for legislation, the title is changed to *Excellence in Schools*. The self-contradiction is removed, and term means simply 'good quality', but there is still a resonance of exclusivity.

All this, Blair claimed, makes sense 'because it works': increasing quality and standards to create an education system which provides the educated workforce for industry in globally competitive markets. Even if it means inequalities, it is worth it. New Labour proved to be an even more enthusiastic proponent of market forces and privatisation than the Conservatives. Assessment and school league tables were strengthened with the setting of targets at all levels: national government targets for literacy and numeracy, as well as targets for LEAs, for schools and for individual pupils. This was remarkable from a political party which, in its original form as old Labour, had acted to abolish grammar schools to set up the universal comprehensive system (see Chapter 3). It had even proposed the abolition of independent private schools. But New Labour was committed to elements of Thatcher's economic policies in the 'New Labour Project' formed by Tony Blair, Gordon Brown and Peter Mandelson during the 1990s. Their aim was to achieve old Labour's ideals of equality in society through strong social services. While old Labour governments under Harold Wilson and Jim Callaghan had never had the economic strength to provide it, Blair's plan was to make the economy successful so that there would be funding for hospitals and schools.

In order to make the economy work, Blair believed, a Labour government had to be seen to be sympathetic to business: it is businesses which produce the money for the economy to work and for welfare services, including education, to be funded. He was not going back to the old days of Labour governments setting high taxes and being opposed to industry. They returned, then, to the economic principle that market forces and low taxation bring high economic returns. The fall of the Berlin wall in 1989 and the collapse of the communist economies of the Soviet Union and Eastern Europe strengthened the global basis of free-market capitalism. With the publication of Francis Fukuyama's (1992) book, *The End of History*, free-market capitalism seemed to be 'the only game in town'. Blair's commitment to quality at any price is encapsulated in his phrase 'standards, not structures', meaning that the format of schools – commitment to equality through the comprehensive school – is not important. What is important is that all children get the opportunity to succeed through good-quality schooling, and *that* is what will bring about equality of education and, through equality of education, equality in society.

〰 Reader tasks

- Interview a head teacher about his/her views on marketisation. How much does s/he have to attend to parental choice? How much time is spent on marketisation? Are the educational processes in the school affected by parents' wishes?
- Ask a head teacher about the school's relationship with the local authority. How much influence does the local authority have on the schools? What is the influence of members of the governing body on the school?

New Labour's economic thinking, while in many ways based on Thatcher's commitment to the market, was different. For the Thatcherite neo-liberals the ideal is a completely privatised society, with a minimal role for governments – rolling back the state. State-funded services are a drain on the economy and demotivate people: much better that people pay for the services which they want, hospitals or schools. For the New Labour project, state-funded institutions are, as Keynes suggested, fundamental to a healthy and successful society and economy. Blair's vision for schooling was derived from the economist Will

Hutton (1992) who criticised Britain for failing to invest in services and allowing too large a differential to occur in society. Rather than abolish independent schools, which was the old Labour solution, Hutton suggested that state schools should be made so good that parents would not need to spend their income on private education. State schools were to be 'in the market' with independent schools. It didn't quite work out like this, however: during the years of Labour government state schools did improve, but because of the flourishing economy during the late 1990s and 2000s, incomes rose and more people were financially able to send their children to independent schools. However, market forces operated and independent schooling began to become more expensive. In 2008 the cost of independent schools had risen to an average of £10,000 a year, an increase of 40 per cent in five years (Milne, 2008). With the downturn in the economy in late 2008 it was predicted that there would be a move back to state schools.

Blair's belief in marketisation led thinking away from the universal comprehensive ideal to the opposite concept: diversity. For markets depend on diversity. To give customers choice, you must give them differences: for clothes, it's colour, cut, fashion trends, price; for cars, it's size, shape, speed, fuel economy, accessories. The more differences, the more people buy, trading in their old Ford Fiesta for something faster with air conditioning. Blair's view was that for the market to operate in education – for schools to be really competitive – there must be diversity. So New Labour policy, embodied in the 2002 Education Act, was to move secondary schools away from their former comprehensive uniformity to 'specialist schools', they could specialise in particular curriculum areas such as the arts, physical education, the sciences or technology. Schools were to apply for 'specialist status' and then would be awarded additional funding to provide specialist facilities (see Chapter 4). The 2005 Education Act encouraged the expansion of faith schools as a further means of diversification (see Chapter 9).

Ball (2008: 119) calls this 'endogenous competition' – schools competing against each other *within* the system. 'Exogenous competition' is to bring external competitors and providers into the system. The Conservative governments had made some moves to introduce external agencies by establishing city technology colleges (CTCs) during the late 1980s and early1990s. These were state-funded independent schools with sponsors from the commercial sector. The idea was to foster close links between schools and commerce and to encourage the involvement of external parties other than the educational professionals. The scheme began with Dixons, the electrical retailers, becoming the first sponsors, and some CTCs do still exist. However, the interest – and the funding – from private sponsors was limited and the scheme never fulfilled its original ambitions. But New Labour was to use the external, or exogenous, model extensively. The privatisation of school meals, cleaning and other services begun by the Conservatives continued, and Labour introduced Compulsory Competitive Tendering (CCT). This meant that all work to be carried out on a school had to be offered to private companies and not carried out by the local authority services. Underlying this is the assumption that state-run organisations cannot be effective compared with the private sector. CCT was intended to introduce 'efficiency' into the public sector.

A scheme introduced by the Chancellor of the Exchequer, Gordon Brown, was the Private Finance Initiative (PFI) for the building of schools. Instead of the local authority finding the capital to build a new school from its council taxes, a finance company could provide the capital for the building, which it would then own and lease back to the LA or the school. This took away the control of the design of buildings from the schools and LAs, but released capital so that schools are built rapidly. It has recently produced criticisms of both architecture and building quality (Stewart, 2008a) indicating that private enterprise might not always be the most efficient or effective, but the idea was to bring private capital into education, and with it the enterprise initiative of industry. However, the biggest offensive by New Labour to introduce external agencies into education was the academies scheme.

First called 'city academies', these are an extension of the city technology colleges in that they are state-funded schools sponsored by commercial organisations. The difference is that, in the case of academies, the sponsor has control of the building, admissions, staffing and the curriculum. Academies are New Labour's biggest commitment to a neo-liberal agenda in education (see Chapter 4). Blair's vision was that good schools using new initiatives could 'regenerate' low-income communities and expel poverty. That he should have tried to do this, not simply by providing additional state-funded resources but by involving the private sector, is typical of the 'Third Way' thinking of New Labour: it is not just *either* the state *or* private enterprise, but a mixture of both – the best of both worlds. The state provides the security of the funding, but privatisation ensures that there is innovation and enterprise. It is also a return to the charitable and philanthropic days of the 1900s when the wealthy could invest their money in good causes. The assumption is that a school run by a private enterprise will be more efficient and more effective than one run by a state body. The same idea is inherent in the policy for School Trusts. Any school, or group of schools, is able to apply for 'Trust Status' (DfES, 2006). The school is not, like an academy, owned by another company, but by the trust which has control of all its property and assets. Membership of the trust can include individuals, businesses or a university who take part in the governance of the school. A trust school is able to devise its own curriculum and set its own admissions requirements.

Another part of the privatisation policies of Thatcher and Blair was to encourage the use of independent 'consultants' to carry out work in the state education system. There had always been a small number of such organisations, such as the Centre for British Teachers (CfBT, 2008). During the 1990s these organisations swelled in number and the so-called 'outsourcing' of services began. Consultants are now employed on a large scale to carry out many of the activities which would have been done by local authorities: supporting and advising schools and academies, advising local authorities themselves, recruiting teachers, carrying out reviews and evaluation of services. Perhaps the most significant work of the independent consultants has been Ofsted inspections. While Ofsted is a government organisation employing a small number of staff in London, all inspections are outsourced to private companies who bid to carry out each inspection. Many of these companies were in fact formed by the local education authorities when Ofsted was launched in 1992. Advisory staff would be paid their salary by the authority, but only if they were able to win sufficient Ofsted contracts to supply the necessary finance. Outsourcing is another means of achieving the effects of marketisation: any work is given to the most efficient company who bids for it. They may be the cheapest, but must also prove themselves to give the best service. Independent consultants have even been employed to replace local authorities. For example, when, in 2001, the City of Leeds Education Authority was found to be failing, Capita Consultants, a large profit-making company, was drafted in to run it.

Many of the smaller consultancies have been set up by former teachers, head teachers, local authority advisers or HMI who have retired to 'go independent'. For many it has been a successful and lucrative move. It is interesting that outsourcing to private companies is largely invisible: an inspection team operates on behalf of Ofsted and it is viewed and treated as such. Only when it goes wrong does the 'source' become visible. This occurred in the summer of 2008 when the American company ETS-Europe, which was employed to administer the annual SATs in England, failed to get papers marked in time and proved to be badly organised with incorrect marking and reports of marking done by hotel bar staff (Mansell, 2008). When hundreds of schools had not received their SATs results by September, the company's contract was ignominiously terminated.

Private enterprise has become firmly embedded in the state education system. It has met some resistance from the teachers' unions and professional associations (NUT, 2008), but over the years there has been acceptance of the transformation of education as part of a government-controlled welfare state to the 'mixed economy' of state control and private enterprise. In 2007 the new Labour Prime Minister, Gordon Brown, argued for an end to the conflict between education as a market and as a social service:

> We need both strong public services and we need a dynamic market economy to have a fair and prosperous society. Arguments about the size of the state and the funding of public services mark important dividing lines in politics, investment in public services in my view is absolutely critical. But we don't believe in a zero sum game in which there is only one winner between state and market forces in advanced economies. Each, markets and government, have their place. (Brown, 2007)

But New Labour differed from Thatcher and Major's neo-liberalism in that there is, despite all the outsourcing and privatisation, a stronger commitment to public service and management by government. While neo-liberals 'leave it up to the market', New Labour's 'Third Way' was to intervene and use competitive methods to ensure that the correct results were achieved.

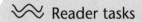 **Reader tasks**

- How does external funding for schools improve children's education?
- Why do you think the government has been keen to limit the role of local authorities in the running of schools?

Conclusion: A Critique of Marketisation – The Credit Crunch

Government policies in the last twenty years have been to employ market forces to introduce efficiency in education and to equip the labour market for a global economy. Thatcher's neo-liberalism assumed that creating a market would deliver it. Blair used marketisation methods to make sure that the education system fulfilled the needs of the knowledge economy. It is now taken for granted that schools, like shops, need to compete for pupils. Parents can search for the best for their children. The reality, of course, is not so simple and Thatcher's dream of free choice for all does not apply to most. Schools have limited admission levels and parents are frequently frustrated at not being able to get their choice, leading to disappointment: children being sent to the school which is *not* the parents' choice. Choice also fails to accommodate those who simply are unable to take their children to schools further away than the local one. The policy also tends to involve children travelling further to school and contradicts 'green' policies on energy conservation and traffic reduction.

These are the practical difficulties, but it might be argued that they are worth the overall effort. For the real motivation for marketing in education is not, in itself, to give choice as a simple ideal. The neo-liberal theory of choice is that it drives up quality and standards through the process of competition. For Labour, it doesn't matter whether parents actually get a choice. What marketisation does is to offer a school and its teachers the possibility of success or the threat of failure and closure, and it is this combination of opportunity and threat which makes for good schools (Tooley, 1999). And, as Barber (2001) says, there should be 'high expectations and standards, no matter what'. But perhaps it is time to reflect on what 'no matter what' entails. With social and philosophical objections Lawton (1992) and Whitty (2002) provide the strongest critique, not just of the practical difficulties, but of the way that markets damage citizenship and community. Whitty argues that the policy treats people as consumers rather than as citizens. Simply 'getting the best for your child' ignores the individual's responsibility to the community. It is not simply a matter of educational provision, but that people should contribute to the community and be politically aware. For the neo-liberal, emphasis on markets and education as a commodity to be bought and sold creates a society of consumers rather than a society of citizens and is a threat to democracy. The effect can be seen in the way society has moved from politics to economics. As Judt (2005) shows, people are less interested in politics and political ideas with low turnouts in elections. They are motivated by what they can acquire through the economy: a society of consumers who express themselves through their possessions rather than through thoughts and actions. This trend to the collapse of community action is typical across the neo-liberal United States, as illustrated by Putnam (2000).

Britain has always been a highly stratified society (see Chapter 10) and the McKinsey Report (2007) finds that 'pupil performance still has a stronger link to socio-economic background than is the case in the world's best systems'. The social class effect on children's education is in spite of more than ten years of a Labour government committed to social justice. Parental choice was introduced to drive up quality and standards between schools, but it can be argued that it simply offers choice to middle-class parents who will manipulate the system to get the best for their children. McKinsey recommends higher-quality teaching as the solution to this problem of differential attainment. However, for the teaching profession, the National Union of Teachers (NUT) representative, John Bangs, argues that the problem lies with parental choice:

> The reason the effect of social background is playing out in the results is not to do with the quality of teaching. It is the result of the rather poisonous cross-party approach to promoting choice and diversity over the last 20 years. When you start introducing choice and diversity you start introducing social division. McKinsey has not recognised the elephant in the room. (Stewart, 2008b: 11)

Marketisation has changed the relationship between schools and their pupils. The relationship previously was one of the professional to the pupil in which the professional held the power. Since the 1988 Act, the relationship has become one of provider and client (customer), similar to the relationship between the private school and its pupils and parents. It is a model which governments have tried to engender in the whole state sector, not just in education, but in health and social services. Like the restaurant waiter, the teacher and the doctor are there to please their customers. The positive aspect to this is that teachers are obliged to create an atmosphere of goodwill in order to retain their pupils. But it does raise questions about whether this relationship is the right one. It gives more power to parents, but are parents the right ones to decide on the needs of their children? The neo-liberal assumption is always that they are.

Neo-liberal assumptions about global capitalism were challenged with the credit crunch and the crisis in international banking in October 2008. Capitalism is based on investing to make profits. The desire to make more profits and bonuses led bankers and financial traders to take bigger and bigger risks in unregulated borrowing and lending. It all felt very good because there seemed to be lots of money. On 11 October, Dominique Strauss-Kahn, head of the International Monetary Fund (IMF), described the global economic financial system as 'close to meltdown': confidence in investment and profits was gone and a return to the slump of the 1930s threatened. The crisis left governments across the world struggling to prop up the financial system and attempting to restore confidence in the money markets by investing billions into their accounts – so-called 'recapitalisation', but it could well be described as 'nationalisation'. It was a disaster predicted by the economist Joseph Stiglitz (2002) who had warned of the dangers of free-market capitalism in which governments are not permitted to intervene. In order for banks to keep up with the impetus and demands of the global economy, and without government intervention to curb excessive borrowing and lending, they were going to take more and more risks. Toynbee (2008: 25) describes the events as 'capitalism collapsing under the weight of its own self-contradictions'. She argued that market forces cannot be left to themselves: in the end, a strong state is needed.

The events challenge the assumptions that free market capitalism is the only way to run society and the economy. The marketisation of education, was based on the neo-liberal philosophy that markets and competition will drive up quality and standards. Suddenly this assumption about free markets seemed doubtful. With the return to the idea of social values, and a glimpse of 'Old Labour', the British Prime Minister, Gordon Brown, remarked that

> ... we do not live by markets alone. I have long understood that markets rely on values that they cannot generate themselves. Values are important in treating people fairly, acting responsibly, co-operating for the benefit of all. And these values that our economy and society need in order to flourish are not born in markets, nor are they born in states. These values – fairness, stewardship cooperation – are learned in families, neighbourhoods and communities and developed in the relationships we enjoy as a society. (Brown, 2008: 6)

Recommended reading

Friedman, T.L. (1999) *The Lexus and the Olive Tree*. New York: Anchor Books. Friedman gives a good account of the way global capitalist economies work.

Gray, J. (1998) *False Dawn: The Delusions of Global Capitalism*. London: Granta. Gray also explains global capitalism, but warns of the dangers of assuming that markets can be left to themselves with no regulation by the state.

Judt, T. (2005) *Postwar: A History of Europe since 1945*. London: Heinemann. Judt's is a readable account of social history since the Second World War and provides a good background to understanding the political background to education.

Tooley, J. (1999) 'Asking different questions: towards justifying markets in education', in N. Alexiadou and C. Brock (eds), *Education as a Commodity*. London: John Catt Educational. Tooley argues the case for the marketisation of schooling.

Whitty, G. (2002) *Making Sense of Education Policy*. London: Paul Chapman, Chapter 5: 'Consumer rights versus citizens rights in contemporary education policy'. Whitty gives a strong critique of New Labour policy on marketisation, arguing that the current changes in education policy are 'linked to a redefinition of the nature of the state and a reworking of the relations between state and society' (p. 93).

References

Ball, S.J. (2008) *The Education Debate*. Bristol: Policy Press.

Barber, M. (2001) 'High expectations and standards for all, no matter what: creating a world-class education service in England', in M. Fielding (ed.), *Taking Education Really Seriously*. RoutledgeFalmer.

Bash, L. and Coulby, D. (1991) *Contradiction and Conflict: The 1988 Education Act in Action*. London: Cassell.

Bottery, M. (2000) *Education Policy and Ethics*. London: Continuum.

Brown, G. (2007) Speech on education policy at the University of Greenwich, 31 October. Online at: http://www.number10.gov.uk/output/Page13675.asp (accessed 4 August 2008).

Brown, G. (2008) *Daily Telegraph*, 28 October.

Callaghan, J. (1976) *Towards a National Debate*. Speech at a foundation stone-laying ceremony at Ruskin College, Oxford, 18 October.

Capita (2008) *Capita*. Online at: http://www.capita.co.uk/Pages/Default.aspx (accessed 10 August 2008).

CfBT (2008) *Centre for British Teachers*. Online at: http://www.cfbt.com (accessed 4 August 2008).

Chitty, C. (2004) *Education Policy in Britain*. Basingstoke: Palgrave Macmillan.

DCSF (2007) *The Primary National Strategy*. London: DCSF. Online at: http://www.standards.dfes.gov.uk/primary/ (accessed 30 November 2007).

DfEE (1997a) *Excellence for All*, Green Paper. London: TSO.

DfEE (1997b) *Excellence in Schools*, White Paper. London: TSO.

DfES (2006) *Trust Schools*. Online at: http://findoutmore.dfes.gov.uk/2006/09/trust_schools.html (accessed 4 August 2008).

Education Leeds (2006) *Education Leeds*. Online at: http://www.educationleeds.co.uk/ (accessed 4 September 2008).

Friedman, M. (1990) *Free to Choose: A Personal Statement*. Chicago: Harvest Books.

Fukuyama, F. (1992) *The End of History and the Last Man*. London: Penguin.

Gray, J. (1998) *False Dawn: The Delusions of Global Capitalism*. London: Granta.

Hayek, F.A. (1991) *The Road to Serfdom*. London: Routledge.

Hutton, W. (1995) *The State We're In*. London: Vintage.

Judt, T. (2005) *Postwar: A History of Europe since 1945*. London: Heinemann.

Lawton, D. (1992) *Education and Politics in the 1990s: Conflict or Consensus*. Lewes: Falmer Press.

McKinsey & Co. (2007) *How the World's Best-Performing Schooling Systems Come Out on Top*. London: McKinsey. Online at: http://www.mckinsey.com/clientservice/socialsector/resources/pdf/Worlds_School_Systems_Final.pdf (accessed 4 August 2008).

Mansell, W. (2008) 'Company that marks Sats beset by mayhem', *Times Educational Supplement*, 16 May, p. 6.

Marx, K. (1948, 1990) *Capital.* London: Penguin.

Milne, J. (2008) 'Independents threaten to slam gates on state sector', *Times Educational Supplement,* 18 July, p. 16.

NUT (2008) *Academies: Looking Beyond the Spin: The NUT's Opposition to the Government's Academies Initiative.* London: NUT. Online at: http://www.teachers.org.uk/topichome.php?id=224 (accessed 2 August 2008).

Ofsted (2005) *Framework for the Inspection of Schools.* London: Ofsted. Online at: http://www.ofsted.gov.uk/publications/index.cfm?fuseaction=pubs.summary&id=3861 (accessed 4 August 2008).

Porter, R. (2000) *Enlightenment: Britain and the Creation of the Modern World.* London: Penguin.

Putnam, R.D. (2000) *Bowling Alone: The Collapse and Revival of American Community.* New York: Simon & Schuster.

Stewart, W. (2008a) 'Academies strangled by poor builders', *Times Educational Supplement,* 25 July, p. 16.

Stewart, W. (2008b) 'Class effect prevents England from joining the world's best educators', *Times Educational Supplement,* 8 August, pp. 10–11.

Stiglitz, J. (2002) *Globalization and Its Discontents.* London: Penguin.

Tomlinson, S. (2001) *Education in a Post-Welfare Society.* Buckingham: Open University.

Toynbee, P. (2008) 'Wanted: a leader who dares draw some bright red lines', *The Guardian,* 20 September, p. 25.

Tooley, J. (1999) 'Asking different questions: towards justifying markets in education', in N. Alexiadou and C. Brock (eds), *Education as a Commodity.* London: John Catt Educational.

Whitty, G. (2002) *Making Sense of Education Policy: Studies in the Sociology and Policy of Education.* London: Paul Chapman, Chapter 5: 'Consumer rights versus citizens rights in contemporary education policy'.

3

Inequalities and the school system

Introduction

This chapter outlines policy on the organisation of schooling from the 1944 Education Act through to the early twenty-first century. It covers the introduction of the tripartite system, the development of comprehensive schooling and the marketisation policies of the last two decades which have led to a wide variety of secondary schools in England. The way education is accessed gives students different sorts of educational experiences and different types of options at the end of their schooling. Government policy determines the opportunities made available to young people in school, higher education and employment. But we need to take account of the entrenched inequalities in wider society which affect people's life chances. The concepts of equity, social justice and equal opportunities are complex, and education is just one factor in determining long-term opportunities and social mobility.

Influence and control in the education system are related to power and inequalities in society. The historical power of Christian groups gave the Church of England influence over schooling and, in the last thirty years, the same legitimacy and power has been given to business through the sponsorship of academies. The Education Acts which changed the shape and organisation of schooling and its governance each say something about which groups in society have the power to influence children's education. Recent developments raise questions about whose interests are being served:

- How does the way schooling is organised affect children's opportunities?
- As systems change, which children are affected?
- What beliefs and ideologies have influenced the ways in which schooling has been organised since the 1944 Education Act?

- Who has the authority to control and influence children's education?
- To what extent can education policy minimise the impact of wider inequalities in society, particularly those associated with class and ethnicity?

The 1944 Education Act

The 1944 'Butler' Education Act made secondary education available to all children. This was not a new idea: socialists had argued for free education for all working people. At the end of the nineteenth century Keir Hardy had urged that education should be free at all stages, without any tests of prior attainment of any age: 'a comprehensive highway along which all could travel' (quoted in Benn, 1992: 135). The Act was introduced towards the end of the Second World War when only a fifth of children received a formal education after the age of 14. The government recognised that it was necessary to develop a postwar society less dominated by class and inequality, and a future in which the benefits of peace would be shared by all sections of society (Batteson, 1999; Newsam, 2008). The Act required state-funded education for pupils up to the age of 15 and reflected the intention to provide 'instruction and training as may be desirable, in view of their different ages, abilities and aptitudes'.

Three types of schools – grammar, technical and secondary modern – became known as the 'tripartite system'. They were designed to provide the intellectual technicians and general workers in the growing postwar economy. The assumption was that children with different abilities and aptitudes required different types of curriculum. The 11-plus examination was used to allocate children to the particular education that was most suitable for them, promoting differential opportunities appropriate to individual needs. The grammar school offered an academic curriculum, the technical schools were to educate future scientists and engineers in mechanical and scientific subjects; secondary modern schools were to train pupils in practical skills for work. In reality there were few technical schools and, with strict quotas on admission to grammar schools, the majority of children were sent to secondary modern schools. The 1944 Act permitted a system of 'direct grant schools', independent schools which received a grant from the Ministry of Education in exchange for accepting a number of selected pupils on free places. The 1944 Act did permit comprehensive schools, but very few were developed. So opportunities for diverse secondary schooling were present at the inception of the tripartite system (Glass, 1959) and have continued to develop throughout the rest of the twentieth and into the twenty-first centuries.

The tripartite system created a hierarchy of status between the three schools, but this was not the original intention. It was intended to provide for individual pupils' needs and skills for a postwar industrial economy. Both Labour and Conservative politicians believed that education for all children would help remove class barriers and provide a means of social mobility for able working-class children. But it soon became clear that the tripartite system largely benefited middle-class children and that selection at 11 was not offering equal opportunities. This was not only of concern to the Labour Party, but also to those middle-class parents whose children did not get into grammar schools. Various writers in the 1950s and 1960s revealed a strong class bias in 11-plus selection (Floud et al., 1956; Silver, 1973). Douglas (1964) found that children on the borderline of passing were more likely to get grammar school places if they came from middle-class families because the questions were culturally biased. During the 1960s such criticism led to the 11-plus becoming more of an IQ test. The sociologist A.H. Halsey (1965) claimed that one quarter of pupils were incorrectly allocated. Working-class children were seen to be disadvantaged as they tended to go to secondary modern schools and grammar schools were dominated by children from the middle class. The pupils, including girls, from working-class backgrounds who did get access to the grammar schools achieved significant social mobility with a considerably higher percentage receiving secondary and university education (Adonis and Pollard, 1997). The idea that 'able' working-class children need to be 'rescued' from their local environment provides a recurring theme of the last one hundred years.

There were regional variations, but about 25 per cent of pupils attended grammar schools and the majority were in secondary modern schools. Grammar schools became associated with high-status education and secondary moderns as low-status schooling (Newson, 1963). Rather than a means of giving children the appropriate education, the 11-plus came to be a test to be passed or failed – even people today consider themselves failures because they did not pass. There were significant differences in the opportunities provided by the different schools with grammar schools offering qualifications for university, the professions and the best-rewarded jobs. Children attending secondary modern schools were not given the opportunity to gain qualifications until 1965 when the Certificate of Secondary Education (CSE) was introduced. Selective education reinforced a system and society already fractured by inequalities.

The Development of Comprehensive Education

The Labour government of 1964 encouraged local authorities to abolish the 11-plus and move to a non-selective system allowing all children the opportunity to gain access to further and higher education. Anthony Crosland, Secretary of State for Education in 1965, believed that 'comprehensivisation' would break down class barriers in society. It would help pupils to mix socially, while offering greater opportunities to those who would have gone to secondary modern schools, a sharing of similar experiences within the community:

> A comprehensive school aims to establish a school community in which pupils over the whole ability range and with differing interests and backgrounds can be encouraged to mix with each other, gaining stimulus from the contacts and

> learning tolerance and understanding in the process ... The Secretary of State therefore urges authorities to ensure, when determining catchment areas, that schools are as socially and intellectually comprehensive as is practicable. (DES, 1965: para. 36)

The debate between selection and comprehensive schools is based on different understandings of the role of education. The 1944 Act had assumed that different types of schools with different curricula are needed to equip pupils according to their aptitudes. The comprehensive model was committed to education for tolerance and understanding in a shared community, not just about equipping young people with skills.

Circular 10/65 was sent to each local authority requesting proposals for comprehensive schools. It was only a request, and some Conservative local authorities chose to keep their tripartite systems. The continuation of selective grammar schools in some parts of England, along with the continued existence of independent schools, meant that full comprehensivisation never happened. But the 1968 Education Act continued the policy and, by 1970, 115 of the LEAs had had their reorganisation plans approved. Attitudes varied between those who saw it as equality of opportunity and those who believed the closure of grammar schools meant the 'levelling' of standards rather than raising them for all. Although there was an expectation that a Conservative government would undermine comprehensives when they returned to power in 1970, the system was sufficiently entrenched to prevent a wholesale dismantling. Comprehensive schools continued as local policy rather than under central direction.

Virulent attacks on the principles and philosophy of comprehensive education came from right-wing politicians and academics. The influential 'Black Papers' (Cox and Dyson, 1969; Pedley, 1969) argued that standards achieved in comprehensive schools were poor and that they were used to achieve social and political objectives at the expense of educating pupils. Margaret Thatcher, as Secretary of State for Education in 1970, removed the demand for comprehensivisation by withdrawing Circular 10/65, replacing it with Circular 10/70 which allowed each local authority to decide its own policy. The see-saw between central direction and local choice continued with the Labour government elected in 1974 reversing Conservative policy through Circular 4/74. It continued its commitment to comprehensives and the 1976 Education Act formally rejected the selection of pupils by ability, bringing an end to the tripartite system in name but not in reality. There are still over a 160 state-run grammar schools in England and any threat to their existence opens up a groundswell of support for them (Chitty, 2003). By the mid-1970s, the comprehensive system incorporated about 90 per cent of secondary education compared with around 20 per cent in 1968. Nearly all new schools were built as comprehensives and were the accepted pattern of secondary education for children in the state-maintained sector.

The removal of grammar schools led to an increase in the proportion of the age group attending independent schools and high-achieving pupils being 'creamed off' the state sector. This has now stabilised at around 7–8 per cent (Independent Schools Council, 2008), but recent data on the differences in educational achievement between the independent and state sectors show that the ideal comprehensive system never existed. In 2007 31,347 candidates from 476 independent schools took A levels. Of the 101,649 entries from these candidates:

- 99.4 per cent of all entries (101,020) received pass (A–E) grades compared to a national average 96.9 per cent;
- 50.0 per cent of entries (50,854) were awarded the top A grade compared to a national average 25.3 per cent;
- 76.1 per cent of entries (77,332) were graded A or B compared to a national average of 49.7 per cent. (ISC, 2008)

The type of neighbourhood and socially mixed comprehensive school envisaged by Crosland was never going to be easy to achieve. The system was manipulated by middle-class parents, even to the point of moving house to be within the catchment area of a particular school. Faith schools used their right to select pupils as a way of selecting middle-class parents and pupils (see Chapter 9). Adonis and Pollard (1997) suggest that the middle-class manipulation of the comprehensive system enabled them to hijack the best educational opportunities to a greater extent than would have been the case through a selection process. In other words, comprehensive schooling increased, rather than diminished, inequality.

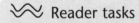 Reader tasks

- The old Labour vision for schooling was of a universal comprehensive system. Do you think that this could ever work?
- Are there any reasons for selecting pupils for different schools on the grounds of aptitude or ability?

1979 and The Rise of the Market

The Conservative governments from 1979 were concerned with standards and parental choice rather than social justice and equal opportunities, and Margaret Thatcher introduced market forces and competition to raise standards of educational achievement (see Chapter 2). Alongside the continued existence of the independent sector, new types of schools challenged the ideal of the neighbourhood comprehensive. The remodelling of the comprehensive system to include elements of selection began with the Conservatives' introduction of city technology colleges in 1986. These were reforms to what was viewed as a deficit model of comprehensive education by both Conservative and Labour governments. Many of the concerns expressed by the Conservative governments of the 1980s and 1990s were reinforced by the New Labour government from 1997 which considered that comprehensive education needed to be modernised:

> In education, we reject both the idea of a return to the 11-plus and the monolithic comprehensive schools that take no account of children's differing abilities. Instead we favour all-in schooling which identifies the distinct abilities of individual pupils and organises them in classes to maximise their progress in individual subjects. In this way we modernise the comprehensive principle, learning from the experience of its 30 years of application. (Labour Party Manifesto, 1997)

This approach takes up the theme of both Conservative and Labour governments' policies since the 1980s: a comprehensive system cannot provide one solution for all pupils. The argument reached its notorious limit when schools were described by the Prime Minister's Press Secretary, Alistair Campbell, as 'bog standard comprehensives'. Instead, diversity was needed to meet a variety of pupil needs and to fulfil the market-driven concept of parental choice. Ball (2003) refers to this as a loss of civic values and the consequences of individualising education and educational systems. The 1996 Education Act stated that pupils were to be educated in accordance with their parents' wishes:

> ... the Secretary of State, local education authorities and the funding authorities shall have regard to the general principle that pupils are to be educated in accordance with the wishes of their parents, so far as that is compatible with the provision of efficient instruction and training and the avoidance of unreasonable public expenditure. (DfES, 1996: para. 9)

The New Labour government of 1997 quickly published a White Paper entitled *Excellence in Schools* (DfES, 1997). It reinforced the Conservative assumption that parents needed data to choose schools. There had been concerns about this approach since the 1988 Act and there were various criticisms about the reliability of data and league tables (Plewis and Goldstein, 1998). But the Labour government had no intention of turning away from testing and league tables. In July 1998 the School Standards and Framework Act (DfES, 1998) claimed to be concerned with standards but in fact focused on the development of new categories of maintained schools and did not mention comprehensive education. It set out a number of new categories of schools: foundation schools, voluntary schools and community and foundation special schools. It gave parents the right to express a preference for a school except where it was a foundation school, voluntary aided or wholly selective. The Act legitimated further levels of selection and a diverse school system which gave foundation and voluntary schools control over their admissions.

The right to control aspects of admissions was further extended to specialist schools, introduced by the Conservative legislation in 1993. The 1998 Act had permitted specialist schools to admit up to 10 per cent of their pupils on aptitude. A further incentive was given to schools to apply for specialist status and they were offered £100,000 if it could be matched by private funding. It was clear at this stage that both the Prime Minister and the Secretary of State for Education were hoping for a radical extension to the specialist schools programme. The Beacon Schools programme was also established which was intended to identify high-performing schools across England with a view to sharing effective practice in other schools to raise standards. All these developments were based on assumptions that the appearance of being given higher status and being partially selective would increase the attractiveness of a school.

Tomlinson (2005: 103) comments that by January 2000 the drive towards a diverse educational system had led to 13 kinds of schooling: independent schools, grammar schools, church and faith schools, specialist schools, advanced specialist schools, city academies, city technology colleges, 'fresh start' schools, 'contract' schools, trust schools and some comprehensives and secondary moderns. Under the School Standards and Framework Act (DfES, 1998), grant-maintained schools, which had a degree of independence from the local authority, were abolished. They could choose to become foundation schools or to rejoin the local education authority as maintained community schools. Foundation schools did not continue to receive direct funding from central government as had been the case with grant-maintained schools, but school governors controlled admission, as in grant-maintained schools. In March 2000, (city) academies were added and were intended to replace seriously failing schools. They were to be funded by central government and managed by associated sponsors of voluntary, church or business organisations, with no LEA input (see Chapter 4). Underlying all these developments was a political belief that the secondary school system needed to be 'modernised'; informed parental choice was the mechanism to encourage good schools and force weak schools to improve. Diversity and choice in secondary education was to raise standards across the whole school system.

In 2005, after eight years in government, New Labour published a White Paper (DfES, 2005) which was one of the defining policies of its third term. It argued that education reforms needed to go further and to provide yet more power to parents in driving up standards. In his foreword Tony Blair asserts that business sponsors bring a new energy to schools: 'the drive that their business and educational sponsors bring to their development backed by their willingness to innovate and use their freedoms imaginatively' (DfES, 2005: 3). There is a commitment to more diversity in school governance and greater powers for individual schools. Every school would be able to acquire self-governing trust status; independent schools would be encouraged to enter the new system, and the role of academies was reinforced (see Chapter 4). The 2005 White Paper saw the future of education as individual schools having a much greater say in the way they are run, the power of local authorities would be diminished, new admission policies would widen access to successful schools and failing schools would close as successful ones grew. Every school would become a self-governing and independent state school, broadly on the model of city academies, and would work with business employers and the voluntary sector. This would be achieved, in part, through the dynamic of parental choice.

The White Paper was the final step in the Labour government's reforms since 1997. The paper did not argue for a return to an explicit system of selection, but the potential for schools to develop their own admission policies opened that door. The possibility of all schools becoming trusts would provide an enthusiasm and drive to develop specialisms, to employ teachers and to own assets. Also contained within the White Paper was the possibility that parents would have the powers to force their child's school to become independent. Continuous pressure from parents, as 'consumers' of education, would create a constant drive towards improvement. Popular schools would be encouraged to expand, so addressing the lack of places in good schools; companies would be allowed to take over schools if they adopted charitable status and local authorities would have a duty to encourage diversity. Private schools, including independent faith schools, would be entitled to become academies – self-governing state schools. It was a heady mix of reforms driven by parental power and the attractions of diversity and choice.

The 2005 White Paper reversed two decades of Labour policy on secondary education. The 11-plus had failed in the 1960s because it excluded most children from the best grammar schools. The 2005 White Paper substituted social selection by parents for that associated with the 11-plus so attacked by traditional Labour governments. The White Paper also continued the erosion of local government powers which the Conservative Acts of 1989 and 1993 had begun. The city technology colleges set up with private money were based on a view that schools were better free from the stifling hand of local education authorities.

The National Union of Teachers (NUT) had opposed the 2005 Education White Paper on the grounds that plans for choice and diversity would damage schools, and that the balance was shifting from parents choosing schools to schools choosing pupils. To counter this, the 2006 Act introduced a new school admissions code of practice with strict limits on schools' ability to select pupils. It brought tensions within government: the Education Secretary, Ruth Kelly, wanting to enhance social mobility, recognised the need for statutory procedures on admissions; others saw a binding code of admissions as interfering with the government's commitment to school autonomy. The 2006 Education and Inspections Act (DfES, 2006b) changed some of the 2005 White Paper proposals, reflecting values and assumptions that were once seen as representative of the Conservative rather than the Labour Party. Trust schools were a major addition to the Act. They were to be under the majority control of an external interest, whether a private company, religious sect or other institution. Trust schools have the right to own and control land and buildings that had belonged to the local council. They determine their own ethos, retain the right to determine their own admissions criteria within the Admissions Code and have the right to influence their curriculum. Members of governing bodies are appointed, not elected, and are not accountable to the local community the school serves. The Act also provided powers to form trusts made up of a number of schools with a single 'super head' as chief executive overseeing the other heads (DCFS, 2008a). There were major objections from traditional Labour supporters, MP Jon Tricket commenting:

> In place of the civilising values of co-operation, community cohesion and equity which prevail in the relationship between schools, now the market principles of competition, fragmentation, success and failure will be introduced. (Trickett, 2006: 7)

The Act attempted to counter opposition by attaching 'new safeguards' to trust status. They were required to ensure that they operate in the best interests of local children, contribute to raising standards at the school and promote community cohesion. Where a trust appoints the majority of governors, it must set up a parent council. Trust schools were to be inspected by Ofsted, like other publicly funded schools (DCSF, 2008a). The 2006 Act continued the move away from accountability to central government and local authorities, but at the same time gave local authorities a number of strategic functions, most significantly in matters of equality:

- a duty on local authorities in England to promote fair access to educational opportunity;
- a strengthened Code on School Admissions;
- a ban on selection by ability;
- a ban on admissions interviewing of parents or pupils;
- new powers for admissions forums;
- a duty on local authorities to provide free transport for disadvantaged families.

The 'fair access' section makes clear the intention to prohibit selection 'by stealth':

> The new Code will prohibit oversubscription criteria that seek to select by stealth (such as the use of supplementary application forms) and provide clear guidelines on uniform and transport policies that might undermine a fair admission system and disadvantage children from poorer families. (DfES, 2006a: 2).

Types of schools

By 2007 the English secondary education system was truly diverse:

- ... 62 per cent of secondary maintained mainstream schools, city technology colleges (CTCs) and academies were community schools, 16.6 per cent were foundation, 16.3 per cent were voluntary aided, 3.3 per cent were voluntary controlled, 1.4 per cent were academies and only 0.3 per cent were City Technology Colleges.
- ... 82.3 per cent of secondary maintained mainstream schools, CTCs and academies had no religious character, 10.1 per cent were Roman Catholic, 6.0 per cent were Church of England, 1.2 per cent were another Christian faith and the remainder were Jewish, Muslim or another faith.
- ... there were 176 secondary modern schools, 3,059 comprehensive schools and 164 grammar schools.

(DCSF, 2008b: 9)

Diversity has a price in terms of which pupils get access to which schools. Pupils eligible for free school meals (FSM), with special educational needs (SEN) or from minority ethnic groups are not distributed evenly among different types of school. The following snapshots from the government's own statistics (DCSF, 2008b) indicate:

- Pupils that attend an academy are more likely to be eligible for FSM, come from a minority ethnic background and speak English as an additional language, compared to pupils attending schools with other governance arrangements. They are also more likely to be classified as SEN and the KS2 prior attainment for pupils entering academies is lower compared to those entering other school types. Voluntary controlled schools have the lowest incidence of pupils with the above characteristics (p. 3).
- Looking at schools by their admissions arrangements, grammar schools have a lower than average incidence of pupils eligible for FSM and pupils classified as SEN (p. 4).
- Voluntary aided schools and CTCs had lower intakes of FSM pupils than their local areas (p. 90).
- Black African, Bangladeshi, Black Caribbean and Pakistani pupils were under-represented in grammar schools compared to local areas (p. 88).

(DCSF, 2008b)

Admissions

The 2005 White Paper led to considerable debate about admissions policy and, in the end, the 2006 Act (DfES, 2006b) determined that all maintained mainstream schools would be bound by the same School Admissions Code, SEN Code of Practice and exclusions guidance as all other state-funded schools. This still allowed schools that controlled their own intake to influence their admissions.

The majority of schools are community schools owned by local authorities which control their admissions. The majority of 'new' forms of school fall into the specialist schools category and have remained community schools.

Of the 3,385 state secondary schools in England in 2008 2,153 are in this category; they are able to select 10 per cent of their pupils on the basis of their specialism. Grammar schools select all of their pupils through the 11-plus exam; they are funded by local authorities, which control admissions. Secondary moderns take pupils not attending grammar schools and are funded by the local authorities, which control admissions. Foundation schools, which are mainly former grant-maintained schools, are funded by the local authority but owned by the governing body which controls admissions. Voluntary controlled schools are almost always church schools, and the lands and buildings are often owned by a charitable foundation. However, the local authority has primary responsibility for admission arrangements. In voluntary aided schools (many of which are church schools) the governing body decides on admission arrangements. Most aided schools are linked to either the Church of England or the Roman Catholic Church, but can be linked to a variety of organisations. Private and independent schools are registered fee-paying schools, with one-third of pupils receiving assistance, funded by pupils' fees with admissions under the control of the school.

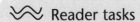

Reader tasks

- Do you agree with the idea of different types of schooling and parental choice?
- Is there a way of preventing middle-class parents from gaining additional advantages for their children through the school system?
- Do you agree that there is a role for independent schools?

The End of the Comprehensive System?

Policies since 1997 have undermined traditional comprehensives to the point where they are now a rare breed, and traditional Labour supporters have seen their version of comprehensive education destroyed in the name of diversity and choice. Chitty (2003) suggests four errors which led to the demise of the comprehensive system. The first was the attempt to sell the idea that comprehensives offered a grammar school education for all. He quotes Hargreaves (1982):

> The slogan was a sophisticated one for it capitalised on the contradictions in the public's mind: parents were in favour of the retention of the grammar schools and their public examinations, but opposed to the eleven-plus selective test as the basis of a 'once-for-all' allocation. If the new comprehensive schools could be seen by the public as 'grammar schools for all', then the contradictions could be solved. (p. 66)

This approach helped to get comprehensivisation accepted, but had negative consequences. The closure of grammar schools led to fears that standards associated with them would also be lost. Chitty's second point is that Crosland and others made unrealistic claims for greater social mobility, that working-class children would have new opportunities. Assumptions that social class differences could be challenged by pupils attending the same school left supporters open to the accusation that comprehensives were about social engineering rather than educational achievement. This was hardly surprising when the initial circular presented precisely that argument. Benn and Simon (1970: 64) argued that 'a comprehensive school is not a social experiment; it is an educational reform', a position also taken by Chitty who argues that 'what really matters is developing the right teaching strategies in order to enable every child in the school to be successful and fulfilled' (Chitty, 2003: 14).

The third mistake identified by Chitty relates to the curriculum. He suggests that there was a complete absence of a debate about the content of secondary schooling with no discussion about the curriculum and assessment process (see Chapter 5). The reports which followed the growth of comprehensives in the 1950s, 1960s and 1970s did not examine issues of pedagogy, selection and assessment, which meant that the majority of comprehensives 'simply attempted to assimilate the two existing curriculum traditions handed down from the grammar and secondary modern schools' (Chitty, 2003: 14). Lawton (1973: 10) laments 'the consistent failure to re-think the curriculum and plan a programme which would be appropriate for universal secondary education'. Finally, Chitty refers to the power of the media with opponents such as Cox and Dyson gaining their support. Their attacks on comprehensives and progressive education built on fears of the move away from grammar schools and the greater social interactions that characterise the comprehensive system.

Another advocate of the comprehensive system, Tim Brighouse (2003: 4), argues that the comprehensive ideal was 'to give equal value to all sorts of human potential and activity within certain moral limits and principles'. But the comprehensive movement drew together contradictory approaches to the curriculum and schooling. He suggests there was probably only basic agreement on the idea that selection at 11 was unreliable, that it contravened ideas of social justice and inhibited the aim of providing equal opportunity for all. In the urban conurbations which made up two-thirds of the educational system, the comprehensive school had effectively disappeared. He quotes Newsam's thesis that in London, and the other great conurbations, the comprehensive ideal has been an illusion – 'a cruel deception where all concerned have tended to collude in a game of the emperor's clothes' (Brighouse, 2002: 21). Such disappointments allowed claims for new systems and more diversity to dominate policy over the last thirty years.

Brighouse argues that within country and small market towns which cover only one-third of secondary children, it is possible to still see comprehensive provision. But in large conurbations, the hierarchal structure of a wide range of schools does not conform to any comprehensive pattern, and the model of comprehensives advocated by early pioneers is further away than it was in the initial stages of comprehensivisation. Chitty (2003) also worries that the present secondary diversity is far worse than the divided system of the postwar period and will ultimately lead to a substandard education for thousands of young people.

Conclusion

The New Labour government of 1997 was not going to undo policies of choice and diversity introduced by the Conservatives. Tony Blair and other New Labourites wanted to show a break with the past and traditional models of Labour. This meant not only that the Conservative changes remain in place, but that legislation over the next ten years reinforced diversity in the name of parental choice as the lever for raising standards. Differences in governance had been a characteristic of the school system before the recent Conservative and Labour legislation, but changes in the 2006 Act affected ownership of school property, the ability to control the hiring of staff and, in particular, the level of independence given to schools in admissions policy. Two policies in particular have had a major impact on the ideologies about control of state-funded education: specialist schools and academies. The next chapter looks at these in more detail to see how policy translates into practice.

Recommended reading

Brighouse, T. (2003) 'Comprehensive schools then, now and in the future: is it time to draw a line in the sand and create a new ideal?', *Forum*, 45 (1): 3–11.

Gorard, S. (1997) 'Market forces, choice and diversity in education: the early impact', *Sociological Research Online*, 2 (3). Online at: http://www.socresonline.org.uk/2/3/8.html (accessed 23 February 2009).

Heath, N. (2004) 'Comprehensive schooling: in need of definition?', *FORUM: for promoting 3–19 comprehensive education*, 46 (2): 73–6. Online at: http://dx.doi.org/10.2304/forum. 2004.46.2.8 (accessed 1 September 2008).

References

Adonis, A. and Pollard, S. (1997) *A Class Act: the Myth of Britain's Classless Society.* London: Hamish Hamilton.

Ball, S.J. (2003) *Class Strategies and the Education Market: The Middle Class and Social Disadvantage.* London: RoutledgeFalmer.

Batteson C.H. (1999) 'The 1944 Education Act reconsidered', *Educational Review*, 51 (1): 5–15.

Benn, C. (1992) *Keir Hardie.* London: Hutchinson.

Benn, C. and Simon, B. (1970) *Half Way There: Report on the British Comprehensive School Reform.* London: McGraw-Hill.

Brighouse, T. (2002) 'Collegiates are the future', *Times Educational Supplement*, 4 October, p. 6.

Brighouse, T. (2003) 'Comprehensive schools then, now and in the future: is it time to draw a line in the sand and create a new ideal?', *Forum*, 45 (1): 3–11.

Chitty, C. (2003) 'The Right to a Comprehensive Education', Caroline Benn Memorial Lecture 2002, revised and reprinted in *Forum*, (2003) 45 (1): 12–16.

Cox, C.B. and Dyson, A.E. (eds) (1969) *Fight for Education: A Black Paper.* London: Critical Quarterly Society.

DCSF (2008a) *What Are Trust Schools?* London: DfES. Online at: http://www.standards. dfes.gov.uk/sie/si/eips/trusts/ (accessed 15 August 2008).

DCSF (2008b) *Composition of Schools in England.* London: DfES. Online at: http://www. dcsf.gov.uk/rsgateway/DB/SBU/b000796/index.shtml (accessed 15 August 2008).

DES (1965) *The Organisation of Secondary Education*, Circular 10/65. London: DES.

DfES (1996) *Education Act.* London: DfES. Online at: http://www.opsi.gov.uk/acts/acts1996/ ukpga_19960056_en_1 (accessed 11 September 2008).

DfES (1997) *Excellence in Schools: A White Paper.* London: DfES.

DfES (1998) *School Standards and Framework Act 1998.* London: DfES. Online at: http:// www.opsi.gov.uk/Acts/acts1998/ukpga_19980031_en_1 (accessed 18 September 2008).

DfES (2002) *14–19: Extending Opportunities, Raising Standards* (Consultation Document), Cmnd 5342. London: HMSO.

DfES (2005) *Higher Standards, Better Schools for All – More Choice for Parents and Pupils – A White Paper.* London: DfES. Online at: http://www.dcsf.gov.uk/publications/schoolswhitepaper/ (accessed 18 September 2008).

DfES (2006a) *A Short Guide to the Education and Inspections Act.* London: DfES. Online at: http://www.dcsf.gov.uk/educationandinspectionsact/docs/Guide%20to%20the%20Education% 20and%20Inspections%20Act.pdf (accessed 23 February 2009).

DfES (2006b) *Education and Inspections Act.* London: DfES. Online at: http://www. opsi.gov.uk/acts/acts2006/pdf/ukpga_20060040_en.pdf (Accessed 1 August 2008).

Douglas, J.W.B. (1964) *The Home and the School.* London: MacGibbon & Kee.

Floud, J., Halsey, A.H. and Martin, F.M. (1956) *Social Class and Educational Opportunity.* London: Heinemann.

Glass, D.V. (1959) 'Education and social change in modern England', in A.H. Halsey, J. Floud and C. Arnold Anderson (eds) (1961) *Education Economy and Society.* London: Collier-Macmillan, pp. 391–413.

Halsey, A.H. (1965) 'Education and equality', *New Society*, 17 June, pp. 13–15.

Hargreaves, D.H. (1982) *The Challenge for the Comprehensive School: Culture, Curriculum and Community.* London: Routledge & Kegan Paul.

Heath, N. (2004) 'Comprehensive schooling: in need of definition?', *FORUM: for promoting 3–19 comprehensive education*, 46 (2): 73–6. Online at: http://dx.doi.org/10.2304/ forum.2004.46.2.8 (accessed 10 September 2008).

ISC (2008) *Pupil Numbers.* London: Independent Schools Council. Online at: http://www.isc. co.uk/FactsFigures_PupilNumbers.htm (accessed 31 July 2008).

Labour Party (1997) *Labour Manifesto.* London: Labour Party. Online at: http://www.labour-party.org.uk/manifestos/1997/1997-labour-manifesto.shtml (accessed 2 March 2009).

Lawton, D. (1973) *Social Change, Educational Theory and Curriculum Planning.* Sevenoaks: Hodder & Stoughton.

Ministry of Education (1959) *15 to 18.* London: HMSO.

Newsam, P. (2008) 'Education Act 1944', *Microsoft® Encarta® Online Encyclopaedia.* Online at: http://uk.encarta.msn.com/encyclopedia_121503282/education_act_1944.html (accessed 18 August 2008).

Newsom, J. (1963) *Half Our Future: A Report of the Central Advisory Council for Education (England).* London: HMSO.

Pedley, R.R. (1969) 'Comprehensive disaster', in C.B. Cox and A.E. Dyson (eds), *Fight for Education: A Black Paper*. London: Critical Quarterly Society, pp. 45–8.

Plewis, I. and Goldstein, H. (1998) 'Excellence in Schools: a failure of standards', *British Journal of Curriculum and Assessment*, 8: 17–20.

Silver, H. (ed.) (1973) *Equal Opportunity in Education*. London: Methuen.

Tomlinson, S. (2005) *Education in a Post-Welfare Society* 2nd edn. Buckingham: Open University.

Trickett, J. (2006) 'Make up your mind about education', *The Guardian*, 15 March, p. 3.

Specialist schools and academies

Introduction

Two controversial New Labour initiatives were the development of specialist schools and the introduction of academies. Both were based on the belief that non-education sponsors – businesses and charity groups – add value to schools by bringing new energy, enthusiasm and resources into the education system. This chapter discusses two possibilities:

1. Specialist schools and academies have undermined comprehensive principles and created a divided and hierarchal secondary education system.
2. They have been successful in tackling educational disadvantage and under-achievement.

Specialist Schools

Specialist secondary schools developed from the Conservative government's city technology colleges (CTCs) which began in 1994. Labour built on the approach making models of sponsorship a part of their plan to raise standards in secondary education. The specialist school programme was based on the assumption that business involvement in education would have a positive effect by bringing the entrepreneurial skills and approaches which have been effective in business, as well as providing additional resources and support to enhance standards. Schools would undergo a change in culture and ethos and the benefits were to be sufficiently powerful for ministers to argue that specialist status should be available to the majority of schools. It was intended that by 2008 all eligible schools should become specialist to play a role in revitalising education in areas of socio-economic disadvantage (DCSF, 2008a).

The plan succeeded: in 2001 there were 700 specialist schools and by 2008 there were 2,695, representing 85 per cent of all secondary schools. Subject specialisms were spread across the curriculum, and some schools had a second.

Initially all schools applying for specialist status were required to raise £100,000 in sponsorship from businesses, charities or other private sponsors. This was reduced to £50,000 in 1999 and it became possible for a school to make a case on the grounds of its particular circumstances that £20,000 was sufficient. The introduction in 2002 of the Partnership Fund helped schools which found it difficult to gain sponsorship. The additional funding was a reason for applying for specialist status, and research shows that it is not just used to support the specialist area but is diverted to other departments (Gorard and Taylor, 2001). West et al. (2000) found that a third of head teachers reported that specialist funding had released existing funds to support non-specialist subjects and 10 per cent reported that specialist funding was supporting whole-school initiatives. In this respect, there are clear advantages to specialist status and disadvantages to not having it (West et al., cited in Castle and Evans, 2005).

Initial concerns were that giving more to some schools would penalise those which did not meet the eligibility criteria; these were the schools with serious weaknesses or in special measures and in most need of additional resources and support. Various changes to the eligibility criteria still left vulnerable schools unable to access the additional resources that came with specialist status. In June 2008 schools that were at risk of falling below a 30 per cent target for students achieving five good GCSEs were told they could be stripped of their specialist school status and the funding that goes with it. The 638 schools were placed on an 'at risk' register called 'the National Challenge' list. Schools were to get tailored support to rise above the 30 per cent target, but were told that they would be closed and replaced with an academy within the year if they did not make substantial progress by the following December. Curtis (2008a) reported that schools suffered a collapse in applications after being put on the register (see p. 57).

One of the concerns about this differentiation of schools was whether specialist schools would become more selective and increase social segregation. As schools were required to raise sponsorship there were fears that specialist schools would be easier to develop in areas with middle-class parents, and there is evidence that diversity and choice strategies are doing just this. Taylor et al. (2005) have demonstrated that, on average, 29 per cent of schools in England had attracted a more socially privileged intake between 1999/2000 compared to 1994/5. The shift was most marked in grammar schools, comprehensive schools with sixth forms and, among specialist schools, language colleges and foundation and voluntary aided (VA) schools. While there was provision within the Schools Standards and Framework Act of 1998 for specialist schools to select up to 10 per cent of their pupils in their relevant specialism, this was not widely taken up.

Research into the performance of specialist schools presents conflicting findings. Ofsted's evaluation of specialist schools in 2005 showed that they do well against a range of indicators:

> Being a specialist school makes a difference. Working to declared targets, dynamic leadership by key players, a renewed sense of purpose, the willingness to be a pathfinder, targeted use of funding and being part of an optimistic network of like-minded schools all contribute to an impetus and climate for improvement.
> (Ofsted, 2005: 3)

However, Glatter (2004) found no evidence to support the positive summary given by Ofsted. The explanation for their superior performance lay in the additional resources they received and the type of schools able to apply for specialist status. Jesson's (2001, 2003) work, though, supports the Ofsted judgement. In reports produced for the Specialist Schools Trust, he found that specialist schools produce superior examination results. His data have been challenged, particularly in the causal connection between school type and superior performance: variables not included in his analysis such as the nature of schools selected to become specialist could have been responsible for differential performance. The debate is not so much to do with the actual performance of pupils in specialist schools; the evidence from research is reasonably consistent in finding that pupils at specialist schools do slightly better at KS3 and GCSEs than pupils with similar characteristics at non-specialist schools. The issue is whether performance is affected by the specialist school status. Castle and Evans (2006) argue that 'there is no proven causal link between the improved performance of these schools and their specialist status' (p. 28). League tables indicating that specialist schools have improved their grades faster than traditional comprehensives may be the product of the increased funding that specialist schools receive, rather than curriculum specialisation. In February 2007 a *Times Educational Supplement* analysis found there were more underperforming schools inside the specialist schools movement than outside it (Stewart, 2007a).

The debate about specialist schools highlights fundamental differences in approaches to raising standards and achieving the best opportunities for all pupils. Critics of the specialist school system argue that diversity and competition have had more negative consequences than positive (Gorard and Taylor, 2001; Taylor et al., 2005). The choice between a range of specialist schools can actually result in less choice for pupils from disadvantaged backgrounds with limited mobility. School differences become inequalities of status. The Ofsted (2005) evaluation found that, compared to other schools, specialist schools do well against a range of indicators, including leadership and management, quality of teaching and improving standards. However, they also found that the rate of improvement in pupils' performance in the specialist subjects was levelling off. There is evidence that new specialist subjects or courses were introduced in the great majority of specialist schools and that specialist subject entries at GCSE were higher per pupil in each type of specialist school than for all schools, suggesting an extension of the range of opportunities for pupils attending specialist schools. The government provided a strong defence of the policy and signalled its determination to extend specialist status to all schools that qualify (DCSF, 2008a).

Specialist schools worked in collaboration with less successful schools to boost their performance (DfES, 2005a, 2005b). From 2004, schools were able to apply for additional funding as High Performing Specialist Schools

(HPSS) and in 2005 the Training School Programme was incorporated into the HPSS programme. The assumption behind the development of HPS schools was that they would have the capacity to lead others and should form collaborative networks with the wider community which could include local authorities and other relevant agencies to share and disseminate good practice. An evaluation of the HPS schools found effective collaboration with partner primary schools, but that partnerships with local secondary schools, the wider community and local businesses was less well developed (PricewaterhouseCoopers, 2008), suggesting that the transfer of expertise across the secondary sector is problematic. The government introduced other initiatives aimed at reducing the divisive effect of specialist schools through:

- supporting schools which found it difficult to gain sponsorship;
- identifying aspects of community work as a form of specialism;
- emphasising the collaborative aspects of the specialist schools mission;
- establishing measures to support choice for less affluent parents through financial help with travel costs to a school of their choice.

The aim for every secondary school to become a specialist school appeared to address issues of disparity of resources and the impact of specialisms on choice. But the move by the Schools Minister in 2008 to increase the competitive element by linking targets at GCSE to specialist school status reinforced the divisiveness of the system and reinforced the hierarchy of schools.

Reader tasks

- Do you agree with the policy of creating specialist schools? What is the evidence that they have improved pupils' education?
- Do specialist schools help pupils from disadvantaged backgrounds?
- Make a list of the characteristics of schools that are likely not to be granted specialist school status and consider the implications of this for school admissions and resources.
- Interview your fellow students to see the impact of attending specialist schools and whether they perceive there to be any advantages associated with specialist school status.
- In what way do specialist schools contribute to providing a diversity of choices for parents and is this of equal value for all children?

Academies

From 1997 onwards a current of opinion within New Labour wanted to provide alternatives to traditional comprehensive schools, particularly Tony Blair's education adviser and Schools Minister, Andrew Adonis:

> the comprehensive school revolution ... destroyed many excellent schools without improving the rest ... The demise of grammar schools was carried out in the name of equality but ... served to reinforce class divisions. (Macleod, 2007: 8)

The drive towards more choice and parental involvement led to new forms of educational provision. Academies emerged as a new way to provide routes to educational success and to break existing patterns of deprivation and underachievement. Designed to replace failing comprehensive schools in urban areas, they were to be state-funded independent schools owned by private sponsors. In March 2000, Secretary of State David Blunkett said: 'We will use the full range of fixed distinct legislative powers to enable new promoters to take over or replace weak and failing schools with the new academies'. Five years later the Prime Minister, Tony Blair, confirmed his belief in their role: 'Academies are helping to overcome the effects of generational disadvantage and years of failure' (Mansell and Luck, 2005: 4). Such claims were often disputed on the grounds that many of the schools which had been closed and replaced by academies were not actually failing at the time of closure. At the point when the government initially set a target of 200 academies to be open by 2010, there was little research to demonstrate their benefits, in particular the value of private sponsorship, but this did not dent the commitment to the initiative. The commitment to academies was an interesting case of government policy being derived from pure political vision rather than empirical evidence.

The academies initiative was launched by the Labour government towards the end of its first term in March 2000. Like specialist schools, they are a development of the Conservatives' city technology colleges: state funded but privately sponsored independent secondary schools operating outside many of the normal regulations for state schools and outside local authority control. This continued Thatcher's attack on the slow, cautious bureaucracy of local authorities. It was part of New Labour's long-term strategy:

> The Department's Five Year Strategy, published in 2003, committed the Government to having 200 Academies open or in the pipeline by 2010, with 60 in London. The Government is committed to establishing 400 academies and regards the scaling up of the programme as a national imperative, supported by the growing body of evidence that Academies are working. There are currently 83 academies open in 49 local authorities, with a further 50 to open in each of the next 3 years. As a result, we expect to exceed the 2010 target of 200 Academies either open or in the pipeline. (DCSF, 2008b)

Each is registered as a charitable company, funded by central government. Their admissions are agreed with the Secretary of State as a condition of the funding agreement, to be consistent with the Code of Practice on School Admissions and with admissions law. All academies are bound by the same SEN Code of Practice and exclusions guidance as other state-funded schools. New academies are also required to follow the National Curriculum programmes of study in English, Mathematics, Science and ICT. Academies, like the majority of secondary schools, have specialist school status, with a specialism in one or more subjects. They are not bound by national teachers' pay or conditions of service but are subject to Ofsted inspections.

In many ways academies are an exciting approach to challenging deprivation and underachievement. The assumption was that significant resources should be used to develop a new approach to underachievement, including the replacement of existing schools. The combination of new schools and sponsors would bring in expertise and new approaches would provide a more exciting environment for children, engaging them in a way that was new and radical. Instead of local authority influence, they would draw in new partners from the world of business to challenge deprivation and underachievement. However, from their inception there was a barrage of concerns about the legitimacy of external groups in state-funded education. This was pushed further with the government's requests to leading private schools to contribute more to the state sector. A few independent schools formalised relationships with local academies and could apply to the government through the one million a year funding scheme which has been provided to encourage independent/state schools partnerships support projects, including exchanging trainee teachers and classroom materials. There was a prospectus to encourage independent schools to sponsor academies, although without needing to provide funding: 'We want successful independent schools to sponsor academies for their educational expertise and commitment, not their bank balances' (DCSF, 2007: 7).

Academies got off to a slow start, with only three opening in September 2002, but soon became a flagship in Tony Blair's drive to introduce choice into public services (see Chapter 2). The issue which caused most controversy was the degree of influence sponsors could have in return for only a small percentage of the £23 million building costs, and none of the running costs (NAO, 2007). Sponsors were initially required to pay 20 per cent of the school's capital costs, but that changed to £2 m, or less than 5 per cent. The remaining capital costs are met by the taxpayer, along with subsequent running costs. To date few sponsors have handed over the full amount, but the financial contribution was always seen as part of a wider package. The DCSF comments on sponsors: 'All of them bring a record of success in other enterprises which they are able to apply to their academies in partnership with experienced school managers' (DCSF, 2008c).

Sponsors appoint the majority of an academy's governing body, which appoints its senior management. The private sector, or charitable sponsor, always appoints the majority of governors, even when a local authority is co-sponsor. It is not surprising that concerns were expressed at the degree of control associated with sponsors who, having donated only a few hundred thousand pounds, were able to spend tens of millions of pounds of taxpayers' money. The opportunity to sponsor academies has been taken up by Christian charities who, at the beginning of 2006, announced a major expansion after winning support from the car manufacturer Honda and the mobile phone company Vodaphone. The United Learning Trust, an Anglican charity, will have a portfolio of 12 open or proposed academies, establishing it as the biggest single supporter of the academy system. In April 2006, 36 out of a hundred academies either already opened or in development were backed by Christian organisations (Paton, 2006).

The government's own description of the academy scheme stresses the aim of tackling disadvantaged areas and pupils:

> The Government sees Academies as engines of social mobility and social justice, and there is a growing body of evidence that they are working. As Academies are established in disadvantaged areas where generations of pupils have been denied access to a first-class education, they are the key element in the drive to raise standards; raising aspirations and creating opportunity in some of the most disadvantaged communities in the country. (DCFS, 2008d)

The same enthusiasm can be seen in the words of Sir Cyril Taylor, chair of the Specialist Schools and Academies Trust, who, three years after their inception, was claiming:

> The academies programme is intended to transform schools in areas of high social disadvantage, which historically have had a weak educational performance. Far from being economically unsound, the academy programme will prove to be a wise use of the nation's resources, producing untold social benefits as well savings to the taxpayer. (Taylor, 2005: 21)

Academies bring into sharp focus many of the issues about equality discussed in Chapter 3, and raise questions about how education policy can be used to address issues of social and educational deprivation. The intractable nature of these problems led to a belief that new ways to organise and manage education were needed. Academies were radical in the degree of innovation associated with them. They were predicated on the idea that organisations outside the education sector would bring something new and exciting which could transform schools. They were to be set up in areas of particular deprivation and to be financed better than average schools. The commitment to provide additional resources for such schools would have probably drawn support across the political spectrum. However, accusations of the abrogation of rights and responsibilities to non-educational private sponsors and the disassociation from local authorities have made academies deeply contentious.

Academies, Standards and Achievement – The Evidence

A key issue for the academies policy is the extent to which the investment in new buildings, new forms of management, new governance and sponsorship promote higher levels of achievement in areas of deprivation. In March 2006 league tables showed that seven academies were among the worst schools in the country. Of the 13 privately sponsored academies that had been open long enough to be included, seven appeared in a table of the bottom 200 state schools for Key Stage 3 (Ross and Paton, 2006). But evaluations of the performance of the academies have shown that it is still early to comment on their potential to raise educational standards. A National Audit Office report (NAO, 2007) pointed out that all academy students entered for GCSEs had previously attended another secondary school, and it was difficult to claim that results were due to the academy. Nevertheless, they pointed to some signs of success from academies at GCSE level:

- GCSE performance in Academies has improved compared with predecessor schools;
- GCSE performance in Academies in 2006 was broadly similar to that in comparable schools;
- GCSE performance is improving faster in Academies than in other types of school, including those in similar circumstances, and the gap between the best and worst performance of individual academies has narrowed;
- taking account of both pupils' personal circumstances and prior attainment, GCSE performance in academies is substantially better, on average, than other schools.

(NAO, 2007: para.8)

The same report also notes that A-level results were well below national average, but that this is due to academies lacking sixth forms in their early years.

The government commissioned an evaluation of the academies programme from its inception. The fourth report by PricewaterhouseCoopers (2007) stresses that the diversity and complexity of pupil profiles in academies and the length of time that they had been open made it difficult to make general statements that applied across the board. The prior attainment of pupils entering academies is among the weakest and is nationally recognised as one of the difficulties facing such schools. One of the issues is that the proportion of pupils eligible for free school meals has changed over the life of an academy. Although intended for pupils in deprived communities, the report indicates that, in eight of the 12 academies opened in 2002 or 2003, the proportion of pupils eligible for FSM declined: one had moved from 51 per cent of pupils eligible for FSM to 12 per cent, indicating that academies were attracting pupils from less deprived circumstances. Of the academies that opened in 2004 there was an *increase* in the proportion eligible for FSM, indicating diversity of intake among academies (PWC, 2007: 8). The report also included evidence that academies excluded disproportionately high numbers of pupils, raising fears that they were transferring difficult pupils to neighboring schools.

PWC's overall conclusion is 'progress in terms of pupil achievement has generally exceeded corresponding improvements at a national level and amongst other similar schools' (para. 9). The report also shows that policy on academies was not static and that a number of changes had occurred. One was a change in relationships with local authorities. There was an increase in academies developing partnerships with local communities and schools, which raised questions about the extent to which academies will remain independent. The PWC report also explores the experiences of pupils from black and minority ethnic (BME) backgrounds. It finds a proportionately greater increase in the percentage of pupils from BME backgrounds in academies compared to other schools. Again, though, there is variance, and the percentage of white pupils in individual academies ranged from 18 per cent to 97 per cent (para. 3.7). Academies were also admitting a higher proportion of pupils of BME origin from outside the local postcode districts (para. 3.8). In terms of the educational opportunities for pupils from deprived backgrounds, academies had a significantly higher proportion of pupils eligible for FSM, having English as an additional language and with special educational needs. The overall conclusion is that 'on average performance from 2000 to 2006 was considerably better than that of similar schools' (para. 4.12). However, the gap between the worst performing and the best performing academies was large, and in some the overall trend in performance was down. The variance in performance suggests that the development of an academy does not in itself improve poor educational performance.

The PWC evaluation suggests that sponsors' involvement is a positive element and that additional expertise and resources from the wider business community are brought to the schools. They also point to the issues of co-sponsorship from local authorities. NFER research found that:

- Academies appeared to be situated in areas where the community populations included higher proportions of children eligible for free school meals (FSM); with special educational needs (SEN); of black or ethnic minority origin; and of lower Key Stage 2 (KS2) ability.
- Academies admit higher proportions of pupils eligible for FSM than the proportion living in the local postcode districts.
- Academies admit higher proportions of pupils with SEN compared to the proportions living in the local postcode districts.
- Academies admit a lower proportion of pupils of higher KS2 ability compared to the proportion living within the local postcode districts.

(Chamberlain et al., 2006)

The PWC (2007) report found that '*all Academies are proactively focussed* on raising pupils' aspirations as a key driver to improvement' (original emphasis). It also found that:

The general picture in relation to pupil performance in Academies is one of overall improvement against a range of indicators at Key Stage 3, Key Stage 4 and post-16 levels. Furthermore, academies' progress in terms of pupil achievement has generally exceeded corresponding improvements at a national level and amongst similar schools. (para. 9)

By 2007, for the 36 academies with underperforming predecessor schools (not including former city technology colleges) the proportion of pupils gaining five or more GCSEs at A*–C had almost doubled, from 22 per cent in 2001 to 43.7 per cent in 2007. For the 20 academies with results in both 2006 and 2007 the percentage achieving five or more GCSEs at A*–C increased by 8.1 percentage points, which is more than three times the increase of 2.6 percentage points seen nationally in state-funded schools. Including English and Mathematics, academies have increased the percentage achieving five or more A*–C GCSEs by 5.1 percentage points – two and a half times greater than the increase of 1.8 percentage points seen nationally.

Comparing academy results in 2007 (37 academies) with those of predecessor schools in 2001, academies had improved their KS3 performance at twice the national average in English, Mathematics and Science. The proportion of pupils achieving level 5 increased:

- in English by 22 percentage points (37.9 per cent to 59.9 per cent);
- in Mathematics by 18.9 percentage points (from 40.1 per cent to 59 per cent);
- in Science by 15.1 percentage points (36.7 per cent to 51.8 per cent).

(DCSF, 2008e)

The strength of the government's commitment to its academy programme was made dramatically clear in May 2008 when it announced the strategy to improve results through the National Challenge programme. The 638 schools not currently achieving the required level were told that they would be replaced with an academy if they did not meet this target. National Challenge schools were to receive extra funding to help them improve. Extra resources were welcomed by the profession, but there were concerns about the impact of the marketised competitive model. A head of a successful school commented:

> My biggest criticism would be their obsession with individual schools and in a competitive model, because all of our experience shows that if you selectively improve some schools what you do is to move the more difficult students around, but you don't address the underlying issues. If you are serious about having real improvement across the board then you need to recognize that schools function in an ecological way. (Addley, 2008)

The impact on schools of being designated as failing had implications for applications to the schools and was associated with the threat that they could be stripped of their specialist school status and the funding that went with it. John Dunford, General Secretary of the Association of School and College Leaders, was quoted:

> People are mystified. It makes it very much easier for selective schools, which don't face the problems those in the National Challenge face, to get specialist status and extra funding. It is a new unfairness, added to the wider unfairness of the 30 per cent floor target in the National Challenge. (Curtis, 2008a).

〰 Reader tasks

- What are the arguments for the view that academies can improve the education of pupils in deprived socio-economic areas?
- Sponsorship of academies gives religious organisations, such as the United Learning Trust, the opportunity to influence pupils' education. Do you agree with this?

Critique of Academies

A number of assumptions lie behind the academies initiative. The first is the belief that organisations outside the field of education bring additional skills and expertise to the educational process and help to raise standards. Independence from local authorities and the community of local authority schools was seen as another means of raising standards. However, because of the degree of the government's ideological commitment to the scheme, the academy model proceeded at a pace which did not allow for the lessons from the initial evaluations to be acted upon. Opponents see academies fragmenting local community networks of education, increasing competition between schools and absorbing unfair amounts of public funding. They raise critical questions about who controls education and whether schools should receive differential funding.

Questions have been raised in the media about the way sponsors have used their position. In 2007 an investigation by the *Times Educational Supplement* (*TES*) revealed that an academy awarded a contract involving £20 m of public money to a company owned by its sponsor without offering it to other bidders. The *TES* claimed that this was the second time that Vardy academies had paid organisations or individuals with connections to Sir Peter Vardy for work that had not been put out to tender (Stewart, 2007b). A number of newspapers also commented on the initial outlay from sponsors being effectively returned to them through various business deals and the provision of services to the academies.

Critics argue that any success academies have achieved is due to massive public investment, not the involvement of private sponsors. The strength of opposition is indicated by the existence of the Anti-Academies Alliance whose honorary president has a website expressing very strong opposition to academies (Purchase, 2008). Concern has also been expressed that Academies do not have to comply with teachers' pay and conditions of service and are allowed to pay lower salaries. That worry does not apply to their heads: in 2007 figures obtained from Companies House revealed that academies were paying significantly more than the top level of the school leadership pay scale: the average salary of an academy head during 2005–6 was over £105,000 compared with the average of £69,525 for a typical secondary head (Abrams, 2007a).

It has also been suggested that the financial cost both to taxpayers and to sponsors is problematic. A report from *New Philanthropy Capital* which advises donors to charities suggested that they would be better spending the £2 m of academy sponsorship on other educational projects and that academies are a high risk investment for wealthy donors (Ross, 2006). One of the most powerful criticisms of academies is the £8 m difference between the cost of building an academy and the cost of building a conventional school (Ross, 2006). The National Audit Office (NAO, 2007) does not suggest such a wide cost differential, although it does recognise that academies are more expensive. Another concern has been whether the stakeholders – staff, students and parents – actually want an academy. Frequently only a small proportion are involved in voting. A parent commented, 'one of the biggest problems is that the funding agreement between council and sponsor is in essence secret because the sponsor has so much control' (Benn, 2007).

Opinions about academies are often polarised. Academies were presented by the Labour government as a model for a different type of education system: a vision of education in partnership with external sponsors. The injection of resources and the rebranding of the schools were intended to provide a new start in areas of deprivation and to be an incentive for middle-class parents to send their children to these schools. The culture of schools would change, raising standards and opening opportunities for working-class pupils. In particular, partnerships with high-status public schools, such as Marlborough College, would attract middle-class parents. Such a model of change has less to do with the teaching and learning opportunities than with changing the way in which schools are perceived. The solution to demoralised schools in areas of deprivation was seen to be a brand-new building and new management. The government view was that:

> Sponsors challenge traditional thinking on how schools are run and what they should be like for students. They seek to make a complete break with cultures of low aspiration which afflict too many communities and their schools. We want this to happen, which is why we entrust the governance of academies to them. (DCSF, 2008c)

Academies were another attempt at restructuring secondary schools in England with the explicit intention of addressing low educational achievement and disadvantage. Previous attempts ranging from grammar schools to city technology colleges, grant-maintained schools and even specialist schools have mainly benefited the middle classes, not the urban poor. There is, as always, a fear that academies will be taken over by the already advantaged and educated parents who know how to make choices for their children and are tempted by new buildings and a different model of governance. Academies are an ambitious attempt by the government to create a new type of education opportunity which could either drive up standards, as the government has argued, or help develop a two-tier system dividing pupils by social class.

Recent additions to the network of academies appear to share the ethos of the early CTCs in specialising in business, enterprise and other vocational specialisms. But policy towards the development of academies is itself constantly changing with attempts at greater local community collaboration and universities as sponsors. In February 2008 the Higher Education Minister, Bill Rammell, argued that universities should be put at the heart of plans to expand academies, urging every university in the country to pair up with a struggling school under the academies scheme. He argued that the need to address widening participation in higher education needed stronger links between schools, colleges and universities: 'For Universities, direct engagement with secondary education is the natural next step in widening participation' (quoted in Curtis, 2008b). By the end of 2007, 21 universities had started sponsoring academies. In September

2007 Lord Adonis, the Schools Minister, announced a string of private schools as sponsors of academies. This was seen as an attempt by New Labour to move away from a picture of academies striking up partnerships with any organisation able to 'put up the money', with its implications of a cavalier approach to pupils' education.

Fundamental issues remain. Academies remain independent from the local authority and the wider educational community. External sponsors remain outside the democratic process and are not accountable to the community. Such concerns have not, though, affected parents' views. Attractive buildings and resources have made the new schools oversubscribed before they have opened. But the Headspace surveys have shown head teachers overwhelmingly opposed to the expansion of the academy programme (Crace, 2006). This opposition has remained constant throughout all five surveys, rooted in concerns about the impact on other local schools and the inequitable distribution of resources.

It is not surprising that the development of academies has been contentious. The *TES* regularly reported on conflicts such as the attempts by Sir Peter Vardy to develop three academies in Sunderland and the opposition from Sunderland Council which had its own plans to sponsor three academies. This led to a model of shared sponsorship between business interests and Sunderland Council, which ensured that the council retained some control over the schools. It meant that Sunderland academies had the same admission codes as other local authority schools and were part of the same admissions process. There are also issues about unequal funding. Abrams (2007b) reported that academies received almost the same income per pupil as leading independent day schools. Academies were receiving state funding of just over £9,000 per pupil, but the DfES argued that recurrent grants were paid on the same basis as their state neighbours. It denied the academies were more generously funded and said that accounts were not comparable because of differences between the funding across the academic year for academies, while other schools cover the financial year. Academies also received start-up funding and a wide range of discretionary grants. The annual revenue funding also included an element to cover services provided to other schools by local authorities, money for the cost of school meals and start-up grants.

The debate about academies has in part been fuelled by claims about the extent to which they are value for money. Opponents could see from the National Audit Office report (NAO, 2007) that they cost more than other schools, overran their budgets by an average of £3 million and were not collaborating with neighbouring secondary schools. However, the same report showed that academies were improving the standards of education and raising the achievements of pupils from deprived backgrounds. The report also recognised the need to get good value for money from the large capital investments made in academies, and argued that they are on course to deliver value for money, despite problems of low standards in English and Mathematics and that permanent exclusion rates were nearly four times higher than the national average.

Conclusion – Trust Schools

> Academies have polarised opinion: for some they are a chance to turn schools that are serving areas of deprivation into a new and exciting initiative which would change the whole culture of the school and pupils' aspirations. For others they exacerbate a tiered schools system where issues of exclusion and a not-yet-proven relationship between academies and school improvement are major concerns. Many critics of the academy programme share the belief in the need to address poor educational achievement and areas of deprivation but argue that academies should be returned to the maintained sector and made accountable to the communities they serve. This is a major point of difference. For those who believed in comprehensive education it has become difficult to see Labour engaged in anything but its destruction and the introduction of a selective system with tiers of education.

There is hope for those who care about local accountability in the development of trust schools (DSCF, 2008e). Unlike academies, trust schools remain part of the local education authority and are funded like other maintained schools; they follow the National Curriculum and are inspected by Ofsted. They emphasise collaboration with a range of other partners such as schools, universities, businesses and the wider community. This has led both Labour and Conservative politicians to talk in glowing terms about the development of cooperative trust schools which would be owned and controlled by the local community. The model assumes that the collaborative ethos means work with local organisations to engage parents and to give a voice to pupils. Sponsors are partners involved in a formal working relationship over time. In September 2008 the Schools Minister proposed that a hundred schools in the coming two years would become cooperative trust schools owned and controlled by the local community. He talked of wanting to see 'this model rolled out across the country, cultivating cooperative schools and the democratic, innovative opportunity they represent' (quoted in Wintour, 2008). This leaves concerns about state-owned schools entering into such arrangements with the private sector and their contribution to the imbalance in educational provision, but acts as a counter to the loss of local authority influence associated with academies. Nevertheless trusts are another form of branding within the secondary system and may well become another rung in the hierarchy of schools.

〰 Reader tasks

- What factors appear to have been significant in developing academies and the model of sponsorship associated with them?
- What do you see as the advantages and disadvantages of the academy model for pupils in an area of high deprivation and low educational achievement?
- What impact could the development of academies have on other schools?

Recommended reading

Castle, F. and Evans, J. (2006) *Specialist Schools – What Do We Know?* Sheffield: RISE. Online at: http://www.risetrust.org.uk/specialist.pdf (accessed 1 August 2008). A useful article that explores a range of evidence about the effectiveness of specialist schools in raising achievement and the likely impact of additional funding.

Chitty, C. (2008) 'The School Academies Programme: A new direction or total abandonment?', *FORUM: for promoting 3–19 comprehensive education,* 50 (1): 23–32. This article is by one of the strong advocates of comprehensive education and a critic of academies. He considers whether academies are changing from their original model but remains concerned about loss of local accountability.

PricewaterhouseCoopers (2008) *High Performing Specialist Schools Interim Evaluation.* DCSF. Online at: http://publications.dcsf.gov.uk/eOrderingDownload/DCSF-RBW034. pdf. A clear and valuable second evaluation of specialist schools that identifies achievements and concerns associated with specialist status.

Tomlinson, S. (2005) *Education in a Post-Welfare Society.* Buckingham: Open University. A through exploration of policy developments and the political context behind New Labour's education policies.

References

Abrams, F. (2007a) 'Pay premium for academy principals', *Times Educational Supplement,* 25 May, p. 8.

Abrams, F. (2007b) 'Academies rake in the cash', *Times Educational Supplement,* 18 May, p. 18.

Addley, E. (2008) 'A result for Labour – but could do better', *The Guardian,* 22 August, p. 17.

Benn, M. (2007) 'What kind of future is this?', *Education Guardian,* 23 October, p. 3.

Castle, F. and Evans, J. (2006) *Specialist Schools – What Do We Know?* Sheffield: RISE. Online at: http://www.risetrust.org.uk/specialist.pdf (accessed 1 August 2008).

Chamberlain, T., Rutt, S. and Fletcher-Campbell, F. (2006) *Admissions: Who Goes Where? Messages from the Statistics.* Slough: NFER.

Crace, C. (2006) 'Non-believers', *Education Guardian,* 5 December, p. 2.

Curtis, P. (2008a) 'Education: government damaging troubled schools, say unions', *The Guardian,* 18 August.

Curtis, P. (2008b) 'Universities urged to back more academies to reduce class bias', *The Guardian,* 11 February, p. 8.

DCSF (2007) *Academies and Independent School: Prospectus.* London: DCSF. Online at: http://www.standards.dcsf.gov.uk/academies/pdf/independentschoolsprospectus.pdf (accessed 12 August 2008).

DCSF (2008a) *What Are Specialist Schools?* London: DCSF. Online at: http://www. standards.dcsf.gov.uk/specialistschools/what_are/?version=1 (accessed 12 August 2008).

DCSF (2008b) *Current Projects of the Academies Programme.* London: DCSF. Online at: http://www.standards.dcsf.gov.uk/academies/projects/?version=1 (accessed 12 August 2008).

DCSF (2008c) *Sponsorship*. London: DCSF. On line at: http://www.standards.dcsf.gov. uk/academies/what_are_academies/sponsorship/?version=1 (accessed 12 August 2008).

DCSF (2008d) *Why Academies?* London: DCSF. Online at: http://www.standards.dcsf.gov. uk/academies/what_are_academies/whyacademies/?version=1 (accessed 12 August 2008).

DCSF (2008e) *Academies Are Working*. London: DfES. Online at: http://www.standards.dcsf.gov. uk/academies/what_are_academies/working/?version=/1 (accessed 12 August 2008).

DCSF (2008f) *What Are Trust Schools?* London: DfES. Online at: http://www.standards. dfes.gov.uk/sie/si/eips/trusts/ (accessed 12 August 2008).

DfES (1998) *School Standards and Framework Act 1998*. London: DfES. Online at: http://www.opsi.gov.uk/Acts/acts1998/ukpga_19980031_en_1 (accessed 12 August 2008).

DfES (2005a) *Higher Standards, Better Schools for All*. London: DfES. Online at: http:// publications.dcsf.gov.uk/default.aspx?PageFunction=productdetails&PageMode= publications&ProductId=Cm%25206677&pdfs/DfES-Schools%20White%20Paper. pdf (accessed 21 February 2009).

DfES (2005b) *The Government's Response to the House of Commons Education and Skills Committee Report: The Schools White Paper: Higher Standards, Better Schools for All*. London: DfES. Online at: http://publications.dcsf.gov.uk/default.aspx?PageFunction=productdetails& PageMode=publications&ProductId=DCSF-215709276 (accessed 21 February 2009).

Glatter, R. (2004) Submission to House of Commons Select Committee on Diversity and Choice. Online at: http://www.publications.parliament.uk/pa/cm200405/cmselect/cmpubadm/ 49-ii/49we03.htm (accessed 21 February 2009).

Gorard, S. and Taylor, C. (2001) *Specialist Schools in England: Track Record and Future Prospect*. Cardiff: Cardiff University School of Social Sciences.

Jesson, D. (2001) *Educational Outcomes and Value Added Analysis of Specialist Schools for the Year 2000*. London: Technology Colleges Trust (http://www.tctrust.org.uk).

Jesson, D. (2003) *Educational Outcomes and Value Added by Specialist Schools*. London: Specialist Schools Trust.

Macleod, D. (2007) 'Adonis denounces comprehensive school revolution', *The Guardian*, 25 January.

Mansell, W. and Luck, A. (2005) 'The schools that did not fail', *Times Educational Supplement*, 7 October, p. 4.

NAO (2007) *The Academies Programme*. London: National Audit Office. Online at: http://www.nao.org.uk/publications/0607/the_academies_programme.aspx (accessed 23 February 2009).

Ofsted (2005) *Specialist Schools: Second Evaluation*. London: Ofsted. Online at: http://www. ofsted.gov.uk/Ofsted-home/Publications-and-research/Browse-all-by/Documents-by-type/ Thematic-reports/Specialist-schools-a-second-evaluation (accessed 12 August 2008).

Paton, G. (2006) 'Onward Christian sponsors', *Times Educational Supplement*, 7 April, p. 6.

PricewaterhouseCoopers (2007) *Academies Evaluation: 4th Annual Report*. London: PWC. Online at: http://www.standards.dfes.gov.uk/academies/pdf/FourthAnnualPwCReport final.pdf?version=1 (accessed 15 August 2008).

PricewaterhouseCoopers (2008) *High Performing Specialist Schools Interim Evaluation* London: DCSF. Online at: http://publications.dcsf.gov.uk/eOrderingDownload/DCSF-RBW034.pdf (accessed 30 August 2008).

Purchase, K. (2008) 'Foreword', *A Good Local School for Every Child*. Anti Academies Alliance. Online at: http://www.kenpurchasemp.co.uk/index.php?section=viewsto&id=0057 (accessed 10 September 2008).

Ross, T. (2006) 'Academy investment is "high risk"', *Times Educational Supplement*, 28 April, p. 4.

Ross, T. and Paton, G. (2006) 'Flagship school bottom of KS3 table', *Times Educational Supplement*, 13 March, p. 13.

Stewart, W. (2007a) 'Specialist results not so special', *Times Educational Supplement*, 16 February, p. 8.

Stewart, W. (2007b) 'Academy cash switch', *Times Educational Supplement*, 28 September, p. 6.

Taylor, C. (2005) 'Only the weak shall enter this kingdom', *Times Educational Supplement*, 21 October, p. 21.

Taylor, C., Fitz, J. and Gorard, S. (2005) 'Diversity, specialisation and equity in education', *Oxford Review of Education*, 31 (1): 47–69.

West, A., Noden, P., Kleinman, L.M. and Whitehead, C. (2000) *Examining the Impact of the Specialist Schools Programme*, Research Brief No. 196. London: DfEE.

Wintour, P. (2008) 'Balls to set out vision of 100 schools becoming cooperative trusts', *The Guardian*, 11 September, p. 11.

5

The curriculum and state knowledge

Introduction

This chapter examines the state control of knowledge in the school curriculum. For the first three-quarters of the twentieth century it seemed that what children learned in school was of little interest to politicians or the government. But for the last thirty years the curriculum has become one of the hottest political issues. We look at how the curriculum has changed over the years and why recent governments have made children's knowledge central to government policy.

The Development of the State Curriculum in England

Elementary Schools and the Basics for the Working Class

The first state elementary education in England from 1870 had a closely defined curriculum known as 'the four Rs': reading, writing, 'rithmetic and religion. The curriculum in the board schools was based upon the Church foundation model: literacy and numeracy to equip the poor with basic skills for employment, with religion to propagate Christian moral values in society. It was not designed to produce the leaders of the nation and the cultural elite who were being educated in the fee-paying public schools. Those schools taught a rich and balanced curriculum based upon a broad range of subjects: mathematics, sciences, the arts and humanities. Elementary education was for the poor: an upcoming workforce and military personnel (see Chapter 3). It is difficult to know quite how successful the curriculum was in the board schools, but it has been judged to be effective by the quality of diaries and letters written home by soldiers in the First World War. The notion of 'basics for all' still lingers over the political discussions of the curriculum, rooted in the notion that literacy and numeracy are all that are required for the working classes. The curriculum was 'gendered' with differential provision for girls and boys (see Chapter 8). The curriculum in the nineteenth and early twentieth centuries did not just *reflect* the social structure of society, it shaped and replicated it, keeping the working classes and women in their places.

The Twentieth-Century Hands-Off Policy

Following the Balfour Act in 1902, the curriculum of elementary schools had been left to teachers: there was no curriculum directive from government, and the local authorities who controlled schools did not see it as their role to intervene either. The reluctance to establish a national curriculum for schools continued with the 1944 Education Act.

The twentieth century brought Keynesian economics and the beginning of the welfare state, and the 1944 Act was one attempt to bring social equality. The Act made secondary education available to all regardless of class and the ability to pay, bringing a broader curriculum to some working-class children by giving them access to secondary and higher education. However, Chapter 3 shows that the 11-plus selection process favoured middle-class families. The Act had little impact on the curriculum which was left unmentioned, with just one exception: schools should teach Religious Education and include a daily act of corporate worship of 'a broadly Christian kind'. The state saw its role as defining religious and moral direction, but not the knowledge to be taught, confirming the influence which the Christian Church still had on education.

The state neglect of the curriculum reflects its satisfaction with what teachers were doing. It shows also, perhaps, a lack of awareness by politicians about the importance of knowledge in state schools. Until 1944 all governments in the twentieth century had been Conservative or Liberal in which most MPs and ministers had attended public schools and received a curriculum with which they were satisfied. However, Lawton (1992) suggests another reason for the lack of a state curriculum: the fear of the politics of totalitarian regimes which dominated Europe during the 1930s. The Second World War had been engendered by nationalism and the extreme ideologies of left and right. The Nazi regime under Hitler in Germany and the Communist government in Soviet Russia under Stalin had made schools into propaganda machines to support state ideology. Politicians in the UK, anxious not to be seen to be anti-democratic, were reluctant to impose national control of the school curriculum. Rather than indifference to the curriculum, it might be that politicians saw the curriculum as *too* powerful and potent a force for them to engage with. This becomes significant when we look at the creation of the National Curriculum in England and how it was to be made 'democratic'.

While the government had no direct influence on the school curriculum during the first three-quarters of the twentieth century, the 1944 Act did affect the primary curriculum. The 11-plus selection comprised tests of IQ, literacy and mathematics and, in the later years of primary schools, teachers prepared children to pass them, resulting in a curriculum in which other subjects were marginalised. The 1944 Act left secondary schools to carry on with the subject-based curriculum which they had inherited from the public schools, with mathematics, English and science at its core. Grammar schools would teach a strong humanities curriculum, including Latin, and the technical schools would have more emphasis, for boys, on science and engineering. Secondary modern schools had a watered-down version of the subject curriculum.

The lack of any government policy on the curriculum left things as they were, with many children lacking access to certain subjects. The introduction of the technical schools could have been an initiative to strengthen the curriculum towards technology and industrial production. But Chapter 3 shows that technical schools were not popular and the majority of children who passed the 11-plus went to the high-status grammar schools for the traditional humanities-led curriculum. There was no government drive to harness the school curriculum to industry and the economy. The failure of the secondary technical schools, and consequently of the technology curriculum, was probably due to the hierarchical status of the tripartite system of the 1944 Act. Grammar schools were seen to replicate the public schools' high-status humanities curriculum. Technology was viewed by the British, in contrast with the rest of Europe, as a low-status form of education (Hutton, 1995).

The 1960s and Curriculum Integration

It was the 1960s that brought changes to the primary curriculum, but by the professionals in the schools, not the state. We see in Chapter 6 how the Plowden Report (1967) affected teaching methods, but also the curriculum. Plowden was a government commission of inquiry about what was considered to be good primary education. Essentially, it recommended the 'progressive' model of primary education which had been developed in early years teaching and recommended a broader curriculum than the literacy and numeracy model which had been perpetuated by the 11-plus. Plowden criticised subject-teaching as inappropriate for young children:

> The conventional ways of categorizing these phenomena as biology, branches of physics such as optics, electricity and magnetism, chemistry, engineering and so on are neither natural nor, except very crudely, understandable classifications to young children of primary school age. If, for the terms used above, rabbits, railway engines, telescopes, TV sets and aeroplanes are substituted, these are at once seen to be things about which children show a spontaneous curiosity and ask endless questions. (para.668)

Plowden signalled a move from the narrow literacy and numeracy curriculum and the abolition of the subject-based model. It produced a wave of thinking among teachers about topic-teaching and recommendations for changing the curriculum on integrated 'topic-work' lines which continued into the 1980s (Gunning et al., 1981). 'Integration' was 'child-centred' in shaping the curriculum to make sense to children, with the idea that 'subjects' are abstract, adult concepts that mean little to children. Primary schools tried to distinguish themselves from secondary education by rejecting the rigid timetabling of secondary subjects and specialist teachers in favour of an integrated curriculum with a single 'generalist' teacher.

These developments were of their time. The 1960s and 1970s saw a cultural change in society from the rigid and formal social mores of the nineteenth and early twentieth centuries. There was a rejection of authority and Victorian family values coupled with a desire for 'freedom', which the child-centred model nicely fitted. Children should be free of the tyrannical constraints of formal schooling; the progressive integrated curriculum and more creative work provided that 'freedom'. Another factor was the development of teacher training during the 1960s and 1970s with the introduction of BEd degrees (see Chapter 7), which encouraged trainee teachers to think about progressive primary education and often recommended the integrated curriculum. The Labour government's move to comprehensive schools with Circular 10/65 (DES, 1965) was consistent with Plowden on the curriculum; the abolition of the 11-plus allowed teachers to adopt a wider curriculum and to stop teaching to the 11-plus test. It was a sign to teachers that the old elitist structures were disappearing, and they felt strengthened in developing more adventurous approaches to their teaching and to the curriculum.

Politics and the Curriculum

Resistance to teachers' control of the curriculum began in the 1970s with the publication of the so-called 'Black Papers' (Cox and Dyson, 1969) which accused primary school teachers of not providing a sufficient basic curriculum and of an overemphasis on art and creativity. The papers were written from a right-wing elitist perspective and were critical of the underlying philosophy of freedom for children as well as the move from traditionalist assumptions about the subject-based curriculum. However, this was not only a right-wing view, and the first of the government criticisms of the curriculum came with the speech made by the Labour Prime Minister, Jim Callaghan (1976) at Ruskin College. Callaghan launched 'the great education debate' by questioning the content of the curriculum, saying that it did not service the needs of industry and the economy. In 1973 Anthony Crosland, Labour Secretary of State for Education, borrowing a metaphor from his predecessor David Eccles, had famously complained that the school curriculum was 'a secret garden in which only teachers and children are allowed to walk'. Callaghan's criticism was about the content of the curriculum; but more than that, it was a complaint that only professionals were able to define it: no one else was allowed into the garden. Callaghan called for a 'democratic' approach to the curriculum, stressing the need for parents and the world of business to be involved.

The next move from government came in the HMI Survey of Primary Education (DES, 1978) in which inspectors criticised integrated topic work for lacking academic rigour and frequently being little more than children copying out sections of text books. The DES document, *A Framework for the School Curriculum* (DES, 1980) called for assessment and monitoring by local authorities. During the 1980s a series of pamphlets from HMI (1984) were the first attempts at a state definition of the curriculum; the fact that the documents came out subject by subject was an indication of a return to the subject-based curriculum, and the title of the series, *Curriculum Matters*, was intended to indicate that the curriculum now *did* really matter. The HMI definitions were not statutory: schools could, and did, choose to ignore them. It was challenging the progressive notion that children's learning should be dictated by their interests, and gave the 'positivist' view that knowledge exists as a set of subjects, is 'out there' and is to be learned. But these early attempts to bring the profession into line to teach a government-led curriculum were to fail. It needed the full force of state legislation with a national curriculum, and this arrived with the 1988 Education Act. Britain was a late starter, but it made up by creating probably the world's most detailed and rigorous national curriculum, and one that was to be assessed by nationally standardised tests: a pincer movement on the professionals.

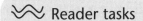

Reader tasks

- List the reasons for government's interest in the curriculum.
- Do you think that the state should define the knowledge to be learned in schools?

The Development of the National Curriculum

The introduction of the National Curriculum was to be a properly democratic process, approved as statutory legislation by the House of Commons and the House of Lords. And for it to be democratic, as Jim Callaghan had suggested, everyone with an interest should be able to contribute to its formation before it reached Parliament. To get a nation of 60 million people to agree on what should count as knowledge was going to be a tall order, and it took some four years from the conception of the curriculum to its implementation. It produced a remarkable tale of argument, intrigue and manipulation – battles between government and its civil servants, professionals and academics. It was started by the Secretary of State for Education, Kenneth Baker.

The first sign came before the Act with a slim red 'consultation document' in July 1987 (DES and Welsh Office, 1987) announcing that the government was planning a national curriculum of ten 'foundation subjects': a core of English, Mathematics and Science with seven 'other foundation subjects', History, Geography, Technology, Physical Education, Art and Design, Music and, in the secondary school, Modern Foreign Languages. It also proposed four key stages and all the subjects would be assessed with national tests at the end of each key stage, at the ages of 7, 11, 14 and 16. We saw in Chapter 2 that the radical neo-liberal thinkers in the Conservative government saw no need for, and even opposed, a national curriculum. They saw it as unnecessary legislation in what was needed to bring education into the marketplace. The new National Curriculum was to apply to the maintained sector – state schools – and was not intended for independent private schools. This was a sure sign that the reason for the National Curriculum was about the marketisation of schooling. Independent schools did not need a national curriculum because they were already in a market.

The document provoked consternation, particularly among primary school teachers, for three reasons. First, a government defined curriculum itself was disconcerting for a profession which had long been used to deciding on children's learning. Second, it was a subject-based curriculum derived from the traditional public school and grammar school model, with subjects defined from 5 to 16. It was a blow to those professionals who had worked to develop new models of a thematic or integrated curriculum. The third shock was the proposal for testing at the end of each key stage. The grammar school selection test had been seen as stressful and divisive, and primary school teachers, freed from it in the late 1960s, had rejected formal testing as detrimental to children's learning. The proposal was to have national testing in all ten of the subjects. The government's entry into the 'secret garden' of the curriculum looked like breaking down the gate and tearing up the flower beds to plant rows of carrots and cabbages. The response of the profession was typified in a publication by the Association of Teachers and Lecturers with a title addressed to the Secretary of State: *Take Care, Mr Baker* (Haviland, 1988).

The subject-based curriculum demonstrates 'neo-conservative' thinking in the Conservative Party: the desire to 'conserve', or to return to, the traditional model of the curriculum which those powerful members of the government had experienced in their public or grammar schools. Typical of the right-wing Hillgate Group (1989) which had the ear of the Prime Minister and Secretary of State, it was an explicit rejection of professional thinking about the curriculum and was criticised by academics for the lack of any proper epistemological basis (White, 1990). Another matter was that none of the ten subjects included anything about politics, the study of society or philosophy. It was to be a safe and C/conservative curriculum: facts and skills with nothing to question or challenge society as it exists.

Neo-conservatism came with a mixture of naivety and cynicism. It was naive in the sense that the civil servants at the DES who drew up the document seemed to be simply unaware of alternative possibilities for knowledge and the curriculum. It was also naive in its assumptions about national testing; the idea that every subject could be assessed on a national basis at the end of each key stage showed ignorance of what would be involved. The cynical action was to send the document out as a 'consultation paper' in July with responses required by 1 September, a short period when teachers were on holiday. Resistance to the proposals were clearly not welcome and they were indeed limited; the decision on the ten subjects was taken summarily by Baker after the 1987 consultation paper.

The next document to arrive was the Report of the Task Group on Attainment and Testing (TGAT, 1988). That the work on assessment was done before the curriculum indicates the priority which the government gave to testing in the national curriculum scheme. Chaired by Paul Black, an academic expert on assessment at King's College, London, the report was intended to set the framework for each subject in the curriculum. It designated the term 'attainment targets' which were to be the strands of each subject to be assessed, such as 'Speaking and Listening', 'Reading' and 'Writing' in English. Black visualised the difficulty of national tests for each of ten subjects in each key stage and was conscious of primary teachers' dislike of sitting their children down to pencil and paper tests. He proposed national SATs and it is interesting that the term was first defined as 'Standard Assessment *Tasks*': they should be classroom activities, such as building a model lighthouse. The activity would be observed to assess pupils in a variety of subjects such as Science, Technology, Art and Design, as well as *speaking and listening* in English. They were intended to avoid a large number of separate tests and children hardly needed to know that they were being assessed. Of course, Black's proposal was never implemented – testing became pencil and paper assessments in the core subjects only, and the 'T' in SATs came to stand for 'test'. This is another example of the conflict between a professional and a government view of assessment. Black's model was based on a complex and sophisticated judgement about children's learning. The government's view was based on simple data to compare pupils and schools. Black (1992) later revealed his anger at the way his work had been treated, saying 'those who gave dire warnings that the Act would be an instrument of Government control have been proved right'.

If assessment was controversial, decisions about the content of the curriculum were even more so. The 1988 Act gives the sole power of decision about the content of the school curriculum to the Secretary of State. However, the legislation requires that s/he should 'consult with' interested parties and, from late 1988, the consultation process for the ten subjects began. For each subject a 'working group' was set up and asked to draft a proposal for attainment targets and programmes of study based on the TGAT Report. The groups, beginning with English, Mathematics and Science, had to work quickly because Baker was determined to get the National Curriculum up and running in September 1989. It was another naive notion that an agreed curriculum could be created in that time. The groups were sent off to stay in hotels for three or four weekends and to produce draft attainment targets and programmes of study. The National Curriculum Council (NCC) was set up to manage the process on behalf of the government.

The subject working groups comprised some academics as experts in the subject, representatives of industry, commerce, the media and parents. Another snub to the profession was the small number of teachers included, a primary and a secondary representative on each group. Baker selected chairs of the groups who would take an anti-professional line. For example, the chair of the English Working Group was none other than Brian Cox of the 'Black Papers'. Cox was a figurehead of anti-progressivism who, Baker expected, could be relied upon to take a right-wing, traditional position. Despite Baker's manoeuvring, things proved not to be as straightforward as he had expected. There was trouble in the groups with angry debate reflecting strongly held viewpoints and the tensions between the political and the professional (Coulby, 1996).

The chair of the Mathematics group, Professor Roger Blin-Stoyle, resigned after the first report received a hostile reception from Baker. This delayed matters and caused problems. The next surprise was to come from the English group which had decided on three attainment targets for English: 'Speaking and Listening', 'Reading' and 'Writing'. When Baker received the report he was unhappy that Speaking and Listening was a target not just for primary pupils but for secondary too. His neo-conservative, traditional view of the curriculum saw English as the study and writing of literature; conversation, discussion and role-play are only suitable for young children; secondary pupils should be reading Shakespeare and writing correctly. But the arch-conservative, Cox, through discussion with the professionals, had been converted to the importance of oral language for older pupils. When Baker resisted the proposal, Cox threatened to resign. After the Blin-Stoyle resignation this would have been too embarrassing for Baker and would have delayed the timetable. Baker had to yield and accept speaking and listening for secondary English pupils. Like Black, Cox later published his own angry account of the politicisation of the curriculum and the way that the consultation process had been cynically managed (Cox, 1991).

There was no doubt that Baker had tried to implement a consultation process which, in itself, could have been democratic and involved everyone's views. The system was that the first working party report was sent to the Secretary of State for his views, then sent out for wide consultation. The group was then to meet again to make revisions in the light of feedback and produce another report. If that was accepted by the Secretary of State it could go to Parliament for approval and become statute. It meant a flurry of documents, multiplied by ten for each of the subjects. All documents were sent to all schools and were available free to anyone who contacted the DES. It was an enormous paper exercise and the debate was not restricted to the educational world with several cases of widespread discussion and protest.

An example was the proposal for the Music curriculum (DES and Welsh Office, 1991a). It proposed two attainment targets: 'Listening and Appreciation' and 'Performance and Composition'. For years music teachers in schools had worked to develop music beyond simply listening to music and singing to the teacher's piano-playing. The development of composition in the Music GCSE had been particularly successful, showing that all pupils were able to perform and compose music, just as they can draw, paint and write (Glover and Ward, 1998). The proposed attainment targets reflected these professional advances in music. By this time, Kenneth Baker had been replaced as Secretary of State by Kenneth Clarke and his response to the proposal reflected the same neo-conservative traditionalist view. He objected to performance and composition, saying that performance, and particularly composition, could only be for selected 'gifted' pupils, and proposed deleting performance and composition. This angered music teachers, and was taken up by the famous orchestral conductor, Sir Simon Rattle, who, at the beginning of each of his concerts, turned to the audience and deplored the actions of the Secretary of State in removing performance from the curriculum, warning that it would threaten the existence of future orchestras in Britain. Clarke climbed down to accept the two attainment targets.

He lost that battle, but won against the History working group. They had proposed that History should include the study of recent events to make it interesting and up to date (DES and Welsh Office, 1991b). Clarke ruled, however, that anything in the History curriculum must be at least thirty years old. So pupils would not be able to study the then recent Faulklands War of 1982 and the controversial sinking of the Argentine ship, *Belgrano*. Pupils were to be kept from anything which might make them reflect upon the political or social status quo. They should know about the kings and queens of England and be reminded of Britain's greatness in the world: a *nationalist* curriculum as well as a national curriculum (Coulby, 2000). This was consistent with the neo-conservative view of knowledge to be learned and not questioned, and the exclusion from the National Curriculum of anything about the study of society or politics.

Religious Education had been the only compulsory school subject since the 1944 Education Act, and it became the only subject *not* to be part of the statutory National Curriculum in the 1988 Act. The subject was still compulsory in that it had to be offered by schools, although parents were able to withdraw their children from it. The Act states that Religious Education should 'reflect the fact that religious traditions in Great Britain are in the main Christian'. The assertion ignored the multi-faith nature of the population. However, there was a concession: the content of the curriculum was to be defined locally by the LEA through a Standing Advisory Council on Religious Education (SACRE). This was intended to allow areas with different religions to define the curriculum to include other faiths. As Cush (2004) points out, it was 'an uneasy compromise' between the two lobbies: the traditional Christians versus those who saw RE as the understanding of religious world views. It was symptomatic of the continuing powerful influence of the Church of England on education policy. While the detailed curriculum content was still in local hands, in 2004 the DfES published national – but non-statutory – guidelines for RE which recommended a stronger multi-faith approach (DfES/QCA, 2004).

There was an acknowledgement of the need for a culturally different curriculum in Wales and a separate curriculum was devised by the Welsh Office, in collaboration with, but separate from, the Department for Education and Science in London. The curriculum for Wales included all the subjects with the addition of the study of the Welsh language and other variations in the subjects. However, apart from this concession, the National Curriculum was to apply to all children of all cultures and, at the time, there was no attempt to consider the cultural values of minority groups in society. The curriculum was to be one which defined British culture.

After all the debate and the papers, the National Curriculum arrived in schools in the form of ten A4 ring-binders, one for each subject, covering attainment targets and programmes of study for all four Key Stages – not difficult for secondary subject teachers who would have one, or possibly two, but primary teachers grappled with nine folders to find the curriculum they were to teach. There was 'help' with a series of 'Non Statutory Guidance' documents pub lished by the National Curriculum Council; one (NCC, 1989) was intended to guide primary school teachers in making the subjects work together, suggesting that they might even integrate some subjects, and this seemed to be a conciliatory gesture to primary teachers: the new National Curriculum might not be quite so subject-centred as it appeared (Ward, 1990). There was also training in the new curriculum for teachers, although it was patchy and limited. It is important to remember that, at the same time as introducing a new national curriculum, the 1988 Act also brought in local management of schools (LMS) making head teachers into business managers, as against their previous role as the senior teacher. In primary schools head teachers found themselves distracted from the strong academic leadership needed for the new curriculum and assessment (Coulby and Bash, 1991).

It was obvious to many that the new National Curriculum, while missing some critical content in politics and social sciences, was too fat. The teacher's stack of ring binders was both the symbol and the reality of overload and over-prescription. Overload was inevitable in the way it was constructed subject by subject. A working group of experts in each subject was bound to make sure they 'get it all in', leaving a collection of ten full folders of content. Another way to proceed would have been to develop the subject proposals then, in another phase, consider the overall curriculum required for each key stage to ensure that it was balanced and coherent. But it would have taken longer. The process was rushed, disorganised and, therefore, undemocratic (White, 1990). The chaotic knowledge war was played with real bullets, because this was government statute; for a teacher not to follow the National Curriculum orders was to break the law. The bitterness and acrimony of the time was summarised in another account of the process. Duncan Graham took over as chair of the Mathematics Working Party after Blin-Stoyle's resignation and later became chair of the NCC. He was one of the professionals committed to the ideal of a national curriculum, but in his book, *A Lesson for Us All*, (Graham and Tyler, 1993) he writes of his sense of betrayal by self-seeking politicians and civil servants.

Plagued by conflict and discord, the first years of the National Curriculum saw various levels of discontent among professionals. Some welcomed the prescription given to them by the new curriculum, others resented it and there was continuing complaint about the pressure both on teachers' workload and the effects of testing on pupils. In 1992 the NCC introduced revisions to the curriculum orders. This brought not a reduction, but more prescription. One of the changes was stronger intervention in the English curriculum with the imposition of a 'canon of great literature': specified texts, including Shakespeare plays, which pupils should study. It was also argued that insufficient attention was being paid to phonics in children's early reading (see Chapter 6). By 1993 the teaching unions were up in arms: taking away English teachers' choice of books to be studied, coupled with concerns about the overload of assessment at Key Stage 1, brought the National Union of Teachers (NUT) out on strike.

The conflict between the political and professional views of the curriculum can be traced through the 1970s and 1980s. In the 1990s conflict between the politicians in power and the professionals in practice was the hallmark of the National Curriculum, with the professionals marginalised. Secretaries of State varied in their sympathy with the professionals. Kenneth Clarke, who succeeded Kenneth Baker, was determined to maintain a distance from the professionals, fearing that he would be enticed by their arguments and would abandon the neo-conservative right-wing line. He refused to visit schools or to talk with teachers. His successor, John Macgregor, was judged to be too close to the professionals and was replaced in 1993 by the unremitting right winger John Patten. He railed against primary curriculum integration and teachers' opposition to the tests in inflammatory speeches and articles (Patten, 1993). He stood firm against the teachers' protests and the summer of 1993 brought a climax to the conflict. Patten was finally replaced as Secretary of State by the former schoolteacher Gillian Shepherd.

Shepherd's appointment as Secretary of State was in itself a climbdown by the government, now led by John Major. In 1990 the Conservative Party had replaced its uncompromising radical party leader, Margaret Thatcher. Her right wing neo-liberal ideology had pushed the Conservatives into an unelectable position with the highly unpopular poll tax. Major, a pragmatic and less ideologically driven politician, had succeeded against the odds in winning the Conservatives the general election in 1992. As a pragmatist, he was able to see that face-to-face conflict with the professions could not continue and appointing Shepherd, a former professional, was to bring compromise. She appointed Sir Ron Dearing to chair the NCC and bring about a workable curriculum and a better relationship with teachers. He had no political affiliations and, as former Chair of the Post Office, was known to be good at resolving conflict. Dearing (1993) drew up a set of guidelines for the revision of the curriculum, slimming it down to occupy only 70 per cent of children's time in school. In fact, Dearing's changes made little difference: there were still ten subjects with attainment targets and programmes of study. The main effects were in the packaging, with a single document (DfE, 1994) with all the subjects included for primary teachers, and with pictures. The overall process with the kindly Sir Ron and better documents made the whole thing more palatable for teachers.

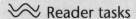 **Reader tasks**

- The National Curriculum brought the government and professionals into conflict. Do you think this was necessary?
- What is your view of the way the National Curriculum was created?

New Labour and the Modernisers

The New Labour government elected in 1997 had no ideological commitment to the neo-conservative National Curriculum, but there was little appetite for radical change. Labour had no real policy on the nature of the curriculum, with one exception, to include something which made young people politically aware and informed about the nature of society. This is a left-wing idea: if people understand society, they are more likely to believe that society should be changed to be more equal; it should also mean that they are more likely to take an interest in politics and to vote. So the new Secretary of State, David Blunkett, commissioned his old university professor of sociology, Bernard Crick, to draw up a curriculum for Citizenship to be included in the National Curriculum (QCA, 1998). Crick proposed three elements: 'Social and Moral Responsibility', 'Community Involvement' and 'Political Literacy'; these underlie the statutory Programme of Study for Citizenship in secondary schools and the optional primary Guidelines for PSHE and Citizenship. The latter were revised by the Qualifications and Curriculum Authority (QCA, 2007) for the economic and global dimensions of learning. It introduced the potential for teachers and pupils to reflect on the nature of society and brought in explicit values rather than the implicitly nationalist values of the rest of the curriculum. It lays emphasis on individual responsibility and civic duty and is portrayed as the means to make young people into active global citizens. However, critics have suggested that the current Citizenship curriculum is unlikely to achieve this in the present political and economic climate (Gibson and Harrison, 2008).

The period following the 1997 election saw a narrowing of the primary curriculum. As we see in Chapter 6, in 1998 New Labour introduced the Numeracy and Literacy Strategies, with the requirement of one hour's teaching of each per day. The strategies marginalised the time for the other foundation subjects in the primary school day: the two hours effectively took up most of the morning, leaving the afternoons for the rest of the curriculum. It was, though, not just a matter of time. Teachers' energies and resources were consumed by the new priorities and, while efforts were made to try to integrate other subjects, like History, into the literacy hour, the high level of prescription in the strategies meant that much of the other curriculum, in particular music and art, tended to be neglected. It is important to understand why New Labour was to sacrifice curriculum breadth for the priorities of numeracy and literacy. As part of their training for the Literacy Strategy, all primary teachers were shown video-taped guidance and examples of good teaching (DfEE, 1998). The first video began with an introduction by the Secretary of State emphasising the need to improve literacy so that Britain can compete in the global economy. Built into the assumption is that working-class people's lives will be improved through education and that they need first and foremost, not a broad and balanced curriculum of the arts, humanities and science, but the 'basic skills' of literacy and numeracy. So New Labour effectively brought a return to the nineteenth-century elementary school curriculum of the three Rs. The tendency to emphasise numeracy and literacy in the curriculum is an international phenomenon, stimulated by the global economy and government's perceived need to ensure that education fulfils the requirements. Coulby (2000), however, points out that, in the global knowledge economy, it is not basic literacy and numeracy that are needed. With the challenges of advances in technology and information, economies need workers with a wide range of skills, particularly in ICT, but also in creativity, imagination and innovation. In the knowledge economy services have replaced goods; problem-solving, adaptation, understanding customers' needs, entrepreneurialism and flexibility are required.

The government maintained its commitment to the core subjects at the centre of the curriculum by retaining SATs tests and league tables in a competitive market. However, Labour did move to engender a more flexible curriculum to encourage the 'creativity' required by the global economy. It was attempted with efforts to revitalise the arts curriculum with a report on the arts in schools (National Advisory Committee on Creative and Cultural Education, 1999) and a speech by David Miliband (2003), the Standards Minister, calling on schools to remember that 'creativity' is essential to a good education for industry. In 2007 the government launched an initiative requiring schools to provide all pupils of school age with five hours per week of high-quality cultural experience: listening to music, visiting art galleries or theatres, or seeing performances from visiting theatre workshops or artists (Creative Partnerships, 2007). The introduction of Modern Languages into the primary curriculum in 2011 is another broadening feature. A government review of primary education led by Sir Jim Rose (2008) published an interim report in December 2008 which appeared to reintroduce the integrated curriculum. While not abandoning the National Curriculum subjects, it suggested that alongside them should run six 'areas of learning':

- Understanding English, communication and languages;
- Mathematical understanding;
- Scientific and technical understanding;

- Human, social and environmental understanding;
- Understanding human physical health and well-being;
- Understanding the arts and design.

While this is not a return to Plowden's critique of subjects being inappropriate vehicles for children's learning, it is a recognition of the need for a more flexible approach to the epistemology of the curriculum and designed to offer more freedom to teachers. It is interesting that Rose's review is entitled *The Independent Review of the Primary Curriculum*, when in fact it is a government-sponsored activity and a response to the Cambridge Review (Alexander, 2007) which was largely critical of state policy. Like all the initiatives on the curriculum it was likely to become a requirement on schools.

The Secondary Curriculum

In secondary education New Labour's influence on the curriculum took longer to take shape. After the inclusion of Citizenship, the real changes have been in liberalising the secondary curriculum. The first was the need to free up space caused by the crowding of too many subjects, and the 2002 Education Act gave pupils the opportunity to drop the study of a foreign language. The second was the attempt to initiate creativity and innovation in the curriculum through privatisation in the academies (see Chapter 4).

There was a view that the post-16 curriculum was too narrow, with most students studying only five AS and three A levels, and that it was insufficiently related to employment. In 2005 the government commissioned Mike Tomlinson, former Chief Inspector of Schools, to review the curriculum and examinations framework for post-16 education. Tomlinson (2004) had recommended the abolition of GCE A levels and replacing them with a broader-based diploma. This would be for pupils at all levels, including those who had previously been excluded from A level study. However, apparently under the instruction of the Prime Minister Tony Blair, the proposal was rejected by the then Secretary of State Ruth Kelly. Blair seemed reluctant to give up the so-called 'gold standard' of A levels and was an example of conservatism: wishing to retain a system which had been successful in the past for an elite.

The government also tried to deal with the issue of vocational education to meet the needs of the economy. The first strategy in 2002 (QCA, 2002b) was to introduce vocational GCSEs offered in the following subjects: Applied Art and Design, Applied Business, Applied ICT, Applied Science, Engineering, Health and Social Care, Leisure and Tourism, Manufacturing. This was extended to the post-16 curriculum in 2008 with the introduction of 14–19 Diplomas, to be available to all pupils. The Diplomas were to be phased in for the following subjects (so-called: 'Diploma lines') from 2008: Construction and the Built Environment, Creative and Media, Engineering, Information Technology, Society, Health and Development; from 2009: Business, Administration and Finance, Environmental and Land-based Studies, Hair and Beauty Studies,

Hospitality, Manufacturing and Product Design; from 2010: Public Services, Sport and Leisure, Retail, Travel and Tourism; and from 2011: Humanities, Languages, Science. The last three are from the traditional subject list, indicating that the Diplomas were to be seen as crossing the academic/work boundary and not as discrete 'vocational-only' subjects.

The 14–19 Diplomas were a compromise solution to sit alongside GCSEs and A levels instead of Tomlinson's inclusive diploma system. They were intended to ensure that all young people stayed in education or training until the age of 18 and to offer curriculum content which would be of direct interest to pupils entering the workplace. The features were to be a focus on the basic skills of English and Mathematics, together with a work placement and an extended project study of the student's choice. The Diplomas were not intended to be vocational awards in themselves, but academic study to prepare young people for future employment. Again, the emphasis on English and mathematics runs through all the government's proposals. An interesting point is the introduction for the first time of 'new' curriculum subjects, such as Leisure and Tourism, and a break from the traditional list of grammar school subjects in the National Curriculum.

The Diplomas were the latest efforts by a government to make the English education system focus on business and commerce. Hutton (1995) describes the difficulties which Britain has always had in making a link between education and commerce. The German education system receives direct funding from industry and a technical education, in engineering for example, is seen as high status and desirable. Hutton describes two features which seem to have operated in Britain to the disadvantage of its industrial base. First, industry has not invested in rewarding apprenticeships for well-qualified and talented students in the way that Germany and France have done. It is as though industrialists want educated people but won't actually make the investment of capital in education and training. This, Hutton suggests, derives from the way capital has operated in Britain to hold land and property, or to invest in quick-profits share-dealing, rather than in long-term investment for industry. The second factor is the class-consciousness in Britain which sees technical employment as low-status: the highest achievers go on to do non-vocational 'academic' subjects. Vocational education has been seen as something suited to low attainers, as Wolf (2002: 56) says, 'a great idea for other people's children'. Attempts were made by the Conservative government in the 1990s to introduce National Vocational Qualifications (NVQ) and General National Vocational Qualifications (GNVQ). But these have proved to be only partially successful and the recent 14–19 Diplomas are another attempt to 'vocationalise' the curriculum.

The announcement about the Diplomas was made in a DCSF (2008) briefing in January. It was a 'top-down', government initiative, with limited involvement of the professions in the planning, and to be implemented very quickly. The DCSF argued that the diplomas were popular with schools and pupils, but this was contradicted by reports in the *Times Educational Supplement* (Mansell, 2008). Many teachers were said to be doubtful about the curriculum and whether pupils would want to take them. In June 2008 serious criticisms were voiced that the curriculum had not been thought through properly; for example, it was noted that the period of work experience need not be in the area of the subject, so that someone taking the construction diploma could succeed without ever setting foot on a building site. Alan Smithers (in Mansell, 2008: 12) described the diplomas as 'a disaster waiting to happen'. They were another case of the government acting rapidly to meet a political imperative with insufficient consultation with professionals. There was general disappointment in schools about Blair's rejection of Tomlinson's recommendations for an inclusive and broad-based diploma. This, together with the concerns about the 14–19 Diplomas, has made some secondary schools turn to the International Baccalaureate (IB) to give a wider curriculum option to post-16 students. The IB is run by a non-profit-making independent organisation which enjoys international recognition of its awards (International Baccalaureate, 2008). It is an indication of the profession making some resistance to the government-directed content of the 14–19 Diplomas.

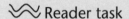 Reader task

Consider whether the 14–19 Diplomas are the right direction for the education system in the early twenty-first century.

The Early-years Curriculum

It was early-years education that saw the developments in educational practice with child-centred methods of learning and teaching in the first part of the twentieth century. The National Curriculum was addressed to statutory school aged children only, and so nurseries and playgroups were safe to continue with the curriculum and methods which they had always used, according to their professional judgements. Many nurseries are not within the maintained state provision, but are in the private sector, making it difficult for the government to have a direct effect on their curriculum. However, when New Labour came to power in 1997 the nurseries were not to be left alone. The year 2000 brought the first government attempt to influence the pre-school curriculum with *Curriculum Guidance for the Foundation Stage* (QCA, 2000). These were not statutory requirements on nurseries, but rather 'advisory goals'. The document was carefully worded to avoid looking like a prescribed national curriculum for nurseries, although the National Curriculum subjects are behind the goals for the five categories of learning:

- Personal, social and emotional development
- Communication, language and literacy
- Mathematical development
- Knowledge and understanding of the world
- Physical development
- Creative development.

Things were not to stop there. The 2002 Education Act brought the requirement for the assessment of young children through the *Foundation Stage Profile Assessment Arrangements* (DfES, 2003), while 2008 saw the introduction of the new Early Years Foundation Curriculum (EYFC) which was no longer 'guidance', but a 'curriculum'. The change from the former guidance was that there were to be specific, and demanding, targets for literacy. By the end of the Foundation Stage (age 5) children should be able to write their own name and read sentences (DCSF, 2008). It was another attempt by the government to ratchet up attainment in literacy – back to the old standards agenda – but this time with the youngest children as the target. The EYFC was judged by many early-years experts and practitioners to be too demanding and a distraction from the play and creative activities which should properly engage children of this age. It provoked further tension between government and the professions. Although the *Times Educational Supplement* (Ward, 2008) reported in their survey that the majority of early-years staff were satisfied with the content of the curriculum, the same edition reported objections from academics and early-years experts. Sue Palmer, who had long been an advocate of the formal teaching of literacy to young children, warns of the danger of professionals' optimism about government initiatives:

> People are innately optimistic. They like to look at the good side. I was one of those people when the National Literacy Strategy was introduced in 1988. There is a surge of optimism when you're working on something new; you think this could really word. But when you realise several years later it's not making the differences you'd expected, you start out trying to make children literate and end up training them to take tests. That is why I felt passionate – because I was fooled and I won't get fooled again. (p. 13)

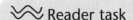 **Reader task**

Examine the current National Curriculum and reflect on whether it is suitable for today's economy and society.

Conclusion: A Critique of State Definitions of Knowledge

The curriculum is a selection of knowledge from all that is available. It is also, as sociologists Berger and Luckman (1967) would say, a definition of what *counts* as knowledge. In this chapter we have examined the way decisions about the school curriculum, and the definitions of knowledge, have passed between professionals and the state. We saw how state education began with a tightly defined curriculum in the nineteenth century, then passed to the hands of teachers and professionals

(Continued)

(Continued)

during the greater part of the twentieth century. The period from the 1980s saw the government wrest control and definition of the curriculum from the professionals, and largely to succeed with the National Curriculum and testing. The late 1990s saw a narrowing of the primary curriculum with a re-emphasis on literacy and numeracy. Recent years have brought some loosening of the curriculum in state schools with more choice for secondary pupils, more 'creative' subjects and the encouragement of curricular initiatives in the academies. However, while the statutory curriculum may have become less tightly controlled, what is taught in schools is now defined by the state through government guidance and direction, and closely monitored through its agents, the QCA and Ofsted. We conclude by considering whether this matters: should the state define and control knowledge?

The Entitlement Curriculum

One rationale for a statutory national curriculum is the ethical one of children's *entitlement*. All children should be entitled to an education which gives them equal access to knowledge. Their access to knowledge, it might be argued, should not be dependent on parents' wishes. Parents might have limited aspirations for their children, believing that education is of little benefit and that children should begin work as soon as possible. Religious beliefs at odds with liberal education might limit the aspirations of girls. Nor, it can be argued, should knowledge be determined by the preferences of individual teachers. In this sense the state-defined National Curriculum is a liberating force for good. All children, not just boys, are now taught science, all are able to learn a foreign language, not just those judged to be 'capable', and social class, formally at least, has been removed from the distribution of knowledge within the state system. Children with special educational needs are entitled to as much of the curriculum as possible, with 'disapplication' only where absolutely necessary. So while the curriculum might not be 'the right' curriculum, and there may be reasons for it being different, at least it gives equality of access to all in state schools.

Another argument in favour of a state curriculum is that knowledge should be determined democratically. The idea is that the government is democratically elected, so the way it determines the curriculum is thereby democratic: what the majority of people have voted for. But there are problems with this. First, is the curriculum that everyone votes for the 'right' curriculum? Does the majority know what is best for children and for the future, or does it need the expertise of professionals to determine what it best? The second issue is how democratic decisions about the curriculum really are. The 1988 Act set up a supposedly democratic consultation process for determining the content of the National Curriculum, but there was political manipulation intended to bias the direction of decision-making and marginalise the professionals. We have also seen that the main direction of government policy on the curriculum has been to relate it to the economy and employment.

Curriculum as Critique

Some would argue that education should give pupils the opportunity to understand a wider range of knowledge and experience and to have a critique of industry and commerce. Apple (1996) points out that the state definition of knowledge is intended to create a 'national culture': a set of beliefs and ideas to which everyone subscribes. A right-wing view of culture is that it is singular, common and national, rather than multifarious and diverse. It leads to a false consensus about what counts as knowledge. A national curriculum, Apple says, tramples on cultural differences. It is not something which should be taken for granted and 'given'. It needs to explain itself and acknowledge where it is coming from. A 'hegemony' is a set of beliefs and ideas to which everyone subscribes unquestioningly – a mechanism which allows the power-ful to control and oppress the weak and poor. The current hegemony in the West is free-market capitalism, and Apple argues that education should pro-vide a critique of the existing hegemony in order to empower social cohesion:

> Cultural politics is ... profoundly ... about the resources we employ to challenge existing relations, to defend those counter hegemonic forms that now exist, or to bring new forms into existence. (p. 21)

He writes of the USA, but the same argument might be employed for the UK, which is also a multicultural society. As Apple would say, in England the National Curriculum and its assessment differentiate pupils along national norms, adding to the disadvantaging of working-class and ethnic minority pupils. It operates as an instrument of market forces rather than a means to achieve social cohesion (see Chapter 9).

Recommended reading

Apple, M.W. (1996) *Cultural Politics and Education*. Buckingham: Open University Press. Apple gives a good critique of state knowledge.

Coulby, D. (2000) *Beyond the National Curriculum: Curricular Centralism and Diversity in Europe and the USA*. London: RoutledgeFalmer. Coulby argues that the National Curriculum with its core subjects is inadequate for the global knowledge economy of the twenty-first century.

Whitty, G. (2002) *Making Sense of Education Policy: Studies in the Sociology and Policy of Education*. London: Paul Chapman, Chapter 2: School knowledge and social education. Whitty explains the school curriculum in terms of the sociology of knowledge.

Wolf, A. (2002) *Does Education Matter? Myths About Education and Economic Growth*. London: Penguin. Wolf challenges the assumption that education improves the economy and gives some evidence that it doesn't.

References

Alexander, R. (2007) *The Primary Review: Children, Their World, Their Education.* Cambridge: University of Cambridge Faculty of Education.

Apple, M.W. (1996) *Cultural Politics and Education.* Buckingham: Open University Press.

Berger, P. and Luckman, T. (1967) *The Social Construction of Reality: A Treatise on the Sociology of Knowledge.* Harmondsworth: Penguin.

Black, P. (1992) 'Prejudice, tradition and the death of a dream', *Times Educational Supplement,* 28 August, p. 3.

Board of Education (1927) *Handbook of Suggestions for the Consideration of Teachers and Others Concerned with the Work of Public Elementary Schools.* London: Board of Education.

Callaghan, J. (1976) *Towards a National Debate.* Speech at a foundation stone-laying ceremony at Ruskin College, Oxford, 18 October.

Coulby, D. (1996) 'The construction and implementation of the core national curriculum', in D. Coulby and S. Ward (eds), *The Primary Core National Curriculum: From Policy to Practice,* 2nd edn. London: Cassel.

Coulby, D. (2000) *Beyond the National Curriculum: Curricular Centralism and Diversity in Europe and the USA.* London: RoutledgeFalmer.

Coulby, D. and Bash, L. (1991) *Contradiction and Conflict: The 1988 Education Reform Act in Action.* London: Cassell.

Cox, C.B. (1991) *Cox on Cox: An English Curriculum for the 1990s.* London: Hodder & Stoughton.

Cox, C.B. and Dyson, A.E. (eds) (1969) *Fight for Education: A Black Paper.* London: Critical Quarterly Society.

Creative Partnerships (2007) *Find Your Talent.* London: Arts Council England.

Cush, D. (2004) 'Cultural and religious plurality', in S. Ward (ed.), *Education Studies: A Student's Guide.* London: RoutledgeFalmer.

DCSF (2008) *Early Years Foundation Stage.* London: DCSF. Online at: http://www.standards. dfes.gov.uk/eyfs/site/4/4.htm (accessed 9 November 2008).

Dearing, R. (1993) *The National Curriculum and Its Assessment: Final Report.* London: Curriculum and Assessment Authority.

DES (1965) *The Organisation of Secondary Education,* Circular 10/65. London: DES.

DES (1978) *Primary Education in England.* London: HMSO.

DES (1980) *A Framework for the School Curriculum.* London: HMSO.

DES (1984) *English from 5 to 16: Curriculum Matters 1 – An HMI Series.* London: HMSO.

DES and Welsh Office (1987) *The National Curriculum 5–16: A Consultation Document.* London: DES.

DES and Welsh Office (1991a) *National Curriculum Working Group Music Interim Report.* London: DES and Welsh Office.

DES and Welsh Office (1991b) *National Curriculum Working Group History Interim Report.* London: DES and Welsh Office.

DfE (1994) *The Primary National Curriculum.* London: DfE.

DfEE (1998) *The National Literacy Strategy.* London: DfEE (with accompanying videotape).

DfES (2003) *Foundation Stage Profile Assessment Arrangements*. London: DfES. Online at: http://www.opsi.gov.uk/si/si2003/20031327.htm#muscat_highlighter_first_match (accessed 4 August 2008).

DfES/QCA (2004) *Religious Education: The Non-statutory National Framework*. London: DfES/QCA. Online at: http://www.qca.org.uk/libraryAssets/media/9817_re_national_framework_04.pdf (accessed 9 October 2008).

Gibson, H. and Harrison, D. (2008) 'Education for democracy: political contexts for learning citizenship', in S. Ward (ed.) *A Student's Guide to Education Studies*. Abingdon: Routledge.

Glover, J. and Ward, S. (1998) *Teaching Music in the Primary School*, 2nd edn. London: Cassell.

Graham, D. and Tyler, D. (1993) *A Lesson for Us All: The Making of the National Curriculum*. London: Routledge.

Gunning, S., Gunning, D. and Wilson, J. (1981) *Topic Teaching in the Primary School*. London: Arnold.

Haviland, J. (1988) *Take Care, Mr Baker: Powerful Voices in the New Curriculum Debate*. London: ATL.

Hillgate Group (1989) *Learning to Teach*. London: Claridge.

HMI (1978) *National Primary Survey*. London: HMSO.

Hutton, W. (1995) *The State We're In*. London: Vintage.

International Baccalaureate (2008) Online at: http://www.ibo.org/ (accessed 4 August 2008).

Lawton, D. (1992) *Education and Politics in the 1990s*. Lewes: Falmer Press.

Mansell, W. (2008) 'Diplomas on shaky ground', *Times Educational Supplement*, 6 June, p. 1.

Miliband, D. (2003) Speech to the National Campaign for the Arts, 27 March

National Advisory Committee on Creative and Cultural Education (1999) *All Our Futures: Report to the Secretary of State for Education and Employment*. London: DfEE.

NCC (1989) *Curriculum Guidance 1: A Framework for the Primary Curriculum*. York: NCC.

Patten, J. (1993) 'Battle for your child's mind: militant campaigns to disrupt the tests', *Sunday Express*, February.

Plowden, B. (1967) *Children and Their Primary Schools: A Report of the Central Advisory Council for Education*. London: HMSO.

QCA (1998) *Citizenship and the Teaching of Democracy in Schools: Final Report of the Advisory Group on Citizenship* (Crick Report). London: QCA.

QCA (2000) *Curriculum Guidance for the Foundation Stage*. London: QCA.

QCA (2002a) *Programme of Study for Citizenship*. London: QCA.

QCA (2002b) *GCSEs in Vocational Subjects*. London: QCA.

QCA (2005) *GCSE Criteria for Science*. London: QCA.

QCA (2007) *Programme of Study for Citizenship*. Online at: http://www.qca.org.uk (accessed 8 October 2008).

Rose, J. (2008) *The Independent Review of the Primary Curriculum: Interim Report*. London: DCSF. Online at: http://publications.teachernet.gov.uk (accessed 9 December 2008).

TGAT (1988) *Task Group on Assessment and Testing: A Report*. London: DES.

Tomlinson, M. (2004) *14–19 Curriculum and Qualifications and Reform: Final Report of the Working Group on 14–19 Reform*. London: Working Group on 14–19 Reform. Online at: http://www.dcsf.gov.uk/14-19/documents/Final%20Report.pdf (accessed 20 October 2008).

Ward, H. (2008) 'The aims are good, but hitting targets will be hard', *Times Educational Supplement*, 1 August, p. 13.

Ward, S. (1990) 'The core National Curriculum in an integrated context', in D. Coulby and S. Ward (eds), *The Primary Core National Curriculum: Policy into Practice.* London: Cassell.

White, J. (1990) *Education and the Good Life: Beyond the National Curriculum.* London: Kogan Page.

Wolf, A. (2002) *Does Education Matter? Myths About Education and Economic Growth.* London: Penguin.

Working Group on 14–19 Reform (2004) *14–19 Curriculum and Qualifications Reform: Final Report of the Working Group on 14–19 Reform.* London: Working Group on 14–19 Reform. Online at: http://www.14-19reform.gov.uk (accessed 7 November 2008).

Teaching and assessment

Introduction

In this chapter we examine the effects which government policy has had on the work of teachers' professional practice in classrooms. Teaching has provoked political and media controversy, with teachers criticised for the methods they have used. Teaching is probably unique in that no other profession is subjected to the same level of scrutiny or criticism. Through its mechanisms for accountability in education – Ofsted, the Qualifications and Curriculum Authority (QCA) and the National Teaching Strategies – the government in England has probably taken control of teachers' practice more strongly than in any other country in the world.

The Development of Pedagogy in England

Nineteenth-century Chalk and Talk

The 1870 Forster Education Act saw the first state-provided elementary schools in England where teaching methods were simple and 'didactic': the teacher gives a lecture or demonstration followed by, or interspersed with, questions to test pupils' understanding and recollection of the facts. It would be supplemented by written notes, probably on a blackboard, which would be copied down to assist memory. This model of teaching holds a good deal of credibility: it is simple to understand and underlies many assumptions about the nature of teaching in the public mind. It was both required and reinforced by the management of schools and by the system of government accountability.

The didactic model of teaching was reinforced by the state inspection system. Each year the school would be visited by one of Her Majesty's Inspectors (HMI) who would question the class to determine the level of knowledge gained by the pupils and this would determine the level of the teacher's income in the 'payment by results' system. Practice in answering the inspector's questions was essential to the demonstration of pupils' learning and the teacher's pay. This was 'high-stakes' assessment and high-level control. This first phase of state education placed a high level of accountability on teachers and schools. For the first time the government was providing a free education service and it wanted to be able to ensure that its taxpayers were getting value for money.

Early-years Developments

The high-level accountability lasted for a relatively short period. The 1902 Balfour Education Act brought payment by results to an end and, as well as leaving the curriculum free for teachers to determine, it removed the constraints on teachers' practice in the classroom. The removal of accountability left teachers free to develop new methods of pedagogy away from 'chalk and talk' didacticism. This did not happen immediately and it was not until the 1920s that teachers dealing with young children began to change their practice. They were influenced by the thinkers and early-years educators in Europe such as Jean-Jacques Rousseau, Johann Heinrich Pestalozzi and Maria Montessori. Rousseau (1762), not an educator but a philosopher, had an enormous influence on educational thinking. He proposed the notion of the 'natural state' of human beings: they are born good but corrupted by the world. This contrasts with the broadly Judeo-Christian view that people are born in a sinful state and need to be brought to goodness through knowing God. Rousseau's philosophy is central to the 'child-centred' view that we can begin with the child and draw out the inherently good qualities by encouraging development, rather than by imposing an adult model of the world. Pestalozzi (1894) drew on Rousseau's naturalism, arguing that children should be free to learn through independent activity and to explore their own interests. Children should find their own answers rather than simply recall facts. Montessori (1916) developed Pestalozzi's thinking and pointed to the fact that young children, rather than needing to be controlled and regimented, are spontaneous learners and will engage with the natural world, discovering its properties and making sense of their experiences through self-realising activities. Later, the development of child psychology, and particularly the work of Jean Piaget (1926), gave some scientific credibility to this thinking with evidence of a sophisticated cognitive orientation to learning. Piaget's contribution was to demonstrate the different phases through which children pass in their development, moving from the concrete 'operational stage' of the early years to the abstract stage of adolescence.

These European thinkers affected the practice of those working in the early years of education with the development of the *Kindergarten*, the 'child garden'. This term has become common in English now, but it is important to recognise its underlying assumption: that young children, like plants, need to be allowed to grow. The developing child is inherent in the seed; 'feeding and trimming' are the actions to be taken to allow the plant to grow and flourish. It contrasts with the concept of the school as a place where children are forced into socially determined patterns of behaviour: that good has to be drilled into them rather than drawn from them. The early part of the twentieth century saw the development of early-years pedagogy becoming 'child-centred': rather than being made to sit still and listen to teachers and answer their questions, children were asked to engage with materials, to play and to initiate their own learning. Teachers and carers were seen as those who would interact with them, supporting and guiding their development. As well as the psychological and philosophical grounds for these approaches to early-years education, there was a simple human perspective: young children in the nineteenth-century didactic classroom were quite simply bored and unhappy. The child-centred 'Rousseau-ian' model of education was, as much as anything, a part of the attempt to rehumanise schooling and to allow children to behave as children and less as institutionalised clones.

Child-centred early-years education, with play and learning from direct experience, became the norm for infants' schools. These ideas about learning and teaching grew among professional educators and were no part of government education policy. It was a time when professionals were in charge of schooling – a period of social democracy. Local education authorities provided the funding for schools and nurseries and the professionals in them worked in the ways they thought best.

In the later years of primary education, the child-centred model of education was slower to arrive, and this *was* due to government policy. It is not that the government prescribed teaching methods, but the 1944 Education Act indirectly affected pedagogy. The Act introduced the tripartite system and the selection of pupils through the 11-plus examination which tested pupils' intelligence (IQ), literacy and mathematics (see Chapter 3). The 11-plus was based on the assumption that it was possible to assess at 10 or 11 years of age what children would be able to achieve at 15 or 16. The intelligence tests which played a central part in the examination were claimed to have this 'predictive validity': a high or low IQ score remains fixed over time and is unaffected by learning or cultural factors. Such tests had first been designed by Alfred Binet in 1902 to determine the educability of children in France. This idea then became refined over the years to provide a battery of tests which could determine 'g', or general intelligence. The psychological concept of unchanging intelligence is now criticised by those who suggest that intelligence, if it exists at all, can be changed by educational experiences and upbringing (Howe, 1999). However, the notion of fixed inherited ability has run through the English education system. Division by ability defined the structure for secondary schooling. It also defined the structure of the later years of primary schools with streamed 'ability' classes of A, B and C. The separation of pupils by assumed ability was intended to facilitate the preparation of children for the tests at 11: class A were groomed to pass, the others prepared for failure, reinforcing the nineteenth-century didactic model of teaching with safe and secure learning by rote. The methods based on discovery, interaction with the environment and play were never allowed to develop.

Plowden and the 1960s: Revolution and Change

Things were to change with the publication of the Plowden Report (1967), one of the most influential and controversial documents in English education. There are many interpretations of Plowden, often mistaken and exaggerated. Lady Bridget Plowden was commissioned by the government to carry out a survey of primary education and to make recommendations for good practice for both teachers and local authorities. Essentially, she recommended that primary education overall should become more like early-years practice. Rather than being talked at didactically by the teacher, children should be allowed to engage in active learning, to work in groups, to learn from each other and be provided with engaging activities in which they could learn from experience. This child-centred vision was summarised in a well-known sentence from the report: 'At the heart of education lies the child', which was taken by some teachers to mean that children should be taught individually rather than as a class.

The effect of the report was to change the pedagogy of classrooms during the 1970s from the whole-class model of desks facing the front to one in which children sat in groups and teachers attempted to engage with individuals. Plowden had not said that there should be no class teaching, but during this period class teaching became defined as 'not good practice'. Some turned their classrooms into a kind of workshop with an approach called 'the integrated day' where groups worked on different activities, some doing mathematics, some doing art, some doing reading and writing. This was intended to enable the use of resources in different areas of the classroom and to allow choice of activities for children. Individual work would take place in several ways. A particular instance was the learning of mathematics where children worked individually through a structured scheme and would be helped by the teacher with the specific task for the day. The streaming of classes into A, B and C categories was stopped because it was felt to disadvantage low achievers by isolating them and creating pockets of low expectation; during the 1960s and 1970s 'mixed-ability' teaching became the norm in primary schools. The removal of streaming reflected the change from selective to comprehensive secondary education at the same time (see Chapter 3). Developments in primary teaching at this time were inspired by research on children's language development (Tough, 1976) with an emphasis on children's talk as the medium for their learning rather than listening to teachers. 'The child at the heart of education' essentially meant that there should be an understanding of the way children learn and that they should be listened to.

Primary Teaching and Politics

The approach generated by the Plowden Report came to be known as 'progressive' primary education and, during the 1970s, attracted criticism from parents, the press and right-wing academics. Teachers were said to be failing children by not teaching them in the traditional manner; classrooms were turning into places for children to have fun painting and playing, but not getting down to it; exploring and finding out, but not being taught properly. The classic response was in the so-called 'Black Papers' (Cox and Dyson, 1969). Ideological views based on the European philosophy of Rousseau and others were said to be failing children and the nation. A dichotomy began to emerge between those teachers who were said to be 'traditional and didactic' and those who were 'progressive and exploratory'. Politically matters came to a head in 1976 with the affair at the William Tyndale Junior School in North London. Teaching staff at the school had a strong commitment to a Marxist view of education and society in which children should be brought up to resist the oppression of capitalism. In fact, the school was disorganised and chaotic with no proper teaching and pupils were allowed to wander around unengaged in any serious educational activity. There were protests by parents and, after a media storm, the Inner London Education Authority closed the school down. The incident damaged the image of primary education which was depicted in the popular press as revolutionary and out of control (Riley, 1998; Davis, 2002). The William Tyndale School was portrayed as typical of progressive primary education; primary teaching methods were at the centre of news stories and seen as a part of the national decline.

Teaching methods were also a part of Callaghan's (1976) Ruskin College speech. As well as calling for a curriculum which related to industry and the world of work (see Chapter 5), Callaghan made criticisms of teaching methods, suggesting that there might be 'wild men in the primary classroom'. Given the gender distribution of primary teachers, he must have assumed there were 'wild women' too, but his jibe suggested that in his mind were the male head and deputy at William Tyndale. We saw in Chapter 2 that Callaghan's speech was part of the narrative of decline about British society and the economy, placing blame for the economic crisis on the education system, schools and teachers. Primary school teachers' methods were seen as one of the instruments of that failure. It was remarkable that they were seen as such an important feature of society and the economy; it was also wrong-headed.

In fact, research evidence shows that the changes to primary teachers' practice during the 1970s were modest. Although desks had been rearranged in most classrooms and individualised teaching of mathematics and literacy had been introduced, teachers' fundamental pedagogy had changed much less than the media portrayed. An HMI (1978) survey of teaching classified teachers' practice

(Continued)

(Continued)

as 'didactic' or 'exploratory' and found that only 25 per cent of teachers used any exploratory methods. Delamont (1987) found that, while teachers had grouped the tables in the classroom, they did not interact with groups, but spoke with individuals or the class, and that the 'progressive revolution' in the primary classroom had never really happened. Teachers' practice was still basically rather routine and dull. However, the image was created that primary school teachers, or at least some of them, were allowing children to get away with enjoying themselves and not learning, or even worse were sowing the seeds of Marxist revolution (Simon, 1981).

Research on Primary Classrooms

The controversy and news led to a flurry of research activity during the late 1970s and early 1980s to discover whether the so-called 'progressive' or 'traditional' methods were better. The first, by Neville Bennett (1976) of the University of Lancaster, studied 28 teachers and their classes, eliciting data from the teachers about their practice using a questionnaire. Bennett identified 12 different teacher 'types', ranging from the progressive to the traditional. He then tested their pupils at the beginning and at the end of the academic year in mathematics, reading and writing. His first finding was that the traditional teachers' pupils performed better on the tests than the progressives. The results made headline news in the popular press, again showing that progressive teachers were 'failing' pupils. Bennett's study was criticised for its methodology. The first criticism was that it was a 'black box study': Bennett had never observed in classrooms, only gained self-reported questionnaire data from teachers and testing the children at the beginning and end of the year. The second was that he tested only mathematics and English and not the full range of the curriculum where 'progressive' teachers might have been found to be succeeding in subjects such as the arts and humanities. The third criticism was a statistical one. Bennett had used the number of pupils in the 28 classes as the unit of measurement in calculating his results. This gave a large number which made the differences between the teachers statistically significant. It was argued that Bennett should instead have used the number of teachers as the unit of measurement, not the number or children (Gray and Satterly, 1976). Bennett's re-analysis based on the smaller number of 28 found that the differences between teachers was not statistically significant. Needless to say, this technical finding was never reported by the popular press and Bennett's original message, that progressive teachers were failing, was left embedded in the popular mind.

Other research did a better job of assessing the practice of primary teachers. Galton et al. (1980) in the ORACLE Project at the University of Leicester observed the ways that teachers interacted with pupils and identified four main types. They found that many teachers worked with individual pupils and that the ones that engaged the whole class were more successful. The findings made for criticism of the individualised approach, that class teaching works but insufficient class teaching was taking place. The effect of Plowden had been to turn primary school teachers away from class teaching with too much interaction with individuals. Other studies during the 1980s showed similar results: that the effects of different teaching styles and methods could be significant in pupils' achievement. (See Hastings and Chantrey-Wood (2002) for a good summary.) Two studies were particularly significant and had a high impact on government thinking. Mortimore (1988) found differences in achievement in London primary schools due to different teaching methods and to the ways in which schools were led by head teachers. Alexander (1992) carried out an evaluation of primary education in Leeds where the local authority had invested large amounts of money in a project to boost the quality of primary education with additional staff, advisers and resources. He found that teachers were working to a 'progressive' formula stipulated by the local authority which emphasised an attractive environment and group work in classrooms, but which lacked focus on children's learning and the monitoring and assessment of learning. Alexander's critical report on Leeds schools drew the attention of those who were opposed to progressive education and confirmed to the government that there were weaknesses in primary practice which might be addressed.

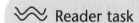 **Reader task**

Should the government have any influence on teaching methods, or should teachers be left to use the methods of their choice?

Government Intervention Begins

In the previous chapter we saw that when the National Curriculum was introduced in 1988 there was to be no government intervention in teaching methods or pedagogy:

- the way in which teaching is timetabled and how lessons are described and organised cannot be prescribed;
- the organisation of the curriculum to deliver national requirements ... is a matter for the head teacher ...

(DES and Welsh Office, 1989: para. 4.3)

This freedom given to teachers over their pedagogy was a surprise at the time because of the criticisms of primary teaching methods in the media during the 1970s and 1980s. However, within a short time, the government's hunger for controlling all aspects of the education system was to extend to prescriptive definitions for teachers' practice. In December 1991 the Secretary of State for Education Kenneth Clarke announced a review of primary teaching (Clarke, 1991). He appointed a commission of three: Robin Alexander, Professor of Education at the University of Leeds who had carried out the critical evaluation of the Leeds Primary Project, Jim Rose, Senior Primary HMI, and Chris Woodhead, then director of the National Curriculum Council and known to be a critic of progressive education. The announcement, made in December, required the report by January of the following year. Such a timetable meant that the commissioners worked over the Christmas period and became known as the 'Three Wise Men'. It was obvious from the membership and terms of reference of the commission that Clarke wanted a report that would be critical of primary practice, and he got it. Alexander et al. (1992) pulled together the findings of the research during the previous fifteen years and recommended that there should be more class teaching, more focus on the core subjects of English, Mathematics and Science and more specialist subject teachers in primary schools. Woodhead later became Her Majesty's Chief Inspector of Schools and, in that role, became a vociferous and powerful critic of primary education, accusing primary teachers of being locked into a Plowdenite progressive ideology. He continued his attack on the teaching profession with the suggestion that there were 15,000 incompetent teachers and that the weaknesses were due to incompetent teacher training (see Chapter 7). It made popular media coverage and Woodhead used it to strengthen his position with the public and the government.

Another feature of government worries about pedagogy was international comparisons of educational success. A report by HMI (1991) on teaching in France pointed to strong qualities in the teaching of numeracy and literacy. Data came from the Organisation for Economic Cooperation and Development (OECD) which organised the Programme for International Student Assessment (PISA, 2000) to compare the educational performance of different countries. A striking feature of the data was the success of Japanese and Taiwanese pupils in mathematics. In his research in Taiwan, David Reynolds explained that their success was due to well-focused class-teaching in mathematics. A high level of expectation was placed on pupils, contrasting with the English model of individualised teaching and differentiation between pupils (Reynolds and Farrell, 1996). The conclusions from the PISA data and Reynolds and Farrell's research ignore the cultural differences between the two nations and it has been argued (Hanson, 2004) that the comparison of teaching methods is too simple to account for the differences in performance. However, it added to the pressure for more class teaching and less individual interaction.

The 'Three Wise Men Report' and the PISA data gave Kenneth Clarke the evidence he needed to move in to change primary practice by insisting on more class teaching and the reduction of individualised teaching methods. There was more sabre rattling about the inadequacies of primary teaching and the Prime Minister John Major in the 1992 general election launched a campaign for 'back to basics'. The idea behind this was that the country needed to return to Victorian family values, and this should include a return to those good old didactic teaching methods of the nineteenth-century classroom. Major's suggestion had some appeal with the electorate and he won the 1992 election. However, it became a disastrous slogan as Major's government became mired in sleaze with a series of ministers having to resign for financial and sexual wrongdoings, making 'back-to-basics' a laughing stock.

Nothing actually happened to change primary pedagogy. The Three Wise Men's report sat on the shelf and schools and teachers carried on as they had done. Evidence about the effects of practice on pupils' performance arrived in a report published for Ofsted (Sammons et al., 1995) on the 'key characteristics of effective schools'. But the government took no action. The reluctance by Clarke and his successors at the DfES at first seems strange, but it was part of the Conservative government's ambivalence about intervention in education. In Chapter 2 we noted that the liberal, and neo-liberal, political position is that governments should intervene as little as possible in people's lives: things should be left to individual choice and the market. The need to set up the conditions for the education market required legislation on the curriculum, testing and inspection. But Lawton (1992) refers to 'the contradiction in the Conservative mind'. On the one hand they needed to create the market, on the other hand they wanted not to intervene. The lack of action on teachers' practice is to be explained by the non-interventionist strand of Conservative thinking.

New Labour, New Strategies

For Tony Blair's New Labour government elected in 1997 there was no such reluctance. Labour policy had always been to use government to improve the health and well-being of the nation. A solution to the nation's problems was to raise the achievement of working-class children who had previously been disadvantaged. This high-level interventionist policy is outlined by Michael Barber (2001) in his article *High Expectations and Standards for All, No Matter What.* Barber was a professor of education at the London Institute of Education who gave up an academic career to become the New Labour's government adviser at the DfES. He drew attention to the failings of the English education system, pointing out that adult literacy is lower than in many other countries. He argued that government should provide a combination of 'high challenge and high support'. The 'no matter what' conclusion to the title of his article is symptomatic of the unequivocal view which the New Labour government took towards intervention. He outlined four principles:

- Expect schools and teachers to do an excellent job: hold them to account for their performance.
- Reward success, challenge failure.
- Recognise that if teachers are to perform excellently they need … encouragement (and) rewards… .
- Recognise that, for some schools and some pupils, the challenge of meeting high standards is more demanding and provide the necessary targeted support.

(Barber, 2001: 20)

It is difficult to disagree with this as a plan of action, but it is based on the assumption that improvement will only come from government intervention: the government must provide the 'challenge', must 'reward success' and provide 'targeted support'. And, of course, the 'support' didn't just mean money and resources, it meant intervention and direction of teachers' practice. As Barber also indicates, a key feature of New Labour policy was to raise the standard of pupils' literacy and numeracy, and this was to be achieved by raising the quality of primary school teaching. The instrument for this was the National Teaching Strategies.

The new Secretary of State for Education David Blunkett wasted no time in implementing the National Literacy Strategy (NLS) (DfES, 1998). It required teachers to take each day a one-hour literacy lesson divided into three parts: a 30-minute session with the whole class on text, word and sentence work, a 20-minute group work session followed by a 10-minute 'plenary' with the whole class, drawing together the key points of the lesson. The National Numeracy Strategy (NNS) (DfES, 1999), introduced the following year, was modelled on the Mathematics teaching which Reynolds and Farrell (1996) had seen in Taiwan: a three-part lesson with a majority of whole-class inter-active teaching, the teacher moving all the children along together, with some differentiation through the short period of group activities. Both strate-gies required a three-part one-hour lesson each day, with 40 of the 60 minutes teaching the whole class.

This was the return to class teaching which had been called for by the 'back-to-basic' advocates. In fact, the strategies were not a return to the nineteenth-century didacticism in that they required 'interactive' class teaching in which teachers and children engage with one another. During the 20-minute group sessions the teacher would work with each group separately. There was no space in the hour for working with individuals: the many hours which teachers had spent hearing individual readers were gone. The strategies were a deliberate attempt to eradicate the individu-alised interactions which had been criticised in the research by Galton et al. (1980) and others. The strategies were accompanied by files of detailed guidance for week-by-week activities while literacy and numeracy coordi-nators in schools were required to attend training sessions on how to implement the strategy and then 'cascade' the training to colleagues in the school. The training sessions included a pack of materials with video tapes of specimen lessons designed to instruct teachers 'how to do it' (DfEE, 1998, 1999).

The teaching strategies were government policy but were not 'statutory' in the way that the National Curriculum was a legal requirement defined by an Act of Parliament. The guidelines and resources were produced cen-trally but enforcing the strategies was left to the local authorities and the hundreds of literacy and numeracy advisory staff who were appointed. There was an interesting point about what powers local authorities had to enforce requirements for teachers' practice, and indeed some schools with strong head teachers refused to carry out the literacy and numeracy hours, claiming that they had high standards of learning in their schools and that the methods they used were superior. Such schools risked the threat of a poor Ofsted report if inspectors did not agree that the methods were satisfactory or the results good enough. But a number of schools did manage to resist the strategies in this way, showing that their results, and their methods, were good enough not to be changed.

There was some initial disgruntled reaction to the notion that teachers should be told how to teach, and there was some irritated response to the model lessons in the videos. Concerns about the pedagogy were expressed as there being insufficient time for children to develop their written work (English, 2002). One of the traditional concerns about class teaching is that slower learners are left behind, and Myhill (2002) questioned whether whole-class teaching benefited underachievers. Critics such as the author Philip Pullman complained that children found the class teaching dull and they lacked the opportunities for spontaneous and creative work (BBC, 2002). The popular children's author Michael Rosen blamed the Literacy Strategy for not encouraging children to read for pleasure (*Daily Telegraph*, 2008). Others criticised the government for 'de-professionalising' teachers by taking away their ability to make their own judgements about the kind of materials and methods to use in their practice (Bassey, 2005).

However, the government was not to be deterred by this kind of criticism which did not damage its ambition to raise standards of basic literacy and numeracy: reading for pleasure wouldn't equip students for jobs in industry. It was also strengthened in its resolve by early research that seemed to demonstrate that the strategies were successful (Sainsbury et al., 1998; Ofsted, 1999): 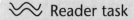teachers were generally positive about the strategies and children's learning did improve. The successes of these early interventions formed the basis of the next years of government policy. The New Labour government of 1997 saw itself as the driving force behind educational development. It employed large numbers of professional advisers who would determine 'the right way' to teach, and it would make teachers work in this way. There was to be a decade of intervention.

〰 Reader task

Do you agree that New Labour's National Literacy and Numeracy Strategies were what primary education needed?

By the 2001 election the government was claiming to have 'transformed' primary schools and wanted to do the same for the secondary sector. The next prescription to come along was the Key Stage 3 Strategy for secondary schools, now known as the 'Secondary National Strategy' (DCSF, 2008a), with a similar prescription for teaching and continuing the primary school model. There was no format for teaching as in the Primary Literacy Strategy, only a set of principles:

1. Focus systematically on teaching and learning.
2. Base improvement activity on evidence about relative performance.
3. Build collective ownership and develop leadership.
4. Involve collaboration with other organisations.
5. Create time for staff to learn together.
6. Embed the improvement in the school's systems and practices.

(DCSF, 2008a)

The government seemed to shy away from the detailed prescription that it had given to primary colleagues. Resistance and criticism were minimal and the government pressed on with reforms. (See Stobart and Stoll (2005) for a critique of the Key Stage 3 Strategy. See Ofsted (2005) for a positive evaluation of the Secondary Strategy, indicating that it changed and improved secondary teaching.)

The government's confidence in defining the practice of teachers grew over the years from 2000. In 2003 the NLS and NNS were followed by the Primary National Strategy. This included the former strategies but was in some ways a more diluted form of intervention. In fact, it appeared to be a considerable change from the detailed direction of the former strategies. It was couched in the form of guidance and advice and suggested that teachers should take more control of the curriculum and their teaching methods (DfES, 2003). It looked as though the government was backing off: leaving teachers to determine their methods, even encouraging them to be diverse and 'innovative' and creative in their approaches.

However, it was not long before the strong arm of intervention returned in the form of instructions about the teaching of reading. A professional debate about methods of early reading ran through much of the twentieth century. Briefly, it concerns whether children learn to read by first learning the sounds of letters and then applying them to the analysis of written words to gain meaning (the phonics approach) or whether they begin with the context of a text, inferring the letter sounds from the meaning of the words (the meaning approach); this approach emphasised 'reading with real books' rather than the contrived texts of reading schemes written to teach phonic rules. In some ways the debate reflects the traditional and progressive approaches to primary teaching. Traditional teachers would favour the more obvious and direct phonics method, whereas progressive teachers would recognise children's interest in meaning and context. Part of the right-wing criticism of progressive educators was that 'reading with real books' failed to teach children the basics of reading and many lacked the basic skills to enable them to succeed in the school system and then in work. In fact, much of the rhetoric about teachers' practice was misinformed. Just as Delamont (1987) found that most teachers were traditional in their approaches, HMI (1991) in a survey of reading in primary schools found that there was little 'reading with real books', that teachers used a variety of approaches and that 95 per cent of teachers used reading schemes.

The rhetoric about failure in the teaching of reading continued and the lack of phonics teaching came to be viewed as the culprit. Developments in the direct teaching of phonics emerged in the form of a scheme known as 'synthetic phonics'. This systematic teaching of letters and sounds received considerable publicity, including a television series, by its energetic proponent Ruth Miskin. In a typical example of the way that the government responded to popular assertion in the media, it commissioned Jim Rose to examine the case for phonics teaching in schools. The Rose Report (2006) indeed found that there should be synthetic phonics teaching in schools and, again, primary school teachers were required to make this their principal method in the teaching of early reading. Chapter 7 analyses the government's control of teacher training, but it is notable here that, during 2007–8, teacher-training providers were subjected to a high level of scrutiny and pressure to ensure that they were training future teachers in the methods of synthetic phonics. Each received a letter from the Schools Minister, Lord Adonis, requiring evidence that phonics teaching was being carried out.

Another attempt by the government to influence teachers' practice has been *Teachers' TV*. This appears to be a benevolent offering to teachers, with tips for the curriculum and lessons, but the editorial line inclines towards the government's view of learning and teaching. It is available for most of the day as a digital broadcast and online (Teachers' TV, 2008).

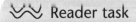 Reader task

Interview some established teachers about their views of policy on teaching. Do they think that there is too much government direction of their practice? What do primary teachers think about the teaching of phonics and the Primary National Strategy? What do secondary teachers think about the Key Stage 3 Strategy?

High-stakes Assessment and Target Setting

The 1988 Education Act brought the national assessment system with teacher assessment and standard assessment tasks (SATs). As we saw in Chapter 2, the main reason for such a comprehensive national system of assessment was to provide information to parents in order to have 'customer choice' of schools. When elected in 1997, New Labour was to increase the stakes in testing by developing a system of target-setting. David Blunkett's vision was to raise standards of literacy and numeracy through the teaching strategies and by setting targets for five years hence when 80 per cent of children were to reach level 4 in literacy and 75 per cent level 4 in numeracy SATs. Target-setting became the central feature of government planning for education. Blunkett promised that if the targets were not met by the end of the first five years of

Labour government in 2002 he would resign as Secretary of State. In fact, by that time he had already been moved to become Home Secretary and was succeeded by the luckless Estelle Morris who had to deal with the embarrassment when the targets were not met.

Target-setting for children's achievement was to operate at all levels: the government set national targets, local authorities had targets for their regions, schools had targets and each individual pupil had targets. Of course, along with the targets went the methods by which targets were to be delivered in the form of the National Teaching Strategies. So targets were the means by which government enforced its model of teaching upon the profession. Rather than simply a means of determining the level of a child's achievement, assessment became an instrument of enforcement (Stobart, 2008). This approach to assessment also makes it 'high stakes': a return to the culture of payment-by-results of the nineteenth century. Blunkett's promise to resign was a token of high-stakes assessment, and it was to enter the culture of the teaching profession in different ways.

 Reader task

Interview parents about assessment. Do they think their children are over-assessed?

An attempt to produce a return to 'payment-by-results' came through a series of actions to reward teachers for high-quality teaching: performance-related pay (PRP). As Ball (2008) notes, the publication of the White Paper *Schools: Achieving Success* in 2001 marked a change from the 'discourse of derision' and criticism of teachers. Schemes to value and reward teachers were created. In a system of 'threshold payments', teachers at the top of the salary scale received an additional £3,000 per year, so long as they met the required standards as judged by the head teacher (TDA, 2007). Another is the designation of Advanced Skills Teacher (AST). An AST should be:

- producing high-quality teaching materials;
- disseminating materials relating to best practice and educational research;
- providing 'model' lessons to a whole class, or a target group of pupils, e.g. gifted and talented (G&T), SEN, English as a second language (EAL), etc., with staff observing;
- supporting a subject leader with regard to schemes of work, policies or management skills;
- observing lessons and advising other teachers on classroom organisation, lesson planning and teaching methods;
- helping teachers who are experiencing difficulties;

- participating in the induction and mentoring of newly qualified teachers;
- leading professional learning groups;
- supporting professional development.

(DCSF, 2008b)

The Advanced Skills Teacher concept was first introduced in Australia, and Smyth and Shacklock (1995) point out that it became a means by which the government, who defined the standards for the AST, thereby defined the nature of teaching. Both the AST and the Threshold schemes have had the effect in England of tightening the government's definition of good teaching.

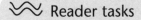 Reader tasks

- What are the advantages and disadvantages of national tests?
- Was the government right to abolish Key Stage 3 testing in 2008?

Critique of Education Policy on Teaching and Assessment

Here we examine some of the critiques of government policy on teaching. The first is the idea that teachers' practice is easily defined and non-problematical. The view that educational research on teaching and reflection on practice are just a waste of time is summarised by Chris Woodhead in his 2001 Annual Report as Chief Inspector of Schools:

> We know what constitutes good teaching and we know what needs to be done to tackle the weaknesses: we must strengthen subject knowledge, raise expectations, and hone the pedagogic skills upon which the craft of the classroom depends ... Why, then, is so much time and energy wasted in research that ought to be straightforward ... If standards are to continue to rise, we need decisive management action, locally and nationally, that concentrates attention on the two imperatives that really matter: the drive to improve teaching and strengthen leadership ... The challenge now is to expose the emptiness of education theorising that obfuscates the classroom realities that really matter. (Ofsted, 2001: 21)

This view is popular with the media and reflects the anti-intellectualism and vilification of research that runs through the right-wing critiques of education. That teaching can be reduced to a list of skills is criticised by, for example, Mahony and Hextall (2000). They describe the way that teaching has been transformed from a professional activity which depends on informed and sophisticated judgements in different contexts and with different individuals into one in which a series of prescribed activities will deliver standards. Bottery (2000) refers to the 'proletarianisation' of teaching: carrying out a set of prescribed activities, which the government defines and everyone knows is correct, de-professionalises teaching. 'Proletarianising' means that it can be done by anyone 'trained' and equipped with the skills, like repairing television sets. As we saw in Chapter 5, the narrowing of the curriculum has become an international phenomenon linked to economic globalisation. Smyth (2000) points out that the proletarianisation of teaching has followed a similar pattern. The teacher is no longer an individual professional trusted to make judgements about the needs of the community and individuals; instead he or she becomes a technician employed to carry out national government policy.

The precise definition of teachers' practice and the high-stakes inspection of schooling have ensured that over the years the profession has developed a culture of compliance. Ticking the boxes and specifying the learning outcomes have become the daily fare of teaching. It is interesting to reflect on whether the profession might have resisted this onslaught on its independence. Bottery (2000) offers an explanation of why this hasn't happened. He refers to Foucault's (1979) 'panopticon' prison where prisoners are observed all the time. The effect of relentless observation is complete compliance and then the removal of the need for observation because the prisoners police themselves to ensure compliance. It is not that schools are inspected by Ofsted 'panoptically'. However, the effects of Ofsted inspection are such that the effects of observation continue before and after the inspection visit: observations by local authority officers preparing the school for inspection, and regular observation by the head teacher and senior staff to ensure that teaching methods are compliant.

The national assessment system was designed to remove the professional role from teachers. SATs are employed because teachers' judgements are not to be trusted. And, of course, in the high-stakes context of assessment in which their salaries and jobs depend on the success of their pupils, the temptation for teachers not to assess correctly is increased. Where assessment used to be a matter of the teacher's professional judgement about the child, it became a weapon in the competitive market wars. High-stakes assessment is criticised by researchers in the Cambridge Primary Review. Harlen (2008) argues that standardised tests are not necessarily more accurate than teacher assessment. They are conducted on a narrow basis – a short test taken on a particular day – and so are a poor measure for an individual pupil. The validity of the test for the individual is compromised by the need for high reliability in reporting the achievement levels of the population: one-third of pupils get the wrong level for them as individuals. SATs are limited to what can be easily measured rather than the more sophisticated learning of the individual which can be judged by the teacher. Harlen continues that government policy on assessment corrupts and distorts both teaching and children's learning. The need for measurable outcomes for the education market damages the teacher–pupil relationship. In order to ensure that pupils perform well, teachers 'teach to the tests', ensuring that pupils give correct answers to a narrow range of questions. And, of course, the heavy assessment on testing demotivates low performers. In this way, Harlen concludes, tests have low dependability and negative impact. Testing does not, as the government claims, 'drive up standards'. She argues that teacher assessment is a more valid form of assessment: instead of accountability being based on the aggregate of pupil achievement in tests, it should be based on the achievements of the school as a whole. This can be achieved by a selection of pupils taking a sample of questions from a bank of assessment items, rather than all pupils taking the same tests. Tymms's (2004) analysis of pupils' actual learning as against their performance on SATs concludes that national strategies have not significantly improved pupils' performance. Rather, children have become better at doing tests, providing an illusion of raised standards.

The devolution of political power in the United Kingdom in 2000 meant that not all had to follow the English Westminster model of education and the Welsh Assembly abandoned SATs for pupils in Wales from 2006. This is interesting because it emphasises the particular case of England which continues to have an all-embracing commitment to the neo-liberal model of education for the economy. Resistance to national testing has been the strongest and most consistent opposition to government policy in education. While the National Curriculum and the National Teaching Strategies were broadly welcomed by the public and the media, assessment had opponents from all quarters. A high level of testing was always seen by teachers as damaging to children's welfare with its inherent tendency to encourage competition and failure for many. Community soundings in the Cambridge Primary Review (Alexander, 2007b) found evidence that parents and children were increasingly pressurised by over-testing that was damaging attitudes to school. Another report in the Review (Wyse et al., 2008) finds: 'A decrease in the overall quality of primary education experienced by pupils because of the narrowing of the curriculum and the intensity of test preparation.'

The wave of popular opinion against the national testing regime continues to grow. A House of Commons Select Committee on Children, Schools and Families (2008) recommended the abolition of national SATs and the use of the sampling system which Harlen (2008) recommends. Robinson and Fielding (2008) in the Primary Review point out that the primary school focus on target-setting and testing contradicts the policy in the *Every Child Matters* agenda which promotes the welfare of the child (see Chapter 10). The announcement by the Secretary of State Ed Balls in October 2008 abolishing Key Stage 3 testing in England in 2008 was a sign that the government was beginning to respond to the pressure.

Personalised Learning and Hints of Professional Freedom

The Gilbert Report (DCSF, 2006) appeared to signal a change in the government's perspective on teaching. Chaired by Christine Gilbert, later Chief

HMI, the terms of reference were 'to present to the Secretary of State a vision for personalised teaching and learning in 2020 which enables every child to achieve higher standards; and to make recommendations which would support delivery of that vision'. There is still the emphasis on standards that will meet economic needs. However, rather than the class teaching that we saw in the teaching strategies, the ideal now is 'personalised learning'. Personalised learning and teaching

> ... means taking a highly structured and responsive approach to each child's and young person's learning, in order that all are able to progress, achieve and participate. It means strengthening the link between learning and teaching by engaging pupils – and their parents – as partners in learning. (DCSF, 2006: 6)

For Plowden, education was 'child-centred' whereas personalised learning is 'learner-centred' but it is also 'assessment-centred'. So we seem to have something like 'Plowden with tests'. However, the authors envision a more complex model of teaching and learning with 'open learning' and 'time ... for learners' reflection'; 'learners are active and curious, they create their own hypotheses, ask their own questions, coach one another'. It is certainly different from the Taiwanese model of undifferentiated class teaching, and a long way from 'back to basics' and Woodhead's (Ofsted, 2001) suggestion that we don't need to reflect on, or to research, practice.

Conclusion

Government policy, steered by global economic priorities, has invaded the professional world of the teacher so that he or she is no longer the self-guided and self-motivated professional of the twentieth century. Instead the teacher becomes a technician delivering a government-determined national curriculum to meet the economic needs of the global economy with financial reward for high quality and achievement. This invasive control is probably inevitable in the global economic context and is part of what Bernstein (2001, cited in Ball, 2008: 203) calls 'the totally pedagogised society': everyone is to be engaged in education or training for lifelong learning; every experience is to be a learning experience designed to re-create the individual for the needs of the global society. Bassey pleads passionately for trust in professionals:

> It is time to stop: day by day it is teachers who know best what their pupils need. It is time for Parliament to require government to transfer to them the power to exercise that trust in the best interests of the pupils and parents whom they serve. (Bassey, 2005: 43)

But there is little evidence that what Wrigley (2003) calls the 'high surveillance, low trust' relationship between government and teachers will change. The centralised policy of control is criticised by Alexander who raises the matter of ownership of the education service:

Policy is not all that matters. Teachers do, and must, exercise professional judgement on the basis of what they know about their pupils; a national education system belongs not to ministers and officials, but to all of us. (Alexander, 2008)

This plea reflects the extremes to which government action in 'micro-managing' the education system has gone. Alexander's Cambridge Primary Review assembled a team of first-rate researchers to provide evidence of the highest academic quality on primary education. At the time of writing (late 2008) most of the Primary Review has been published, and many of its findings are critical of the effects of government policy on professional practice during the last twenty years. It was in response to Alexander's independent review that the DCSF set up its own review chaired by Jim Rose. Without seeing the review which will appear in 2009, it is highly likely that it is intended as a counter to Alexander's criticisms and will be another episode in the long-running battle over the professional practice of teachers.

 Reader task

Take any of the Primary Review reports (Alexander, 2007a). How much does it support or criticise government policy?

Recommended reading

Alexander, R. (2007a) *The Primary Review: Children, Their World, Their Education.* Cambridge: University of Cambridge Faculty of Education. Online at: http://www. primaryreview.org.uk/. All the articles in the Cambridge Primary Review are worth reading for a critique of government policy. In particular, the following refer to teaching and assessment:

- Harlen, W. (2007) *The Quality of Learning: Assessment Alternatives for Primary Education*, Primary Review Research Survey 3/4. Cambridge: University of Cambridge Faculty of Education.
- Robinson, C. and Fielding, M. (2007) *Children and Their Primary Schools: Pupils' Voices*, Primary Review Research Survey 5/3. Cambridge: University of Cambridge Faculty of Education.
- Wyse, D., McCreery, E. and Torrance, H. (2008) *The Trajectory and Impact of National Reform: Curriculum and Assessment in English Primary Schools*, Primary Review Research Survey 4/3. Cambridge: University of Cambridge Faculty of Education.

Hastings, N. and Chantrey-Wood, K. (2002) *Reorganising Primary Classrooms.* Buckingham: Open University Press. Hastings and Chantrey-Wood give a good summary of the research on primary classrooms.

Smyth, J. (2000) Teachers' Work in a Globalizing Economy. Lewes: Falmer Press. Smyth shows how government intervention in teachers' practice is a global phenomenon, driven by economic globalisation.

References

Alexander, R. (1992) *Policy and Practice in Primary Education*. London: Routledge.

Alexander, R. (2007a) *The Primary Review: Children, Their World, Their Education*. Cambridge: University of Cambridge Faculty of Education.

Alexander, R. (2007b) *Community Soundings: The Primary Review Witness Sessions*. Cambridge: University of Cambridge Faculty of Education.

Alexander, R. (2008) 'Testament to the power of 10', *Times Educational Supplement*, 16 May, p. 27.

Alexander, R., Rose, J. and Woodhead, C. (1992) *Curriculum Organisation and Classroom Practice in Primary Schools: A Discussion Paper*. London: DES.

Ball, S.J. (2008) *The Education Debate*. Bristol: Policy Press.

Barber, M. (2001) 'High expectations and standards for all, no matter what: creating a world class education service in England', in M. Fielding, *Taking Education Really Seriously*. London: RoutledgeFalmer.

Bassey, M. (2005) *Teachers and Government: A History of Intervention in Education*. London: Association of Teachers and Lecturers.

BBC (2002) *Author Attacks School Literacy Strategy*. London: BBC News. Online at: http://news.bbc.co.uk/2/hi/uk_news/education/1809451.stm (accessed 9 July 2008).

Bennett, N. (1976) *Teaching Styles and Pupil Progress*. London: Open Books.

Bottery, M. (2000) *Education Policy and Ethics*. London: Continuum.

Callaghan, J. (1976) *Towards a National Debate*. Speech at a foundation stone-laying ceremony at Ruskin College, Oxford, 18 October.

Clarke, K. (1991) *Primary Education – A Statement by the Secretary of State for Education and Science Kenneth Clarke*. London: DES.

Cox, C.B. and Dyson, A.E. (eds) (1969) *Fight for Education: A Black Paper*. Manchester: Critical Quarterly Society.

Daily Telegraph (2008) 'Children's laureate Michael Rosen says youngsters not taught reading for pleasure', 9 July. Online at: http://www.telegraph.co.uk/news/uknews/2275469/Children's-Laureate-Michael-Rosen-says-youngsters-not-taught-reading-for-pleasure.html.

Davis, J. (2002) 'The Inner London Education Authority and the William Tyndale Junior School Affair, 1974–1976', *Oxford Review of Education*, 28 (2–3): 275–98.

DCSF (2006) *2020 Vision: Report of the Teaching and Learning in 2020 Review Group*. London: DCSF. Online at: http://publications.teachernet.gov.uk/eOrderingDownload/6856-DfES-Teaching%20and%20Learning.pdf.

DCSF (2008a) *Secondary National Strategy*, London: DCSF. Online at: http://www.standards.dfes.gov.uk/secondary/keystage3/all/respub/sns0506launch.

DCSF (2008b) *The Advanced Skills Teachers' Standards Website*. DCSF. Online at: http://www.standards.dfes.gov.uk/ast/.

Delamont, S. (1987) 'The primary school teacher 1945–1990: myths and realities', in S. Delamont, *The Primary School Teacher*. Lewes: Falmer Press.

DES and Welsh Office (1989) *The National Curriculum: From Policy to Practice*. London: DES and Welsh Office.

DfEE (1998) *The National Literacy Strategy*. London: DfEE.

DfEE (1999) *The National Numeracy Strategy*. London: DfEE.

DfES (2001) *Schools: Achieving Success*, White Paper, Cm 2530. London: DfES.

DfES (2003) *Excellence and Enjoyment: A Strategy for Primary Schools*. London: DfES. Online at: http://www.standards.dfes.gov.uk/primary/about/ (accessed 10 July 2008).

English, E. (2002) 'Pedagogical dilemmas in the National Literacy Strategy: primary teachers' perceptions, reflections and classroom behaviour', *Cambridge Journal of Education*, 32 (1): 9–27.

Foucault, M. (1979) *Discipline and Punish*. Harmondsworth: Penguin.

Galton, M., Simon, B. and Croll, P. (1980) *Inside the Primary Classroom*. London: Routledge.

Gray, J. and Satterly, D. (1976) 'A chapter of errors: teaching styles and pupil progress in retrospect', *Educational Research*, 19: 45–56.

Hanson, M. (2004) Learning and mathematics, in S. Ward (ed.), *Education Studies: A Student's Guide*. London: RoutledgeFalmer.

Harlen, W. (2008) *The Quality of Learning: Assessment Alternatives for Primary Education*, Primary Review Research Survey 3/4. Cambridge: University of Cambridge. Online at: http://www.primaryreview.org.uk/Downloads/Int_Reps/2.Standards_quality_assessment/ Primary_Review_Harlen_3-4_report_Quality_of_learning_-_Assessment_alternatives_ 071102.pdf (accessed 20 October 2008)

Hastings, N. and Chantrey-Wood, K. (2002) *Reorganising Primary Classrooms*. Buckingham: Open University Press.

HMI (1978) *Primary Education in England*. London: HMSO.

HMI (1991) *Aspects of Primary Education in France: A Report by HMI*. London: DES.

House of Commons Select Committee on Children, Schools and Families (2008) *Third Report: Testing and Assessment – 169-I*. London: House of Commons. Online at: http://www. publications.parliament.uk/pa/cm200708/cmselect/cmchilsch/169/16903.htm.

Howe, M.J.A. (1999) *A Teacher's Guide to the Psychology of Learning*, 2nd edn. Oxford: Blackwell.

Lawton, D. (1992) *Education and Politics in the 1990s: Conflict or Consensus*. Lewes: Falmer Press.

Mahony, P. and Hextall, I. (2000) *Reconstructing Teaching*. London: RoutledgeFalmer.

Montessori, M. ([1916] 1964) *The Montessori Method*. New York: Schocken Books.

Mortimore, P. (1988) *School Matters: The Junior Years*. London: Open Books.

Myhill, D. (2002) 'Bad boys and good girls? Patterns of interaction and response in whole-class teaching', *British Educational Research Journal*, 28 (3): 339–52.

Ofsted (1999) *The National Literacy Strategy: An Interim Evaluation*. London: Ofsted.

Ofsted (2001) *Report of the Chief Inspector of Schools*. London: Ofsted.

Ofsted (2005) *The Secondary National Strategy: An Evaluation of the Fifth Year*. London: Ofsted.

Pestalozzi, J.H. (1894) *How Gertrude Teaches Her Children*, trans. L.E. Holland and F.C. Turner, ed. and intro. E. Cooke. London: Swan Sonnenschein.

Piaget, J. (1926) *The Child's Conception of the World*. London: Routledge & Kegan Paul.

PISA (2000) *Knowledge and Skills for Life*. Paris: OECD. Online at: http://www.pisa.oecd.org/Docs/Download/PISA2001(english).pdf.

Plowden, B. (1967) *Children and Their Primary Schools: A Report of the Central Advisory Council for Education*. London: HMSO.

Reynolds, D. and Farrell, S. (1996) *Worlds Apart? A Review of International Surveys of Educational Achievement Involving England*. London: HMSO.

Riley, K.A. (1998) Whose School Is It Anyway? Educational Change and Development. Lewes: Falmer Press.

Robinson, C. and Fielding, M. (2008) *Children and Their Primary Schools: Pupils' Voices*, Primary Review Research Survey 5/3. Cambridge: University of Cambridge Faculty of Education.

Rose, J. (2006) *Independent Review of the Teaching of Reading*. London: DfES.

Rousseau, J.-J. (1762) *Émile*. London: Dent.

Sainsbury, M., Schagen, I. and Whetton, C. (1998) *Evaluation of the National Literacy Project*. Slough: NFER.

Sammons, P., Hillman, J. and Mortimore, P. (1995) *Key Characteristics of Effective Schools: A Review of School Effectiveness Research*. London: Ofsted, Institute of Education.

Simon, B. (1981) 'The primary school revolution: myth or reality', in B. Simon and J. Wilcocks (eds), *Research and Practice in the Primary Classroom*. London: Routledge & Kegan Paul.

Smyth, J. (2000) Teachers' Work in a Globalizing Economy. Lewes: Falmer Press.

Smyth, J. and Shacklock, G. (1998) Re-making Teaching: Ideology, Policy and Practice. London: Routledge.

Stobart, G. (2008) *Testing Times: The Uses and Abuses of Assessment*. London: Routledge.

Stobart, G. and Stoll, L. (2005) 'The *Key Stage 3 Strategy*: what kind of reform is this?', *Cambridge Journal of Education*, 35 (2): 225–38.

TDA (2007) *Professional Standards for Teachers: Post-threshold*. London: TDA. Online at: http://www.tda.gov.uk/upload/resources/pdf/s/standards_postthreshold.pdf.

Teachers' TV (2008) Online at: http://www.teachers.tv/.

Tough, J. (1976) *Listening to Children Talking*. London: Ward Lock.

Tymms, P. (2004) 'Are standards rising in English primary schools?', *British Educational Research Journal*, 30 (4): 447–94.

Wrigley, T. (2003) 'Is "school effectiveness" anti-democratic?', *British Journal of Educational Studies*, 51 (2): 89–112.

Wyse, D., McCreery, E. and Torrance, H. (2008) *The Trajectory and Impact of National Reform: Curriculum and Assessment in English Primary Schools*, Primary Review Research Survey 4/3. Cambridge: University of Cambridge Faculty of Education.

7

Teacher training, Education Studies and the universities

Introduction

Qualified Teacher Status (QTS) is required for teachers in state-maintained schools. While universities teach and award BA/BEd degrees and PGCE with QTS, the QTS element is awarded by the government. Qualifications for doctors, nurses, lawyers and architects are all made either by universities or the by colleges of the professional bodies. Teaching is the only profession whose qualification to practise has been made by a government department and it is a sign of the importance of teacher training to government policy. The latest professional award for the teaching and care of young children, Early Years Professional Status (EYPS), is also awarded by the DCSF. This is a symptom of the strong accountability measures taken by government for those working in education and with young people.

This chapter outlines the development of teacher training, from its origins in schools, to its academic life in colleges and universities, followed by its transformation to state-definitions during the 1990s. The last thirty years have seen strong government intervention across the whole education service, but teacher training has seen probably the most aggressive attack on the theory and practice of teacher education in universities. The chapter concludes with the development of non-teacher-training Education Studies degrees as a response by universities to government controls.

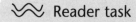 **Reader task**

Do you intend to become a teacher? List the reasons for and against.

The Development of Teacher Education

The earliest form of teacher training in the nineteenth century was the pupil–teacher or 'monitorial' system. It was an apprenticeship model in which a good pupil was trained to become a teacher by watching the experienced teacher at work until he or she was competent to take over. The method has been dubbed 'sitting with Nellie': existing practices were passed on and methods never questioned or changed. Some formal teacher training was begun by the Quakers in 1798. Joseph Lancaster set up in Southwark, a slum area of London, a school called the Lancastrian Institution for Promoting the Education of the Labouring and Manufacturing Classes of Every Religious Persuasion. Teacher training began in these inauspicious circumstances. Hencke (1978) notes that the school 'promoted an odd mixture of radical thought, economy of provision and lack of clear academic objectives which have become the hallmarks of teacher education ever since' (p. 13).

The lack of any academic or pedagogical theory was a characteristic of teacher training throughout the early part of the twentieth century when it comprised a two-year practical training for primary school teachers and none for secondary school teachers. Primary training was principally for single women: those who wished to marry were forced to leave the profession which was seen as one for dedicated spinsters. Courses were free of theoretical material, concentrating mainly upon providing the practical resources which teachers would need to function in the classroom (Ross, 1990). Richardson (2002) explains that the McNair Committee of 1944 had complained that teacher training was impoverished and needed to be improved through a blending of academic and professional study. But it wasn't until the 1960s that the Robbins Committee (1963) recommended the development of a Bachelor of Education (BEd) degree and that the training colleges should be absorbed into the universities. This was a part of the strategy to increase the numbers in higher education, but also to increase the intellectual and academic quality of the teaching profession. However, the merger into the universities was resisted by the local education authorities which then controlled the teacher-training colleges and they remained separate institutions. Universities were linked with the colleges to validate courses and to make awards. BEd degrees were to be taught in the training colleges, but validated and awarded by universities, leaving teacher education formally out of the university sector.

Crook (2002) shows that in the 1960s the validating universities were suspicious of teacher training, believing it not to be a proper academic subject but simply tricks of the trade, and they wanted theory. It was at this point that the subject disciplines were drawn in to form a theoretical basis for education. The philosopher of education R.S. Peters of the London Institute of Education argued that philosophers should determine the subject balance and he met with C.J. Gill, HMI for teacher training, in a closed seminar at the DES to agree the subjects to be included in the new degrees. The proposal was for Psychology, Sociology, Philosophy and Economics to be the theoretical basis. Economics was subsequently dropped and History of Education substituted. Pedagogy was excluded. Simon (1994) argues that the Education Studies programmes developed in the 1960s suffered from being simply academic elements grafted onto teacher training by the universities.

By the mid-1970s, McCulloch notes that the disciplines of Psychology, Sociology, Philosophy and History were well established, but there were soon questions about the relevance of the theoretical disciplines to teaching. The clumsy 'bolting-on' of the academic disciplines and the failure to include pedagogy in the theoretical framework made the new courses appear irrelevant to practice. The failure to take teacher training colleges into the university sector, as Robbins had recommended, meant that teacher training continued to be low-status. The situation improved during the late 1970s and early 1980s when many of the colleges were merged into the new polytechnics and BEd degrees were validated by the Council for National Academic Awards (CNAA). This brought much of primary teacher training into fully academic higher education institutions which were later to become universities.

Criticisms of Theory and the Rise of Government Control

It was the Thatcher government of the early 1980s which began the assault on university teacher education as a part of its attempt to disempower professional academics (Furlong et al., 2000; Cowen, 2002). The charges were that teacher training was a self-serving process for the benefit of academics, irrelevant to the needs of teachers and children and taught by those who were out of touch with classroom practice. Government criticisms of irrelevant theory were echoed by teachers and student teachers (Tomlinson and Hobson, 2001), but also by right-wing academics and political groups (Hillgate Group, 1989; Phillips, 1996). The criticisms strengthened the government in moving against the universities through various regulatory bodies. The first in the mid-1980s was the Council for the Accreditation of Teacher Education (CATE) which required teacher training institutions to submit their courses for audit and approval and to demonstrate their relevance to practice. One feature of CATE was the requirement that all staff teaching on programmes should have 'recent and relevant' experience of teaching in classrooms. This caused a flurry of placements of academics sent out to gain experience in local classrooms, and older staff were bewildered at finding themselves back in the classroom after twenty years in teacher training (Fish, 1988).

The attack on teacher training continued into the Major years of the Conservative administration as part of the 'back-to-basics' policy of the early 1990s. Major's speech to the Conservative Party conference in 1993 announcing the plan to rid teacher training of irrelevant theory about gender and race, and to enable teachers to teach numeracy and literacy, was greeted with rapturous applause. The significance of this was the link between 'the basics' (what we all know to be true and good) and the abolition of theory. It was a powerful populist mixture, attractive both to some practitioners and apparently to the voting public.

Although the CATE criteria had made heavy demands on teacher-training institutions and their courses, it had still left the teacher education curriculum in the hands of the institutions: they had only to justify its relevance. It was still possible in the 1980s to include at least the vestiges of the academic disciplines in courses. With Major, the 1990s brought much stronger controls in the form of the Teacher Training Agency (TTA), now the Training and Development Agency for Schools (TDA). The TTA was first staffed by individuals who openly demonstrated their hostility to the old 'academic' courses and set about explicitly reviling and reforming teacher education. In exchanges between agency staff and academics there was a sense of universities being punished for the theoretical misdemeanours of the past, the discourse often strident and emphatic. Anthea Millett (1999), then TTA Chief Executive, commented on the arrangement for unsuccessful Newly Qualified Teachers, criticising universities for allowing weak students to pass:

> ... some will fall by the wayside ... individual tragedies ... But I am sure that most of us will remember what happened when weak teachers escaped the nets erected in the past ... untold damage to the education of the pupils in their charge. (p. 6)

On the other side, the language from the universities was equally uncompromising. Barton et al. (1994) criticised the new reforms as a part of government attempts to de-professionalise teachers by removing the universities from teacher training. They quote Stuart Maclure (1993):

> [The] sub-plot ... is to take teacher training out of the universities and colleges and ultimately to sever the connection between the study of education in higher education and its practice in schools. This is a deeply damaging idea and must be fought tooth and nail ... the [proposals] must be examined closely for insidious attempts to dismantle the traditional defences of teaching as a profession. (p. 531)

The rancorous nature of the debate at this time is well summarised in an account of a discussion between academics and right-wing politicians at a conference organised by the Universities Council for the Education of Teachers (UCET, 1997).

The New Labour government elected in 1997 brought no respite for the universities and the TTA continued. With the full force of government behind it, the TTA (1998) moved rapidly to take control of teacher education from the hands of the universities through the following moves:

- a set of standards (or competences) to be met by all qualified teachers which were entirely defined by subject knowledge and teaching competence;
- a set of requirements for teacher training, including the length of time to be spent in schools;
- an Ofsted inspection regime which allowed for no deviance from the standards or requirements (Ofsted, 1998);
- a funding mechanism which rewarded only those with good Ofsted grades and penalised those non-compliant with the requirements by removing accreditation and student numbers.

These measures had the effect of removing teacher education from the rest of the unregulated higher education system. Training teachers had become government business and the QTS standards were the means of removing academic theory. To make the process indisputable, the TTA ruled out the features of academic discourse from teacher education: the process became 'teacher training', students were to be known as 'trainees', universities as 'providers', successful teaching as 'compliance with the standards', assessment as 'auditing knowledge'.

There were attempts to remove initial teacher training (ITT) from universities altogether by introducing a variety of school-based modes of training known as School-Centred Initial Teacher Training (SCITT) (TTA, 1995) and the Graduate and Registered Teacher Programmes (GRTP), now the Graduate Teacher Programme (GTP). Where teacher training is carried out in higher education, the university is obliged to work in close partnership with schools and to devolve its funding to school partners to pay for the supervision and assessment of students' teaching experiences. Simple tests of numeracy and literacy which all trainees had to pass before gaining QTS were administered by the TTA; university 'providers' were not to be trusted with tests. The Ofsted inspections of teacher training became progressively invasive; those institutions found by Ofsted to be 'non-compliant with the Secretary of State's requirements' could have their teacher training numbers removed and the department closed down. The 1990s saw confrontation between the universities and the government over teacher education, but by the end of the decade the Standards, the Requirements and the Ofsted inspection framework were firmly and unequivocally in place. Institutions settled into the tireless pursuit of compliance with the latest requirements and standards (TDA, 2007).

〰 Reader task

Look at the latest teacher-training standards (TDA, 2007). Do you agree that they are the way to define teaching?

There are signs that the government may be moving from the 'deprofession-alised' view of teaching as the technical delivery of a national curriculum and to have a more academic basis. The McKinsey Report (2007) compares the teaching profession in the UK with that in other countries and concludes that it is academically under-qualified, recommending that teachers should have a master's degree. The government responded positively, requiring the TDA to set up a national Masters in Teaching and Learning (MTL) to be available for all teachers. At the time of writing the details were beginning to emerge and it was not clear how much control over the degree would be located in the universities, or whether, like initial teacher training, its content would be dictated entirely by the state through the TDA. The move towards a more highly qualified profession is likely to mean a reduction in the number of qualified teachers in schools working with a larger number of teaching assistants and ancillary workers.

〰 Reader tasks

- The debate about who should train teachers continues. If you wanted to train to be a teacher, would you take a university course or a school-based one?
- Do you think teachers should have a strong theoretical base for the work, with a Masters degree in Teaching and Learning, or is practical training all that is needed?

Academic Response to Teacher Training Reforms

While university institutions acquiesced in the hand-over of the initial teacher-training curriculum to the state-defined standards, there has been considerable academic resistance and objection. Mahony and Hextall (1997) question the whole principle of government-appointed 'quangos' such as the TTA in which non-elected individuals, sometimes with no background in education, are appointed and vested with powers over the lives of professionals. Responsibility for decisions is diffuse and unclear. How the assumptions are drawn for the selection of standards and requirements is never explicit. Mahony and Hextall also make the point that there is bound to be tension between the standards as a developmental aid for trainee teachers and as a regulatory mechanism. In a similar vein, Richards (1998) argues that no rationale was given for the teacher training curriculum and that the Standards were based on undiscussed and value-free notions. There was no proposed ideal of the good teacher, merely technicist definitions of skills.

Maguire et al. (1998) criticise the over-explicit detail in the standards which, they argue, is designed to de-professionalise teachers. The set of unquestioned competences is inappropriate to teaching, they suggest, pointing out that the professional teacher operates in largely non-routine situations, especially when children's learning is taken into account. Teachers need to have the freedom and ability to make judgements; the reduction of teaching to a set of rules is inadequate for the education of professionals. They argue also that the emphasis on subject content is misplaced, and that sensitivity to children's learning is important.

Bottery (2000) sees dangers in the very process of compliance and conformity to the reductionist model of initial teacher training. He argues that a culture of compliance with the state-defined curriculum now suffuses initial teacher training and feeds into the profession. The problem is that it removes the ability to apply critique of education policy and practice. Not only is critique removed from the list of skills and knowledge, but the very ability to engage in critique is obviated by the whole process. Bottery recommends that teachers in the twenty-first century need a global perspective on their own practice, on government policies in education and an analysis of the context in which their professional work takes place. He warns of the dangers of a single vision of education, suggesting that:

> Educators may be complicit in the meshing of a primarily technical-rational and implementational culture with a set of centralising government priorities … [This has] produced a monolithic approach to education which has silenced alternative views, and contributed to a greater corporatism and a reduced form of democracy. (p. 155)

The role of the universities in teacher training is couched within the rhetoric of 'partnership with schools'. Partnership is always an attractive proposition in a democratic and free-thinking society, but Crozier et al. (1990) point out that it is also a means of concealing the universities' loss of the curriculum.

Heartfelt and powerfully argued as they are, these protests have made no impression on governments. The 2002 revision to the QTS standards (TTA, 2002) made some concessions to the concept of educational values with a section on 'Professional Standards', and the number of detailed standards was reduced, together with a (large) accompanying handbook of guidance. However, the essence was the same and the machinery for ensuring compliance, the Ofsted Framework (Ofsted, 2004, 2008), made even stronger. The Chief Executive Ralph Tabberer, appointed in 2000 from a higher education background, appeared to signal a softening of the hard-line, anti-university approach of the 1990s (Tabberer, 2000). However, change was slight and significantly there was no concession to change the nomenclature back to 'teacher education' and the 'training' language continues.

Inspection of teacher training grew increasingly rigorous with visits every three years, with a number of universities threatened with 'non-compliance' and the removal of TDA accreditation. From 2008 each teacher training provider had to produce for the TDA and Ofsted a self-evaluation document analysing and providing data from every aspect of its training. Foucault's (1979) 'panoptical' scrutiny described for schools in Chapter 6 is replicated as the demand for accountability increases. It is important to note that while the TDA allocates student numbers in Wales, the specific allocation is under the jurisdiction of the Welsh Assembly and its policy is outlined in the document, *Wales: The Learning Country* (National Assembly for Wales, 2001). Trainees in Wales are not required to take literacy and numeracy tests. While the Welsh teacher training courses are inspected, the regime is less rigorous than the English one and is another example of a 'softer', less regulatory approach than in England.

The University of Liverpool in 2000 found the rigours and trials of compliance with the requirements and standards not worthwhile and withdrew from teacher training. At the time there were rumours that other universities would act similarly, but none did and all continued to offer teacher training under the new regime. The institutional resistance to the government takeover was weak. Had others joined the University of Liverpool in a coordinated act of defiance then the government's grip on teacher training could have been lessened. However, the income and status provided by teacher training was a sufficient incentive for universities to comply with the training requirements and the threatening Ofsted methodology.

Undergraduate Education Studies as a University Subject

Another response of universities to government control of ITT was to develop non-teacher training Education Studies courses funded by the Higher Education Funding Council. Such courses returned control of the Education curriculum to the universities and were not subject to the scrutiny of Ofsted. Education Studies has grown as a major new university subject in the last fifteen years with some 40,000 full- and part-time undergraduate students (HESA, 2008). The growth of the courses appears to derive from two sources: the motivation for universities to re-establish control of the Education curriculum, and the desire of students to study Education without a teacher-training career in mind (Burton and Bartlett, 2006).

Apart from the very small number of original courses of the 1960s at the Universities of York and Lancaster, courses have mainly developed from teacher training. They are either a conversion from an undergraduate teacher-training course, or complementary to an existing undergraduate teacher-training course in the school or faculty. Education Studies has grown as a subject defined by academics without reference to government agencies. Ward (2006), in a study of the development of Education Studies in ten universities, found that the freedom from government control meant that courses had a diverse range of curriculum content, including international education, globalisation, education policy and ecological issues. One common feature of the curriculum in all the courses studies was the 'critique' of policy and professional practice. And this was consistent with another finding: in interviews with academic course leaders, all referred to the benefits of academic freedom, sometimes describing it as 'liberation' from the state control of teacher training. On the other hand, it was found that, while there was freedom from government control, many academics found the need to adjust their courses to the demand of the student market in order to recruit students.

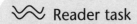 Reader task

Examine the aims for your Education Studies course. What is the knowledge and understanding you are expected to learn, and what are the transferable skills that you are learning? Are they appropriate for you and the career you wish to pursue?

Conclusion

In this chapter we have seen that teacher training was the first of the government's targets for centralised control, well before the 1988 Education Act and the National Curriculum. That fact that it was chosen is probably because it was an easier target with a relatively small number of institutions involved, but it is also a sign of the importance with which teacher training is viewed by governments: teachers still define the nature of education and their quality is central to the whole endeavour. It is interesting, though, that teacher trainers in universities were accustomed to the maximum level of autonomy and academic freedom, and they found the controls the most difficult to stomach. The demand for Education Studies is a product of the growing interest of undergraduate students in education and young people. But it might also be seen as the resistance of the university community to government attempts to remove critical analysis from teacher education. The QAA Benchmark for Education Studies (QAA, 2007) recommends that a key characteristic of Education Studies graduates is that they have an understanding and a critical analysis of government policy. We hope that this book has helped you with that!

Recommended reading

Burton, D. and Bartlett, S. (2006) 'The evolution of Education Studies in higher education in England', *Curriculum Journal*, 17 (4): 383–96. Burton and Bartlett explain the reasons for the rise in non-teacher-training Education Studies.

Crook, D. (2002) 'Education studies and teacher education', *British Journal of Education Studies*, 50 (1): 55–75. Crook gives an interesting historical account of the development of teacher-training as a graduate profession.

McCulloch, G. (2002) 'Disciplines contributing to education? Educational Studies and the disciplines', *British Journal of Educational Studies*, 50 (1): 100–19. McCulloch explains how the disciplines came into teacher training.

Mahony, P. and Hextall, I. (1997) 'Problems of accountability in reinvented government: a case study of the Teacher Training Agency', *Journal of Education Policy*, 12 (4): 267–78. A critique of government control of training and of the role of the Teacher Training Agency.

References

Barton, L., Barrett, E., Whitty, G., Miles, S. and Furlong, J. (1994) 'Teacher education and teacher professionalism in England: some emerging issues', *British Journal of Sociology of Education*, 15: 529–43.

Bottery, M. (2000) *Education Policy and Ethics*. London: Continuum.

Burton, D. and Bartlett, S. (2006) 'The evolution of Education Studies in higher education in England', *Curriculum Journal*, 17 (4): 383–96.

Cowen, R. (2002) 'Socrates was right? Teacher education systems and the state', in E. Thomas, (ed.), *Teacher Education: Dilemmas and Prospects*, World Yearbook of Education 2002. London: Kogan Page.

Crook, D. (2002) 'Education studies and teacher education', *British Journal of Education Studies*, 50 (1): 55–75.

Crozier, G., Menter, I. and Pollard, A. (1990) 'Changing partnership', in M. Booth, J. Furlong and M. Wilkin (eds), *Partnership in Initial Teacher Training*. London: Cassell.

Fish, D. (1988) *Learning Through Practice in Initial Teacher Training: A Challenge for the Partners*. London: Kogan Page.

Foucault, M. (1979) *Discipline and Punish*. Harmondsworth: Penguin.

Furlong, J., Barton, L., Miles, S., Whiting, C. and Whitty, G. (2000) *Teacher Training in Transition: Reforming Professionalism*. Buckingham: Open University.

Hencke, D. (1978) *Colleges in Crisis: The Reorganisation of Teacher Training 1971–7*. Harmondsworth: Penguin.

HESA (2008) *Students in Higher Education Institutions 2006/07*. Cheltenham: HESA.

Hillgate Group (1989) *Learning to Teach*. London: Claridge.

McCulloch, G. (2002) 'Disciplines contributing to education? Educational Studies and the disciplines', *British Journal of Educational Studies*, 50 (1): 100–19.

McKinsey & Co. (2007) *How the World's Best-Performing Schooling Systems Come Out on Top*. London: McKinsey. Online. Available at: http://www.mckinsey.com/clientservice/socialsector/resources/pdf/Worlds_School_Systems_Final.pdf (accessed 20 November 2008).

Maguire, M., Dillon, J. and Quintrell, M. (1998) *Finding Virtue, Not Finding Fault: Stealing the Wind of Destructive Reforms*. London: ATL.

Mahony, P. and Hextall, I. (1997) 'Problems of accountability in reinvented government: a case study of the Teacher Training Agency', *Journal of Education Policy*, 12 (4): 267–78.

Millett, A. (1999) *The Implications for Teacher Training of the Government's Green Paper – 'Teachers: Meeting the Challenge of Change'*. London: TTA.

Musgrove, F. (1968) 'The contribution of sociology to the study of the curriculum', in J.F. Kerr (ed.), *Changing the Curriculum*. London: University of London Press.

National Assembly for Wales (2001) *Wales: The Learning Country*. Cardiff: National Assembly for Wales.

Ofsted (1998) *Framework for the Inspection of Teacher Training*. London: Ofsted.

Ofsted (2004) *Framework for the Inspection of Teacher Training*. London: Ofsted.

Ofsted (2008) *Framework for the Inspection of Teacher Training*. London: Ofsted.

Phillips, M. (1996) *All Must Have Prizes*. London: Little, Brown.

QAA (2007) *Subject Benchmark Statements: Education Studies*. Gloucester: QAA. Online at: http://www.qaa.ac.uk/academicinfrastructure/benchmark/honours/educationstudies .asp (accessed 2 October 2008).

Richards, C. (1998) 'Primary teacher education: high status? High standards? A personal response to recent initiatives', in C. Richards, N. Simco and S. Twiselton, *Primary Teacher Education: High Status? High Standards?* Lewes: Falmer Press.

Richardson, W. (2002) 'Education Studies in the United Kingdom, 1940–2002', *British Journal of Educational Studies*, 50 (1): 3–56.

Robbins, Lord (1963) *Committee on Higher Education: Report*. London: HMSO.

Ross, A. (1990) 'The universities and the BEd degree', in B. Thomas (ed.), *British Universities and Teacher Education: A Century of Change*. Lewes: Falmer Press.

Simon, B. (1994) 'The study of education', in *The State and Educational Change: Essays in the History of Education and Pedagogy*. London: Lawrence & Wishart.

Tabberer, R. (2000) 'Salute the new breed', *Times Educational Supplement*, 27 October, p. 8.

Tomlinson, P. and Hobson, A. (2001) *NQT Views of Teacher Training*. Leeds: University of Leeds.

TDA (2007) *QTS Standards and ITT Requirements*. London: TDA. Online at: http://www.tda. gov.uk/partners/ittstandards.aspx.

TTA (1995) *School-centred Initial Teacher Training: Notes of Guidance*. London: TTA.

TTA (1998) *Teaching: High Status, High Standards. Standards for the Award of Qualified Teacher Status*. London: DfEE.

TTA (2002) *Qualifying to Teach: Professional Standards for Qualified Teacher Status and Requirements for Initial Teacher Training*. London: TTA.

Universities Council for the Education of Teachers (UCET) (1997) *The Role of Universities in the Education and Training of Teachers: The Text of a Seminar Held on Wednesday, 12 February 1997 at the Institute of Education, University of London*, UCET Occasional Paper No. 8.

Ward, S. (2006) 'Undergraduate Education Studies as an Emerging Subject in Higher Education'. Unpublished PhD thesis, Bath Spa University.

Gender and educational policy

Introduction

In this chapter we look at an area which has received a great deal of attention in the press over the last few years: gender and educational achievement. Media interest in education tends to focus on the information which interests parents: how different schools have performed in tests and examinations and their place in published league tables. During the last twenty years, discussion has focused on whether schools are able to affect test results, irrespective of the social background of children, with concerns about what is perceived to be boys' underachievement.

To understand equality of educational opportunity we have to look at the way in which gender, ethnicity and social class interact with one another (see DfES, 2007, and Skelton et al., 2007, for evidence of these interrelationships). Research shows that gender is not the strongest predictor of attainment; the social-class attainment gap being considerably wider than the gender gap. Equally, we know that some minority ethnic groups have an attainment gap which is greater than the gap between boys and girls. But gender is an independent and significant predictor of attainment.

Models of masculinity and femininity in society and in the family are the framework within which the school and educational achievement operate. Family relationships and women's roles in society have changed in recent years, but responsibility for domestic labour and childcare often remain with women. This provides a backdrop for looking at how young men and women see their futures, which in turn has consequences for their motivation in the education system. One of the issues to be explained is the dissonance between educational success and success in the labour market.

Two concerns have run through discussions about educational attainment and gender: the extent to which the curriculum is differentiated on the basis of gender and social class, and the extent to which gender influences achievement. The social construction of masculinity and femininity are a powerful influence on the way in which males and females construct their place within schooling and educational attainment. We argue that the school has a role in both constructing and challenging stereotypical views, thereby changing the expectations of young men and women.

Historical Overview

During the nineteenth century there were significant changes for both working- and middle-class men and women associated with their education and employment. The feminist movement that emerged in the 1860s challenged the economic dependence of married middle-class women whose lives had nothing in common with working-class women who needed to work to survive. The Industrial Revolution produced new jobs in 'the service sector' and middle-class women began to enter the labour market. Thus the education of girls was transformed during the nineteenth and twentieth centuries.

The 1870 Education Act made schooling available for all children up to the age of 10. But working- and middle-class girls were prepared for very different experiences in the labour market, and their schooling developed in very different ways. Middle-class girls attended mainly fee-paying establishments during the nineteenth century, which had an emphasis on ladylike subjects that would equip women to be decorative and play their role within a male-dominated household. A few schools for middle-class girls did follow an academic curriculum, but there was a fear that such study could damage physical health and that well-being would be undermined by too much mental work. Delamont (quoted in Measor and Sikes, 1992) has distinguished between approaches to women's education. On the one hand there were 'separatists' who wanted high standards of education for women and girls, and did not argue that they should receive the same curriculum as men and boys. The other group were 'non-compromisers' who believed that the curriculum available to girls should be the same as that for boys and that all should be judged by the same standards. The nineteenth and twentieth centuries did not make it easy for girls to have a career, marriage and a family. The assumptions were that middle-class women were economically dependent on their husbands and their lives revolved around ensuring that they had the necessary skills and graces to meet his requirements in the home. The notion of 'an appropriate education for girls' continued through the twentieth century and was changed only by the National Curriculum of 1988.

Education for working-class girls was to provide a workforce for the development of the economy. But there was also the belief that women had responsibility for the general health and moral well-being of the family. Schools were the place to provide women with the type of information they needed for basic nutrition and childcare. Obedience, thrift and respect for one's elders were seen as relevant for the role of girls engaged in domestic work. It is no surprise that the curriculum for working-class girls and state elementary schools was associated with domestic activities: knitting, laundering, cooking and childcare. The Schools Enquiry Commission of 1868 compared girls' and boys' school performance and suggested that differences were to be attributed to characteristic mental differences between the sexes, reinforcing assumptions about innate differences as well as those arising from social position and domestic roles. As compulsory schooling was introduced girls received a curriculum that emphasised neatness, cleanliness, needlework and domestic tasks to equip them to operate within the domestic context. Women were seen as not only needing to provide for their working men but also providing the emotional support which would help with the coherence and cohesion of society under threat from the alienation and anomie of the industrial workplace.

The Education Act of 1902 gave control of schools to local education authorities and was followed by the Elementary School Code of 1904. This included laundry work, domestic labour and cookery. The elementary schools attended by working-class girls continued to emphasise domesticity (Richards, 1998). The curriculum for middle-class women within high schools had little of those elements within it. Boys and girls were engaged in science and mathematics to differing degrees, with a much stronger emphasis on these subjects for boys. Sharpe (1976) quotes a headmistress in 1907 commenting, 'mathematics should be kept to a minimum for girls; it does not underlie their industries as it does for so many of the activities of men' (p. 17). The 'gendered' curriculum was very explicit at this point.

The 1920s and 1930s saw an economic slump in Europe and America. The 1926 Hadow Report focused on the caring, socialising role for women in the home at a time of economic depression. Women were given the responsibility of ensuring the socialisation of the labour force and providing the appropriate home background. The teaching of housework was the solution to the problems facing the nation: 'They should also be shown that on efficient care and management of the home depends the health, happiness and prosperity of the nation' (quoted in Sharpe, 1976: 19). In the nineteenth century, and for part of the twentieth, the education of girls was inextricably tied to equipping them with the domestic skills needed to become housewives and mothers.

The 1944 Act focused on social class inequalities, but did not question the traditional assumptions about the differences in boys' and girls' education. Measor and Sikes (1992) quote Newsom's comment about girls in 1948: 'The fundamental common experience is the fact that the vast majority of them will become the makers of homes, and that to do this successfully requires the proper development of many talents' (p. 43). The same approach to the curriculum can be seen in the 1959 Crowther Report which emphasised that girls' eyes were set on marriage and the family, while for boys it was careers that mattered (CACE, 1959). The 1963 Newsom Report (CACE, 1963) reinforced the assumption that boys and girls had different interests and that their curriculum should reflect their destinations in life as wives and mothers.

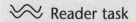 Reader task

Reflect on your own educational experiences. Were they influenced by assumptions that the curriculum should be different for boys and girls?

Changing Attitudes and Policies from the 1960s Onwards

Assumptions about the gendered curriculum were challenged in a number of ways, as changes in the economy brought the need to address a wider perspective on girls' education. The Robbins Report (1963) on higher education pointed to the need for professional women to return to work and argued that greater use should be made of women's skills. During the 1960s and 1970s feminist groups and writers led the drive to expand educational opportunities and the curriculum for women; at the same time the comprehensive movement was challenging inequalities between working- and middle-class pupils in the tripartite system. The 1975 Sex Discrimination Act made it illegal to deny access to employment on the grounds of sex, but this did not actually prevent boys and girls being offered different subject options within schools, and schools found ways to evade the legal requirement.

The equal opportunities legislation of the 1970s and 1980s was significant in the drive to promote opportunities for women, but the real drive for change came from individuals and pressure groups in the women's liberation movement. Feminist writers argued that girls and women were disadvantaged in education and the labour market and were not prepared to accept that there were fundamental differences in the biological capacities of males and females. They gave social explanations for gender differences in educational achievement and considered strategies for change. Various initiatives were developed such as Girls into Science and Technology (GIST) and Women into Science and Engineering (WISE). All these activities challenged the assumption that girls needed a curriculum orientated towards domesticity. At the time girls were seen as underachieving compared to boys. In 1983 the Manpower Services Commission (MSC) launched the Technical and Vocational Educational Initiative which required participating schools to address equal opportunities in relation to gender in order to secure additional funding. This was the first government-sponsored project to address gender inequality.

Moves towards gender equality were significantly enhanced by a Conservative government with the 1988 Education Reform Act and the new concept of 'entitlement' to a curriculum for all pupils (see Chapter 5). While some gender inequalities have continued under the National Curriculum, boys and girls are offered the same core curriculum. We saw in Chapter 3 that at both GCSE and A level boys and girls make different choices, but, particularly in primary schools, the offering is the same. It is a real shift away from the idea that certain sorts of knowledge are appropriate for girls because they would undertake the domestic and childcaring roles deemed to be natural and appropriate for them. It assumes that the Sciences, Technology and Mathematics are as much part of the curriculum for girls as for boys.

The debates during the 1970s and 1980s focused on girls' underachievement rather than their ability to do well in subjects such as English. The National Curriculum and its testing regime exposed the fact that girls were actually achieving at a higher level than boys. Since the 1990s the underachievement of boys has been seen as the problem, initially revealed through the results of GCSE examinations. Since then the gap between female and male attainment has continued to widen in favour of females, and even the traditional advantage of males over females in science areas has largely disappeared.

If, though, we take into account social class, the experiences of working-class and middle-class girls have continued from the nineteenth century to be very different. Despite women's higher educational attainment, patterns of employment and opportunities in the labour market favour men. Working-class and middle-class girls have very different opportunities in the education system. Nevertheless, there are certain realities that all women share. If we look for women in top jobs we see very few. And if we look for men who take responsibility for domestic tasks and childcare we see very few. Women are excluded from top positions and expected to accept the childcare and domestic roles within the family. This has continued throughout the twentieth century and into the twenty-first, in spite of legislation and the National Curriculum. The limitations are, though, not experienced in the same way by girls in different classes. Various studies have shown that, for working-class girls, schooling has been, and still is, focused on the anticipated role of a wife and mother, which is their destiny at the point when they leave school (Griffen, 1985; Lees, 1993).

The focus recently has been on boys' underachievement with reports commissioned by Ofsted and other government agencies to address the problem (DCSF, 2008a). Boys' underachievement has dominated discussions about attainment, particularly in the media; it has a simple attraction and can be presented as something that schools should be able to address. The greater attainment gaps in ethnicity and social class have not been given the same emphasis and media attention, nor are there so many strategies identified to address those issues, even though it is recognised that gender is not the strongest predictor of attainment; social class attainment and some minority ethnic groups present greater attainment gaps than that between boys and girls (DfES, 2007).

The response to boys' underachievement in literacy has been focused on attainment in the assessment system and has failed to identify two big issues. The first is the social relationships between boys and girls, the sexualisation of girls and the power that boys have in their relationship over them. The second is the choices that girls make for themselves framed by their expectations about domestic and childcare responsibilities. Neither of these has the visibility and significance associated with boys' underachievement; yet they are both powerful factors in young people's lives once they leave school and join the labour market. There has been much less attention to areas within the curriculum where girls are less successful. Girls' achievement in mathematics and their under-representation in physics and economics should also be addressed if concerns about pupils' achievements are driven by social justice.

> The high visibility of debates about gender is because of the belief that the problem of the attainment gap can be solved within the school system. Explanations for inequalities have explored the internal processes of the classroom, teacher expectations and interaction, the nature of the curriculum, resources and assessment strategies. The debate usually fails to identify the context within which young people understand themselves: their identities and the way they impact on their willingness to learn. Attention has been given to changes in the labour market and the extent to which that impinges upon boys' sense of masculinity (Mac an Ghaill, 1994) but there has been less interest in the extent to which young girls see themselves tied to a future which gives them the responsibility for childcare, or why women do not achieve the most senior positions in the labour market. While there has been a significant expansion of women working, it has not been accompanied by a shift in the responsibilities that men and women, particularly working-class women, take for childcare responsibilities and domestic tasks.

Gender Differences in Educational Achievement

Recent initiatives to raise standards have been beneficial for both boys and girls. But the rate of increase for females is greater than that for males, and has occurred rapidly, particularly in the proportions who achieve five or more A*–C GCSE passes. Differences vary across pupils' school careers: the achievement of girls in relationship to boys actually widens as pupils get older and, in the last few years, the gap in performance in favour of boys at A level has been eliminated. There are, though, continuing differences in subject entry to A levels with stereotypical female-dominated and male-dominated subjects (Arnot et al., 1998). The gender gap varies across different subject areas, of which the most extreme is for literacy, which is an international pattern. The statistics on educational attainment show that the rhetoric and concern about boys' achievement, particularly in literacy, is valid but there are areas of girls' underachievement which go largely unnoticed.

The data on educational attainment for 2007–8 shows girls outperformed boys in the Foundation Stage Profile. Forty-one per cent of boys reached a 'good level of development' compared to 58 per cent of girls (DCSF, 2008b). At Key Stage 1 there was a gender gap in favour of girls in Speaking and Listening, Reading and Writing, while a higher proportion of boys achieved Level 3 or above in Mathematics and Science (DCSF, 2008c).

At Key Stage 2 boys' performance at Level 4 and above in Mathematics was slightly better than girls', a pattern for the previous three years. Girls continued to outperform boys in all aspects of English at Levels 4 and 5, with a gender gap of 14 per cent for Writing at Level 4 (DCSF, 2008d: Table 2). The differences are also reflected in those who do not achieve well. Thirty-one per cent of boys only achieved Level 3 in writing, compared to 21 per cent of girls; in Mathematics, 14 per cent of boys achieved Level 3 compared to 16 per cent of girls (DCSF, 2008d: Table 3). These statistics illustrate the complexity of gender performance in that both subject and level reveal different stories. The story about boys doing badly in the English subjects is well known, but this evidence shows that, in Mathematics, boys were doing better than girls at Key Stage 2. Evidence from the National Audit Office suggests that not only did boys do better than girls at Mathematics, they also made better progress between Key Stages 1 and 2 (NAO, 2008: 24).

At GCSE, the greater achievement by girls continues particularly at the higher grades (A*–C). In the three years from 2004 to 2006 there was a 10 per cent gender gap in achieving five A*–C grades and a 9 per cent gap in 2007 (DCSF, 2008e: Table 2). The data for 2007–8 reveal a consistent pattern of a greater proportion of girls achieving A*–C grades across all subjects, except for Physics and Biological Sciences. In some instances this is a small difference, as in Mathematics where the attainment gap is 2 per cent, but in English it increases to 13 per cent. It is at this stage that we see the re-emergence of the gendered curriculum. Students make choices at GCSE reflecting different expectations that young men and women have about what are appropriate subjects for them to study. This is visible in subjects such as Physics and Chemistry where a third more boys take them up, and in Home Economics where boys comprise less than 10 per cent. The gendered nature of choice is particularly visible within Design and Technology where over ten times as many boys take electronic products, and the number of girls taking textiles is 40 times greater than that of boys (DCSF, 2008e).

A level information shows that girls are more likely than boys to stay in full-time education and, in a change over the last ten years, girls perform better in the percentage gaining A* grades. The stereotyped gendered choices visible at GCSE become much more obvious at A level. Boys are nearly four times as likely to take Physics, 50 per cent more take Mathematics and twice as many as girls take further Mathematics (DCFS, 2008e). But the gap has decreased since 2001–2. Male subject choices cluster around Physics, Mathematics, Computer Studies and Economics.

Women still predominate in the arts and social sciences. There are nearly three times as many female students taking Psychology and three times taking

Sociology. In Art and Design, Drama, English, French, Spanish and Religious Studies there are over twice as many female than male students. Applied A level results show even greater differences. Applied Engineering was taken by 230 males compared to 10 females, while Health and Social Care was taken by 180 male compared to 4,720 female students (DCSF, 2008f). The overall pass rate by subject and gender shows little difference between boys and girls. But in those achieving grades A and B, female students performed better than males, with 26.8 achieving A or B grades compared to 18.1 per cent of male students. The exception to this trend is in Modern Languages which all have a higher proportion of males achieving grade A. At the other end of the scale, the pattern is reversed with most subjects showing a higher percentage of males achieving grade E. Again there is an exception in Modern Languages, although the differences here are very small (DCSF, 2008e: Table 2m).

~~~~ Reader task

In what ways do you think notions of masculinity and femininity impact on choices made at A level and are these linked to aspirations after schooling?

Access to Higher Education

Historically, women have been under-represented in universities. From 1992 their participation has increased and now more women than men are under graduates in the UK (HESA, 2008: Table 2e). But the link between educational achievement and entry to positions of power and income in the labour market is more complicated. The subjects women take disadvantage them. Data from the Higher Education Statistical Agency (HESA, 2008) show marked differences in the type of courses that men and women take. Men make up less than a quarter of those on Social Work, Education and Psychology undergraduate courses, less than a third on English Studies and less than half on languages. In 2006–7 male qualifiers in initial teacher training made up less than a quarter of students. The subjects with a predominance of males are Physics, where less than 20 per cent are female, Physical Sciences, where less than half are female, and Engineering and Technology where only 15 per cent are female. Architecture has twice as many males as females, as is the case with Economics; in Building less than 10 per cent are female.

There are also marked differences in women's and men's access to universities. At the prestigious postgraduate institution the London Business School, females make up less than a quarter of its students. Women are, though, significantly over-represented in the new universities, and significantly so in the more recently identified new universities which originally were teacher training colleges (see Chapter 7). In these institutions, female students significantly outnumber males, in some cases in the ratio of three to one. While their courses may be of high quality these are not the universities that carry high status and are not yet among the elite with a strong research profile. So both subject choice and type of university will have considerably different impact on male and female students in access to high-status and well-paid work in the labour market.

The impact this has on men and women graduates is part of the explanation for the gender wage gap in favour of men which exists, despite equal opportunities legislation. Research by Chevalier (2006) suggests that there are more complex issues to do with expectations and attitudes towards education and longer-term careers. While differences in education, occupation and expectations helped account for the gender gap, the most important component was the expectation of a career break, which accounted for 10 per cent of the gender wage gap. Women who have preferences for child-rearing have lower wages, even early on in their career:

> Men and women do make different choices throughout their life which significantly affect their wages. However, one should be concerned that the 'choices' made by women stem from fear of discrimination, social pressure and child rearing expectations and one could debate whether these choice variables should be included as explanations of the gender wage gap. (Chevalier, 2006: 4)

Concerns about male participation in higher education stem from a commitment to individual opportunities and from the recognition that greater participation in university education is a government target. The Leitch Report (2006) argued that, if the UK was to become a world leader in skills, it needed to exceed 40 per cent of adults qualified to Level 4 by 2020. Greater participation of men is essential if this target is to be reached. So the gender gap in HE participation, which continues to widen, does matter. The evidence on women and men shows that policy needs to address women's aspirations in the longer term, and male aspirations at the point within their school careers when they are making decisions about continuing into higher education or leaving school.

 Reader task

Girls do well at school. But how do you account for the fact that women are not translating their educational achievements into the labour market?

Gendered Learning

 Children do not enter the classroom as a blank sheet but bring with them a wide range of expectations about how it is appropriate to behave and what is expected of them. Schools either counter such stereotypes or reinforce them. But children also resist and challenge expectations, and select what they chose to adopt and act on in their own lives. Gendered identities affect pupil achievement as they make choices about what is appropriate for them and research has shown that there are strong penalties for children who fail to conform to gender norms (Connolly, 2004). Any attempt to tackle the achievement gap must challenge the ways in which masculinity and femininity are constructed and the way in which boys and girls are positioned in opposition to one another. Strategies should include a holistic perspective: how to support pupils in challenging stereotypes and the behaviours that go with these. This means more than changing assessment mode or single-sex teaching, or changing the proportion of male teachers or focusing on learning and teaching styles. Policy should address the way in which boys and girls behave towards each other and work together, the language which is used to present themselves as feminine and masculine, the sexualisation of the school environment and the way in which it isolates boys and girls. The 'socio-cultural approach' goes beyond the organisation of learning and attempts to challenge the dominant images of 'laddish' masculinity held by the peer group. Tackling this cultural concept could change the whole negative approach to learning held by many boys, but requires the development of teachers' awareness of potentially sexist attitudes and changing the way in which the classroom is organised to engage boys and girls working together. The dominant image of masculinity and the street culture from which it emerges is powerful in creating an alternative culture within schools. Challenging this requires engaging boys in a learning process and getting them to see its value, rather than it being viewed as something which is negative and likely to bring loss of status in their peers' eyes (Younger et al., 2005).

Mac an Ghaill (1994) argued that the loss of working-class manual occupations undermined traditional models of masculinity, leading to an erosion of confidence and a sense that education lacked relevance and value. This negative approach to education is indicated by greater rates of truancy and exclusion (Ofsted, 1996). In other research teachers report that male students exhibit greater behavioural problems in the classroom, with a group culture which sees education as undesirable. A five-year study by Davies and Brember (2001) showed that issues associated with discipline and authority should be given more attention when considering boys' academic achievement. Skelton et al. (2007) comment, 'analysis of the literature and statistics indicates that the 'gender gap in achievement' can only be removed by shifting notions of gender itself; that is, notions of what is appropriate, relevant and meaningful for boys and girls' (p. 2). Challenging the construction of stereotyped gender is at the centre of what is necessary to tackle inequalities in educational achievement. They argue, 'the ways in which teachers, pupils, parents and policymakers construct gender itself must be challenged' (p. 6).

This is a very different notion of the policies needed to address the gender gap. The starting point is for teachers to challenge stereotypes and encourage pupils to challenge them also. Schools need to address language and discourse and the expectations that pupils have of themselves and their own educational success,

(Continued)

> *(Continued)*
>
> particularly what Francis and Skelton call 'oppositional relationships' between boys and girls which require boys to gain status in their own and their peer group's eyes in a way that has a negative impact on their learning (Francis and Skelton, 2005; Mac an Ghaill, 1994; Martino, 1999; Warrington et al., 2000).

Gendered subjects are not just about the future options for individuals, but the wider issue of access and skills in the labour market. While girls are achieving well within the education sector, males remain advantaged in employment opportunities and levels of pay. HESA (2007) found that the median salary of full-time first-degree male graduates was £1,000 higher than that of equivalent female graduates, and the Institute of Chartered Management found the pay gap has widened slightly (Chartered Management Institute, 2007). If schools are to develop strategies to challenge male stereotypes that have negative impact on educational attainment, traditional gender roles may need to also be addressed for the benefit of women.

Future domestic responsibility is a major factor in working-class girls' expectations of themselves and has a bearing on their aspirations in the same way as it does for working-class boys. For secondary pupils their sexual identity contributes to expectations of themselves (Younger et al., 2005). This is not a deterministic position; pupils *do* challenge traditional stereotypes. Studies in secondary schools have shown that girls resist and construct their own lives and femininity, but at the same time they are constantly subjected to language and behaviour from boys which place them in an oppressed position or one where they constantly have to challenge boys' behaviour (Haywood and Mac an Ghaill, 2001). The UK education programme manager of an initiative that aims to stop sexual bullying has pointed to its prevalence: 'The normalisation of girls being called a slut or being subjected to abuse and not taking it seriously has to be challenged' (Bell, 2008).

The Gender Equality Duty legislation of 2007 requires public bodies to eliminate unlawful discrimination and harassment and to promote equality of opportunity between men and women. The 14–19 Gender Equality Project covers a number of projects funded by the DCSF that are piloting strategies to challenge gender stereotypes and to help young people make informed course choices. The interventions are based on the strategies suggested on the DCSF 14–19 website and form part of the Gender Agenda. These projects are based on developing an ethos which 'demonstrates commitment to every individual and which treats staff and pupils with fairness, trust and respect', but they tend to be concerned with interventions in teaching and the organisation of the curriculum rather than challenging the underlying issues about the construction of masculinity and femininity (DCFS, 2008f). Undermining traditional gender stereotypes would benefit both boys and girls and would allow the inequalities that affect girls within the labour and domestic spheres to become part of the debate. As attention has shifted to boys' educational achievements, inequalities have become 'privatised', about individual choice rather than part of the structures of inequality in society. Schools do not address how women can balance family demands and career expectations and how men can be involved in taking a more equal share in childrearing. Without this perspective females will continue to find themselves confronting inequalities in the labour market and the domestic sphere.

Until that happens, success at school will not translate into success, power and prestige for women in the labour market. Education policy should address the needs of girls and their future opportunities as much as those of boys. The power of social class influencing gendered expectations is illustrated by the fact that of students who are not in employment, education or training (NEET), 12 per cent of girls say they expect to be looking after home or family in the next 12 months, whereas this is the case for only 1 per cent of boys (DCFS, 2008g: Chart 6.1.2). Such data reinforce the importance of tackling fundamental concepts of gender and identity if we want to challenge the current attainment gaps for both boys and girls. The structuring of the curriculum on the basis of gender and class which was so visible in the nineteenth and early twentieth centuries remains hidden but still embedded in the school system. Only initiatives that face this directly will change patterns of choice, achievement and career patterns.

〰️ **Reader task**

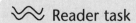

How do you think schools can challenge a 'laddish' culture and encourage greater gender equality in peer relationships?

Conclusion

The analysis at the beginning of this chapter identified the policies that led to different experiences of education for middle- and working-class boys and girls in the nineteenth and twentieth centuries. Such explicit polices have disappeared, but aspirations and achievement are still gendered and framed by class. Boys and girls have won an entitlement to the same curriculum but their own choices remain gendered.

The emphasis in recent years on boys' underachievement has dominated debates and often obscured social class and ethnicity inequalities. Connolly (2006) has argued that recognising the way gender identity interacts with social class and ethnicity produces 'differing and enduring' forms of identity and requires that any programme of intervention be applicable to all boys and all girls. Improvements in female achievement are not shared by all girls and are not across all subjects; this needs to be more directly addressed. Debates about inequality may be more

(Continued)

(Continued)

appropriately focused on which particular categories of boys and girls are under-achieving. Education policy to tackle gender inequalities needs to address the complex processes of construction of gender identity that has negative implications for both boys and girls within families, schools and the labour market.

〰 Reader tasks

- Discuss any experiences you and your friends have had which have been affected by gender stereotypes? How can these be challenged for both boys and girls?
- Interview some of your friends about their experiences of sexual identity and bullying within school. How do they think this could be changed?

Recommended reading

Arnot, M., David, M. and Weiner, G. (1999) *Closing the Gender Gap*. Cambridge: Polity Press. A discussion of explanations of the gender gap and strategies to challenge them.

Connolly, P. (2006) 'Effects of social class and ethnicity on gender differences', *British Educational Research Journal*, 32 (1): 3–23. A careful and precise analysis of the nature of the relationship between social class, ethnicity and gender.

DfES (2007) *Gender and Education: The Evidence on Pupils in England*. Online at: http://www.dfes.gov.uk/research/data/uploadfiles/RTP01-07.pdf. Summarises data on subject choice and attainment, drawing on a wide range of literature to account for gender differences in attainment.

DfES (n.d.) *The Standards Site*. Online at: http://nationalstrategies.standards.dcsf.gov.uk/genderandachievement/. Has a section on Gender and Achievement which gives references to books and journal articles, resources and links.

Skelton, C., Francis, B. and Valkanova, Y. (2007) *Breaking Down the Stereotypes: Gender and Achievement in Schools*. London: EOC. Online at: http://www.equalityhumanrights.com/Documents/Gender/Research/Breaking%20down%20the%20stereotypes%20Gender%20and%20achievement%20in%20schools%20EOC%20research.doc. A detailed review of a wide range of research and data with suggestions for a range of strategies to address the gender gap in achievement.

References

Arnot, M., Gray, J., James, M., Ruddock, J. with Duveen, G. (1998) *Recent Research on Gender and Educational Performance*. London: TSO.

Bell, R. (2008) 'That joke isn't funny anymore', *Education Guardian*, 4 November, p. 3.

CACE (1959) *15–18 The Crowther Report.* London: HMSO.

CACE (1963) *Half Our Future.* London: HMSO.

Chartered Management Institute (2007) *Female Resignations Hit New High Despite Rapid Promotion and Bonus Payouts.* Online at: http://www.managers.org.uk/listing_media_1.aspx?id=10:347&id=10:138&id=10:11&doc=10:3364 (accessed 21 February 2009).

Chevalier, A. (2006) *Education, Occupation and Career Expectations: Determinants of the Gender Pay Gap for UK Graduates,* Working Paper No. CEEDP0069. London: London School of Economics, Centre for the Economics of Education. Online at: http://cee.lse.ac.uk/cee%20dps/ceedp69.pdf (accessed 10 September 2008).

Connolly, P. (2004) *Boys and Schooling in the Early Years.* London: RoutledgeFalmer.

Connolly, P. (2006) 'Effects of social class and ethnicity on gender differences', *British Educational Research Journal,* 32 (1): 3–23.

Davies, J. and Brember, I. (2001) *Closing the Gap in Attitudes between Boys and Girls: A Five-Year Longitudinal Study.* Manchester: University of Manchester School of Education.

DCSF (2008a) *The Gender Agenda.* London: DCSF. Online at: http://www.teachernet.gov.uk/wholeschool/equality/genderequalityduty/thegenderagenda/ (accessed 12 September 2008).

DCSF (2008b) *DCSF: Attainment by Pupil Characteristics in England 2007/08.* London: DCSF. Online at: http://www.dcsf.gov.uk/rsgateway/DB/SFR/s000759/SFR38_2007_Tables.xls (accessed 10 September 2008).

DCSF (2008c) *National Curriculum Assessments at Key Stage 1 in England, 2008 (Provisional).* London: DCSF. Online at: http://www.dcsf.gov.uk/rsgateway/DB/SFR/s000806/index.shtml (accessed 7 September 2008).

DCSF (2008d) *National Curriculum Assessments at Key Stage 2 in England, 2008 (Provisional).* London: DCSF. Online at: http://www.dcsf.gov.uk/rsgateway/DB/SFR/s000804/index.shtml (accessed 12 September 2008).

DCSF (2008e) *GCE/VCE A/AS and Equivalent Examination Results in England, 2007/08 (Provisional).* London: DCSF. Online at: http://www.dcsf.gov.uk/rsgateway/DB/SFR/s000816/index.shtml (accessed 10 September 2008).

DCSF (2008f) *The Gender Agenda – Research and Evidence.* London: DCSF. Online at: http://www.teachernet.gov.uk/wholeschool/equality/genderequalityduty/thegenderagenda/researchandevidence/ (Accessed 8 August 2008).

DCSF (2008g) *Youth Cohort Study and Longitudinal Study of Young People in England: The Activities and Experiences of 16 Year Olds: England 2007.* London: DCFS. Online at: http://www.dcsf.gov.uk/rsgateway/DB/SBU/b000795/Bulletin_tables_final.xls.

DfES (2007) *Gender and Education: The Evidence on Pupils in England.* London: DfES.

Francis, B. and Skelton, C. (2005) *Reassessing Gender and Achievement.* London: Routledge.

Griffen, C. (1985) *Typical Girls.* London: Routledge & Kegan Paul.

Haywood, C. and Mac an Ghaill, M. (2001) 'The significance of teaching English to boys: exploring social change, modern schooling and the making of masculinities', in W. Martino and B. Mayenn (eds), *What About the Boys?* Buckingham: Open University Press.

HESA (2007) *Career Progression of Graduates.* Cheltenham: HESA. Online at: http://www.hesa.ac.uk/index.php/content/view/888/161/ (accessed 14 September 2008).

HESA (2008) *All HE Students by Level of Study, Mode of Study, Subject of Study (#1), Domicile and Gender 2006/07*. Cheltenham: HESA. Online at: http://www.hesa.ac.uk/dox/data Tables/studentsAndQualifiers/download/subject0607.xls?v=1.0 (accessed 10 September 2008).

Lees, S. (1993) *Sugar and Spice: Sexuality and Adolescent Girls*. London: Penguin.

Leitch, S. (2006) *Prosperity for All in the Global Economy – World Class Skills*. London: DCSF. Online at: http://www.dcsf.gov.uk/furthereducation/uploads/documents/2006-12 per cent20LeitchReview1.pdf (accessed 10 September 2008).

Mac an Ghaill, M. (1994) *The Making of Men: Masculinities, Sexualities and Schooling*. Buckingham: Open University Press.

Martino, W. (1999) '"Cool boys", "party animals", "squids" and "poofters": interrogating the dynamics and politics of adolescent masculinities in schools', *British Journal of Sociology of Education*, 20: 240–63.

Measor, L. and Sikes, P.J. (1992) *Gender and Schools*. London: Cassell.

NAO (2008) *Mathematics Performance in Primary Schools: Getting the Best Result*. London: TSO. Online at: http://www.nao.org.uk/publications/nao_reports/07-08/ 07081151es.pdf (accessed 10 September 2008).

Ofsted (1996) *Exclusions from Secondary Schools*. London: HMSO.

Richards, C. (1998) 'The primary National Curriculum', in J.R. Moyles and L. Hargreaves (eds), *The Primary Curriculum: Learning from International Perspectives*. London: Routledge.

Robbins, L.R. (1963) *Higher Education: Report of the Committee appointed by the Prime Minister under the Chairmanship of Lord Robbins*. London: HMSO.

Sharpe, R. (1976) *Just Like a Girl*. Harmondsworth: Penguin.

Skelton, C., Francis, B. and Valkanova, Y. (2007) *Breaking Down the Stereotypes: Gender and Achievement in Schools*. Online at: http://www.equalityhumanrights.com/Documents/ Gender/Research/Breaking down the stereotypes Gender and achievement in schools EOC research.doc (accessed 12 August 2008).

Warrington, M., Younger, M. and Williams, J. (2000) 'Student attitudes, image and the gender gap', *British Educational Research Journal*, 26 (3): 393–407.

Younger, M., Warrington, M. and McLellan, R. (2005) *Raising Boys' Achievements in Secondary School: Issues, Dilemmas and Opportunities*. Maidenhead: Open University Press/McGraw-Hill.

Race, religion and social cohesion

Introduction

Britain is a multicultural, multiracial and multi-faith society. There is a popular view that it has become so because of postwar immigration from the Commonwealth countries: Indian, Pakistan, Bangladesh, the Caribbean, Hong Kong and nations in Africa. However, Britain's diverse population reaches much further back. Like many countries in Europe its population comprises centuries of migrants: Romans, Angles, Saxons, Jutes, Vikings, Normans and Jews. There were black soldiers in the Roman army at Hadrian's Wall. Black people have been resident since the sixteenth century and suffered from early racism when Queen Elizabeth I was said to believe 'there are of late diverse blackamoores brought into this realme, of which kind of people there are allready here to manie' (Fryer, 1984: 10).

This chapter examines the way education policy has attempted to deal with the combined effects of an increasingly diverse population, the inherent racism in British society and the social tensions following 9/11. Government policy on race is not restricted to the Department of Education; because issues of race are seen to affect the nature of society and social cohesion, matters of race and minority groups are also the concern of the Home Office which deals with law and order and policing. Race in Britain is intensely political and at the heart of divisions in society. The first half of the chapter shows how education policy on race and racism has evolved since the 1950s with debates about the nature of multicultural and anti-racist education. The second half examines recent government policy on faith schools and their role in the debate about social cohesion.

Schooling and Race

We first look at the ways in which the education system responded to the social context of black immigration and white racism. Central state policy has often been unclear and practice has been influenced by a mixture of government initiatives, local authority action as well as the professional and academic communities. Throughout, policy and action have been characterised by sharp divisions and bitter controversy.

Assimilation and Integration – White Schools, Black Problems

Tomlinson (1977) and Gillborn (2008) describe the different ways in which the education system responded to postwar immigration. When the first waves of immigration began in the 1950s and 1960s schools in the inner cities found themselves dealing with a diverse range of pupils: children from the West Indies, India, Pakistan and Hong Kong. The first response was to see such pupils as a problem: they didn't speak English, they had different religions, ate different food and knew little of 'British culture'. They were black and seen as a 'racial problem'. There was no national policy on ethnic diversity at the time and the response coming from local authorities and schools soon became known as 'immigrant education'. It is perhaps not surprising that the approach focused on the problem of the pupils and the idea was to try to 'assimilate outsiders' into the existing culture of the school system, mainly by teaching English. Of course, it was essential for pupils to learn English, but the assimilationist approach regarded minority pupils as 'the problem' to be addressed: *they* needed to be changed to fit into existing school practices. They were seen to be a problem for social relations in the community: white pupils and parents would object to their presence. Racism was overt and acceptable in British society, and the perception of black and minority ethnic (BME) children in this way was normal.

'Assimilationism' was more than an attitude; it defined policies on schooling and race. First the language teaching was done in such a way that it neglected the pupil's first language. English was to 'replace' the first language, without having regard to the fact that children used their first language to communicate within their family, or to the psycholinguistic difficulties it brought for children to learn a second language without any relationship to the first (Houlton, 1985). But a wider policy matter was the distribution of black pupils within the schools system. For economic reasons, immigrant families had gravitated towards the low-cost housing areas of the inner cities with high concentrations of pupils in a small number of schools. Schools and local authorities reacted badly to this: schools with a large population of BME pupils were to be avoided. To be properly integrated and assimilated BME pupils should be 'spread around' with smaller proportions in each school. The same perception had been held by authorities in the southern states of America, and the solution there had been 'desegregation bussing' of black children to different schools to dissipate the 'problem' of blacks-only schools. Bradford local authority made a similar proposal in the

1970s to bus BME children to different schools. The proposal was quickly rejected, but it was an indication of the kind of thinking: black and minority ethnic pupils were both a social and educational 'problem'.

While educational policy sought integration through assimilation, there were voices in the wider social and political context which did not advocate integration and the 1960s opposition to immigration was beginning to grow. In 1968, Enoch Powell, Conservative MP for Wolverhampton South-West and Shadow Minister for Defence, gave an infamous speech in Birmingham warning that immigration would lead to racial conflict and that Britain's streets would 'run with rivers of blood'. The speech was highly inflammatory and he was immediately removed from the Shadow Cabinet. However, Powell's speech made him a hero of those opposed to immigration and he particularly appealed to working-class people who felt threatened by the presence of those from other cultures who might take their jobs. These views are now expressed by racist nationalist groups such as the British National Party (BNP). The latent xenophobic fear of 'foreigners' can be subtly fuelled by right-wing politicians. Margaret Thatcher was careful not to speak openly against immigration. However, in a television interview before the 1979 general election which brought her to power as Prime Minister, she spoke of people's concerns about being 'swamped' by different cultures:

> ... by the end of the century there [will] be four million people of the new Commonwealth or Pakistan here. Now, that is an awful lot and I think it means that people are really rather afraid that this country might be rather swamped by people with a different culture and, you know, the British character has done so much for democracy, for law and done so much throughout the world that if there is any fear that it might be swamped people are going to react and be rather hostile to those coming in. (Thatcher, 1978)

This is much less dramatic than Powell's 'rivers of blood' analogy, but it sows fear about immigration and cultural differences.

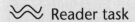 **Reader task**

> Consider your experiences of racism as a pupil in school. Do you recall being subjected to racial abuse, or were you aware of others' experiences?

Multiculturalism and Cultural Pluralism

The mid-1970s brought a change of view about BME pupils among sections of the education community as the concept of a multiracial and multicultural society began to grow. Rather than Britain being a single (white) society and culture into which immigrants should be made to fit, it was recognised that society comprises a number of different 'races' and cultures, and always has done. The Labour government's Race Relations Act in 1976 set up the Commission for Racial Equality (CRE) to support minority groups. In education BME pupils were not to be regarded as a problem. Rather, schools should take account of their different cultural origins and adjust to accommodate them. It should make provision for children to continue to learn and become literate in their first language as well as English. It should take account of their religious beliefs and practices. The curriculum should include the study of BME children's 'cultures': the music of the Caribbean, the history of India, world religions including Islam and Sikhism (Arora and Duncan, 1986). Multicultural education was seen not just as a provision to accommodate ethnic minority pupils. It was intended to enhance the education of all pupils by enriching their learning with knowledge of other cultures and an understanding of the nature of the society in which they were growing up. The school should be a microcosm of a harmonious society in which different peoples live in social cohesion, sharing each other's cultural assets. The school should build close links with its community: sending messages in the community languages, getting members of the community to take part in school activities and gaining the trust of minority parents.

These were the days before the National Curriculum and the content of children's learning was determined by individual schools and teachers, influenced by their local authorities. So multicultural education grew as a movement among informed professionals and changes to the curriculum and approaches in schools were piecemeal. They were largely propagated by the left-wing Labour-controlled local authorities in the big cities. In particular, the Inner London Education authority (ILEA) exerted a strong influence on its schools in areas of ethnic diversity, but some schools simply resisted it. However, during the 1970s and early 1980s multicultural education gained a strong foothold in the consciousness of teachers and local authority officers. While there was still no central government policy on multicultural education, there was recognition that minority ethnic pupils were underachieving in the education system, and in 1976 the Labour government launched a public inquiry into the causes of underachievement led by Sir Anthony Rampton. Its report in 1978 startled both the political and educational world by finding that the underachievement of black and minority pupils was caused by racism among individual teachers and institutional racism in the school system (Rampton, 1981).

Anti-racist Education

Rampton brought into the open the facts that education academics and sociologists had long argued: that the problem in schools was not black pupils, but racism in the system. It gave examples of the ways in which teachers held negative stereotypes of black pupils: for example, that black boys are good at sport and cannot be expected to be good at mathematics. This deficit view of African-Caribbean pupils is a part of the European world view and the covert racism in society. Black writers added their voice and Bernard Coard's (1979) long book title gives the message: *How the West Indian Child is Made Educationally Subnormal in the British School System: The Scandal of the Black Child in Schools in Britain.* Coard argued that teachers' low expectations of black pupils lower their achievement and the system then classifies them as 'sub-normal'.

Black writers also criticised multicultural education. Stone (1981) argued that learning about steel bands and the history of the Caribbean was useless as a curriculum for African-Caribbean pupils. What was required was the traditional curriculum which taught pupils to read and to do mathematics so that they could compete in the employment market. Black people, she insisted, don't want to be depicted as exotically clothed, interesting musicians who eat spicy food; they want proper jobs and power in society. Other criticisms depicted a multicultural curriculum which 'exoticised' the lives of black pupils by learning about 'samosas, saris and steel bands' and which did not recognise the wider racist social context in which black children lived (Troyna, 1984). While black children might at school be in a friendly microcosm of a liberal and tolerant multicultural society, outside the school, or even in the school playground, they would be subjected to racial abuse and violence, as shown in research by Troyna and Hatcher (1992).

It was during the early 1980s that the effects of overt and covert racism began to be recognised and educationists began to address it with 'anti-racist education'. Immigrant education of the 1950s and 1960s had perceived the black child as the problem to be assimilated into white society, multicultural education perceived the ideal of an integrated plural society with mutual respect between ethnic groups and cultures. Anti-racist education rejects the problematisation of the black child, but also questions as naive the notion that ethnic groups can all live together harmoniously without recognition of the power differences between black and white groups; there is need for an understanding of the workings and effects of white racism (Epstein, 1992). Anti-racist education argues that it is not black society and black pupils which are the 'problem', but the racism of white pupils learned from their parents and the power structure of institutional racism which disadvantages black people. In schools, anti-racists argue, action needs to be taken to counter the effects of racism in the classroom and the playground and to eliminate the institutional racism of the school with all-white staff in a local authority controlled by white men. Thus the school should have 'anti-racist' policy to counter racism. This typically would include:

- racial abuse should be explicitly forbidden;
- all incidents of racial abuse should be indentified, recorded and acted upon;
- staff should be made aware of racism and its effects;
- the curriculum should include teaching about race and racism;
- the progress of BME pupils should be monitored;
- the school should endeavour to include black members among its staff.

While multicultural education was seen as the way the school curriculum should be addressed, anti-racist education looked at the school. Schools cannot operate in isolation to address the societal problem of white racism; instead it is the whole political and power structure of society which needs to be tackled. Black people need to be included in the power structure, as MPs, judges, company directors, headteachers and chief executives of councils. This is a left-wing radical idea, and the strongest form of anti-racism is Marxist in its origin (Cole, 2008). In fact, much of the impetus for both multicultural and anti-racist approaches to education came from the left-wing Labour-controlled local urban authorities in England: Liverpool, Leeds, Manchester, Bristol (Avon LEA) and, above all, the ILEA.

However, by the early 1980s when anti-racism had started to grow, the Thatcher government had come to power. While a Labour government had some interest in anti-racism with its ambitions of creating a racially equal society, the 'new right' Conservatives had no time for its radicalising tendencies. Thatcher was interested in economic revolution, getting the trade unions under control and allowing free-market capitalism to operate (see Chapter 2). Not only was she uninterested in restructuring society, she famously stated in an interview with *Woman's Own* (1987) magazine that 'There is no such thing as society: there are individual men and women, and there are families.' However, 'society' was to make itself felt strongly with the so-called race riots across England's inner cities. They began with a police drugs raid on the Black and White Café in St Paul's, Bristol, in April 1980. There was spontaneous resistance to the police among the black community which erupted into street violence, stone-throwing and overturning of police cars. The scenes were replicated in Toxteth in Liverpool and, more dramatically with petrol bombs, in Brixton, South London. The riots were depicted by sociologists as black resistance to white oppression originating in slavery and colonialism and continued by racial disadvantage in 1980s England (Sivanandan, 1982). Thatcher's economic polices brought about a period of economic decline in Britain and the effects of unemployment and poverty were felt most strongly by the black communities in the inner cities. The government commissioned an inquiry into the riots led by Lord Scarman which concluded that the riots were, indeed, the effects of urban poverty and disadvantage (Scarman, 1982): 'complex political, social and economic factors' created a 'disposition towards violent protest' (p. 34). Scarman also pointed to the effects of 'racial disadvantage' and 'racial discrimination', but rejected the notion of 'institutional racism'. He warned, though, that positive discrimination was necessary to prevent racial disadvantage becoming an 'endemic, ineradicable disease threatening the very survival of our society'.

Anti-racist education grew within this highly charged political context of race riots. While the Home Office was concerned about Scarman's warnings of social breakdown, the Thatcher government saw no role for the education system in addressing the issue. Of course, for right-wing politicians, the Brixton riots were confirmation of Enoch Powell's prediction of 'rivers of blood'. From the point of view of policy, it is important to understand that multicultural, and particularly anti-racist, education was born and grew within the education communities: teachers, academics, schools and local authorities. The Labour government had set up the Rampton Commission in 1978, but governments were to take no action to promote different forms of education, and the Conservative government of the 1980s was to set itself firmly against such moves. Anti-racist education was seen by the Thatcher government as left-wing activism designed to undermine free-market capitalism. It was, then, left to the Labour-controlled local authorities to encourage schools to develop multicultural approaches to the curriculum and to create anti-racist policies in their management and governance. This was a symptom of the political differences at the time between national government by the Conservative Party and local authorities which were controlled in the cities by Labour-controlled councils. And, of course, it was at the time the local authorities had control of schools and education policies. The powerful Inner London Education Authority developed the strongest policies on anti-racist and multicultural education in its schools. This was often prompted by active groups of teachers such as 'All London Teachers Against Racism and Fascism' (ALTARF, 1984) and the NUT (1980), supported by the CRE and the Institute of Race Relations (IRR). Local authorities employed advisers for multicultural education who would visit schools to give guidance on the right approaches and set up multicultural education centres. Racism awareness training for teachers was offered. These appointments were paid for by funding which authorities received from the Home Office under section 11 of the Home Office Act, and were the result of the Home Office's interest in social cohesion rather than government interest in educational initiatives.

The Conservative government under Thatcher was suspicious and saw the actions of the local authorities as left-wing activism. There were criticisms that they employed officers and advisers to go into schools as 'race spies', checking on those teachers who did not adopt multicultural or anti-racist policies. When the Rampton Commission published its interim report (Rampton, 1981) the government had expected it to find that black pupils' underachievement was due to cultural effects: black families did not raise their children correctly and therefore failed in the education system. The finding that it was the fault of the system, not the children and their families, identifying the problem for black children in schools as institutional racism was simply unacceptable to the Thatcher government. Its response was to dismiss Rampton as the Chair and to replace him with the more conservative Lord Swann. Swann took another four years to collect evidence before publishing the final report, *Education for All* (Swann, 1985). Again, the findings of the inquiry pointed to the damaging effects of racism and racial disadvantage and its conclusions were that schools should develop a multicultural education which would be suitable for all children, black and white, in a multiracial society. The report was some five hundred pages and priced at £25, a prodigious sum at the time. Apparently to make the report more available, the government circulated to all schools a short summary which made no mention of racism. This was typical of the political manoeuvring of the time with the national government trying to stifle what it saw as 'activists' stirring up racial issues in Labour-controlled local authorities (Ward, 1998). Away from the inner cities and in the Conservative-controlled authorities, anti-racist and multicultural education was seen as irrelevant: as Gaine (1987, 1995) points out, the view was that because they had small numbers of black pupils there was 'no problem here'.

 Reader task

Proponents of anti racist education were critical of multicultural education because it did not deal with the real problems of race in society. Do you agree with them?

Marginalising Race

The Conservative government wished to end the control of local authorities and 'activists', and it did this through the 1988 Education Act. We saw in Chapter 5 how the Act took control of the curriculum from schools and in Chapter 2 how it took control from local authorities through LMS. The move against local authorities was also to limit the equal opportunities policies which were the work of the left-wing authorities. The Local Authorities Act of 1992 broke up the Inner London Authority and a number of other large left-wing authorities into small 'unitary authorities'. Such small organisations simply did not have the resources to sustain the equal opportunities activities which the ILEA had carried out and the local authorities were reduced in power. But the most effective means of eliminating multicultural and anti-racist education came with the National Curriculum and national testing. Chapter 5 explained that this created an overwhelming list of priorities for schools which struggled to implement the new curriculum and to prepare pupils for the new testing arrangements. There was nothing in the new curriculum to require schools to address racism and the statutory orders emphasised an Anglo-centric focus with, for example, little on colonialism and slavery in the History curriculum (see Chapter 5). The government's policy, then, was not to forbid multicultural or anti-racist education, but to marginalise it: schools and teachers put it at the bottom of their pile of priorities. The Conservative government's position was summarised in the speech by the then Prime Minister John Major to the Conservative Party Conference in 1993 when he announced that trainee teachers would be instructed in how to teach children to read and write, not to learn about gender and race (see also Chapter 7). The 1980s and early 1990s might be seen as a struggle by those committed to a just and equal society against a powerful white establishment in which the government overtly and covertly resisted efforts to eliminate racism in the education system.

New Labour and Equal Opportunities

The election in 1997 brought victory for Tony Blair with the New Labour government and something of a revival for multicultural education and anti-racism. As we saw in Chapter 2, Blair's New Labour agenda was strongly focused on raising standards – Barber's 'High expectations and standards for all, no matter what' (2001) – rather than on the traditional Labour mission of equality; multiculturalism and anti-racism were never destined to become high priorities. However, the new government, with the first ever black member of the Cabinet, Paul Boateng, did respond differently from its right-wing predecessor in handling racism in society. The test came with the report of the Macpherson (1999) inquiry into the death of Stephen Lawrence. Lawrence was an African-Caribbean 16-year-old murdered by a gang of white youths while waiting at a bus stop with friends in London. It was a prime example of a racist killing. The white gang had taunted the black young people with racist abuse and then taken violent action. When the (white) police officers were called they treated the incident as provocation by the black people and failed to pursue the white culprits. After years of pressure by Stephen's family and friends, the Macpherson (1999) inquiry into the incident was held. It was found that the police had been negligent and that 'Stephen Lawrence's murder was simply and solely and unequivocally motivated by racism' (para. 1.11). Macpherson regarded the policing as an example of 'institutional racism' where the police's perception of the incident had been framed by their expectations of black people. In addition, the failure by their senior officers to investigate the matter further was evidence that such perceptions were a structural feature of the organisation. Institutional racism was inherent in the London Metropolitan Police Force and should be addressed. Unlike Scarman who had rejected the idea of institutional racism in 1984, Macpherson provided a definition of 'institutional racism' and, even more importantly, the Labour government accepted the findings of the report. The Home Secretary, Jack Straw, agreed that institutional racism was inherent in society and should be eliminated. Previous governments' refusal to understand or to acknowledge racism in society – or even to acknowledge the existence of society – had made the attempts to establish a multicultural and anti-racist education system impossible.

The way seemed clear to move towards social justice in education with equal opportunities for black pupils, and for the education service to contribute to an equal and just society through education about race and racism. The Race Relations (Amendment) Act in 2000 (OPSI, 2000) required all organisations, including schools, to ensure equality of opportunity on grounds of race. This 'duty' is different from previous requirements which had been constructed by local authorities or individual schools in that it is enshrined in legislation. It requires schools to have a policy on race equality, to monitor their activities to ensure that there is no racial

(Continued)

(Continued)

bias and to have an action plan to eradicate inequality. For the first time, there was policy at government level for countering racism. When the Labour government was again elected in May 2001 with a strong majority and the race relations legislation was in place, it seemed that society would progress to equality and pluralism. It was only a few months later, on 11 September 2001, that the world picture was to change.

2001 – Confusion and Retreat

The reaction in Western societies to 9/11 brought a wave of anger and fear about Islam (islamophobia) and an international 'war on terror', led by the combined forces of the British government and the Bush administration in the United States. The struggles of the 1980s and 1990s to gain recognition of the social and educational effects of racism by a right-wing government had been a singular cause. The events of 9/11 brought that straightforward thinking to an end. In 2001 the debate became global as the cultural and religious divide between East and West opened up and began to legitimate articulated opposition to multiculturalism, bringing religion into the centre of the debate. After 2001 the government's recognition of institutional racism, which had been such a step forward in 2000, began to weaken. Gillborn (2008) points out that the Labour government backed away from its commitment to eradicate racism. In 2004 the new Home Secretary David Blunkett described 'institutional racism' as 'a slogan that missed the point'. An internal review of the reasons for black pupils being over-represented in exclusions from schools concluded that it was likely to be due to institutional racism in schools. However:

> The Education Department briefed journalists that 'ministers had concluded that it would be inaccurate and counterproductive to brand the school system racist'. (Gillborn, 2008: 131)

The CRE had been a powerful voice in the anti-racist movement. In 2004 it was formed into a single body to deal with all equality matters, the Equality and Human Rights Commission (EHRC, 2008). This was seen to lower the effectiveness of the old CRE, diffusing race into a generalised human rights organisation. The various equality 'duties' came to be at the discretion of organisations rather than as an absolute requirement.

The challenge to individual and institutional racism is often met with powerful resistance and needs the strength of political authority to carry it through. After the attack on the Twin Towers in 2001, the Labour government weakened in its resolve and yielded to the pressures that suggested that white society would be alienated. Rather than seeking equality by eradicating white racism, which was the thrust of the legislation on the duty for equality in the

Race Relations (Amendment) Act of 2001, government policy softened and turned to 'social cohesion'. It appointed Hazel Blears as 'Communities and Local Government Secretary', effectively the minister for social cohesion. There were warnings that community cohesion was endangered if faith and ethnic groups 'totally dominate' neighbourhoods so that other groups felt 'alienated, insecure or unsafe' (Dawar, 2008). This was not quite Margaret Thatcher's 'we will be swamped' speech; instead 'community cohesion' is threatened. However, it is along the same lines.

Opposition to multiculturalism ranges from the crude insistence of nationalist groups such as the BNP that Britain should be kept for the whites and not be overrun by other cultures to more sophisticated arguments about 'cultural relativism'. Cultural relativism is the view that all beliefs are equally valid and that society should permit people to behave according to the norms of their particular culture. It is argued by those opposed to cultural relativism that society should make definitions of behaviour for all based upon ethical principles. This is an area for conflict and dissent: it has produced debates about whether Muslim women should be allowed to wear the niqab which covers the face when working in schools and whether Muslim girls should be required to undress for PE.

Another source of opposition to a multicultural society during the 2000s was the reaction against 'asylum-seekers'. This became a major issue in the mass media in which the government was accused of allowing supposedly 'bogus' asylum seekers into the country. The government responded to pressure by making severe limitations on immigration. The 7/7 bombings in London in July 2005 reinforced the opposition to cultural pluralism and made the government even more anxious to appear to be managing the 'terrorist threat'. The overreaction by the Metropolitan Police in the shooting of Jean Charles de Menezes, the Brazilian-born electrician who was mistaken for a terrorist, typified the level of anxiety.

During the 1970s and 1980s the reason for the underachievement of minority groups had been seen as 'cultural': the fault of the families and the way they reared their children. A typical view was that Asian pupils did badly because of problems with English, and African-Caribbean boys were brought up by single mothers with absent fathers. The Rampton and Swann commissions dismissed this deficit view of minority families and argued that the problems were caused by institutional racism in schools and society. During the 2000s black pupils were achieving better in the system; more precisely, certain minority ethnic groups were doing well. Pupils of Indian and Chinese origin were scoring well in GCSE results, while those of Black Caribbean and Pakistani origin were still underachieving. Girls were succeeding better than boys and by 2006 the combined effects of gender and ethnicity resulted in 36 per cent of Black Caribbean boys achieving five A*–C passes, compared to 84 per cent of Chinese girls (see also Chapter 10). The differential achievements of minority groups brought into question the simple analysis of black failure caused by white racism.

A surprising critique of the multicultural society came from Trevor Phillips, the high-profile black chair of the Commission for Racial Equality (later EHRC). He spoke against the maintenance of separate ethnic groups, announcing that Britain was 'sleepwalking into segregation' with the creation of racial ghettoes. He argued that multiculturalism was dividing society and that Britain should become more of a singular nation in which there is a greater sharing of the same values:

> The fact is that we are a society which, almost without noticing it, is becoming more divided by race and religion. We are becoming more unequal by ethnicity ... there are some simple truths which should bind us together ... (Phillips, 2005)

He went on to criticise black families for seeing themselves as an oppressed minority, for blaming their failures on white racism and lacking aspiration to achieve.

Government policy since 2001 has been to emphasise the 'British' aspect of the multicultural society. For example, in 2004, it required that those being given British citizenship should require people to demonstrate their ability to speak English. Ceremonies for those gaining British citizenship required people to swear an oath of allegiance to 'Her Majesty Queen Elizabeth the Second, her Heirs and Successors, according to law' (UK Border Agency, 2004). We have seen the move from a strong, but brief, commitment to countering institutional racism in schools and society to a policy of social cohesion which marginalises the attention to racism. In this the Labour government reacted to right-wing pressures in the media and society: for there to be 'social cohesion', there should be an emphasis on 'Britishness' and similarity rather than on the preservation of cultural differences.

One of the major cultural variations in British society has been along religious lines. British history is full of religious tensions and conflict since the sixteenth century. Religious differences have always been a part of the multicultural debate, with demands for the rights of religious groups to maintain their faith and to have it enshrined in the system with Muslim or Sikh schools, or at least to allow for dedicated religious practices within mainstream schools. In the next section we discuss the role of education in social cohesion and whether faith schools are divisive.

〰️ **Reader task**

How would you assess New Labour's policy on race? Do you agree with David Gillborn that it is not designed to eliminate race inequality, but to sustain it at manageable levels?

Faith Schools and the New Labour Agenda

As we saw in Chapter 1, before 1870 schools for the poor were provided by the Church of England; the board schools set up after the 1870 Act were to fill in the gaps left by the church foundation schools. The settlement with the Church allowed it to retain its faith schools, to continue teaching confessional Christianity and to select pupils on the basis of their parents' faith commitment. This arrangement was perpetuated by the 1944 Education Act which designated a dual system of faith schools: voluntary controlled (VC) schools are funded wholly by the state and allowed to carry out denominational worship; voluntary aided (VA) schools make a small contribution to their funding and are allowed to carry out confessional and denominational religious education. This settlement between the state and the established Church was to define the nature of state schooling for the twentieth century and remains unchanged in the twenty-first. Of the 20,000 schools in Britain, just over a third, some 7,000, were faith schools in 2001, the majority being Church of England (4,716) and Roman Catholic (2,110) with 25 Methodist, 32 Jewish and just eight schools of minority faiths (Cush, 2003).

England is an increasingly secular society and, as Toynbee (2006) points out, 'ICM polling shows that 64 per cent of voters think the government should not be funding faith schools of any kind' (p. 6). However, the faith schools phenomenon is growing for two intersecting reasons. The first is the political strengthening of minority ethnic groups in Britain, and in particular calls from Muslims for faith schools to reflect the Christian church provision. The second is the neo-liberal New Labour government policy of marketisation and school diversity which we saw in Chapter 2.

Parekh (2000) suggests that the demand for faith schools is explained by the failure of community schools to meet the needs and interests of ethnic minority groups, particularly of the Muslim population. Gundara (2000) points out that faith schools for Muslims and other ethnic minorities provide a voice and an identity in society. The drive for faith schools by a minority of ethnic groups appears to be the result of traditionalist attempts by parents to cling to religious observance, but even these are probably in the minority. Madood et al. (1994) found that a majority of Muslim families did not seek single-faith Muslim schools, but preferred education in a common school sympathetic to their religious and cultural norms. This suggests that, were community schools fully inclusive, the demand for Muslim schools would be reduced.

During the 1980s and early 1990s applications for Muslim schools were resisted by Conservative governments which either rejected them or left them undecided. While the Conservative government's view would have been in favour of diversity and independence for schools, its assimilationist model of society would have made it opposed to fostering non-Christian traditions.

Walford (2000) shows that the Labour government from 1997 brought a significant change of policy: while there were a small number of rejections, applications for new faith schools in the late 1990s brought approval for Muslim and Seventh-Day Adventist schools. The explanation for this change is that Old Labour's left-wing liberal ideology made it sympathetic to the argument that there should be equality with Christianity to permit schools based on different faiths.

This notion, joined with the New Labour passion for diversity and the market, made for an enthusiastic commitment to non-Christian faith schools and the 2001 Education Act (DfES, 2001) was designed to increase their number. Gamarnikov and Green (2005) show how faith schools fit the New Labour attempt to manufacture social capital from the benefits of a religious ethos. They are part of the neo-liberal agenda to raise standards through diversity and competition between schools. The 2005 Education Act (DfES, 2005) makes for the promotion of faith schools in the 'standards agenda': diversity of schooling will inculcate competition between schools and drive up standards through market forces.

Central to government policy in the promotion of faith schools, and of their popularity with parents, is their academic success which is supposedly a product of their religious ethos. David Blunkett, Secretary of State for Education (1997–2001), was famously said to have remarked that he would like to bottle the ethos of faith schools in order to spread the effects to other schools. However, Schagen and Schagen (2005) demonstrate that the actual difference made by faith schools is very small and that any success is largely determined by differences in pupil intake. Similarly, Gibbons and Silva (2006) find only a tiny gain of one percentile point in achievement at 11 in mathematics and English, and that differences in achievement between schools are explained by admissions policies and the selection of pupils. Gamarnikov and Green (2005) also point out that the faith benefits to educational performance are strictly limited, and that the faith ethos 'is masking the structural equity issues of a market-based system for distributing educational opportunities' (p. 99).

As well as the increase in faith schools there is a covert religious influence through the academies initiative (see Chapter 4). One of the first major sponsors of the city academies was the United Learning Trust, a subsidiary of the United Church Schools Trust (2008) which runs independent schools offering students 'a good education based on Christian principles of service and tolerance' (p. 1). It is interesting that the organisation should have chosen to name a subsidiary with a non-religious title, as though the Christian mission should be obscured in its academies initiative. Less covert is the sponsorship of city academies by the fundamentalist Christian businessman

Sir Peter Vardy, of the Vardy car dealerships. In these academies the influence is perfectly explicit in the teaching of creationism in the curriculum. The Church of England intends to open a hundred additional academies (Taylor, 2007). At the same time, the Head of Education at the Church of England was reported in 2007 as advocating that 'intelligent design', a version of creationism, should be taught as part of the science curriculum in its schools (Stewart, 2007).

 Reader task

Do you agree with David Blunkett that the 'faith ethos' is an asset to children's learning in faith schools?

Faith Schools and Social Cohesion

The year 2001 saw race riots, or 'disturbances', in northern England and some electoral success for the racist BNP in the North West. These events raised the question of whether British society was becoming less cohesive. Mason (2005) of the British Humanist Association suggests that faith-based education contributes to divisiveness. The Cantle Report (2001) into the riots in the North West of England and the Ousely Report (2001) into disturbances in Bradford, West Yorkshire both confirm that young people from ethnic minority groups prefer to be educated in culturally diverse schools:

> We have been particularly struck by the views of younger people, who, in strong terms, emphasised the need to break down barriers by promoting knowledge and understanding of different cultures ... Many of those we spoke to preferred integration on many levels and those who had experienced schools with a mixture of faiths, races and cultures were very positive about their experiences ... (Cantle, 2001: 5.7.1).

> What was inspiring was the great desire among young people for better education, more social and cultural interaction ... Some young people have pleaded desperately for this to overcome the negativity that they feel is blighting their lives and leaves them ignorant of other cultures and lifestyles. (Ousely, 2001: 5.7.2)

Examples of the way in which England is dividing its schools on ethnic and social class lines can be seen in many of the industrial cities and towns of the north. For example, in Blackburn, Lancashire:

> ... there are three overwhelmingly white schools – Darwen Vale High (95.5 per cent white), Darwen Moorland High (91.6 per cent white) and St Bede's Roman Catholic High (96.3 per cent white). The segregation is matched on the other side of the racial divide. At Beardwood High, 94.5 per cent of pupils are Asian. Just 2.5 per cent of the school's pupils are white. Only one school in the borough

reflects the ethnic breakdown of a community whose population is 70.5 per cent white and 26.5 per cent Asian. Of the pupils who go to Witton Park High, 71.7 per cent are white and 26.6 per cent are Asian. (Watts, 2007)

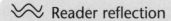 Reader reflection

Do you think faith schools add to, or detract from, social cohesion?

Conclusion: The Inclusive School

The 'community school' has been used as the term for a non-faith school (Wrigley, 2006) but a genuine community school would include those of all faiths, cultures and incomes. A proper conceptualisation of the community school is needed and Gokulsing (2006) offers this possibility. He opposes the state funding of faith schools and suggests that there are other ways for schools to support minority ethnic citizens: the National Curriculum should teach about religions, but the teaching of religious faith should be kept for the home. Such a school could achieve all that is claimed for the faith school: high achievement, high moral standards, good behaviour, religious tolerance and cultural diversity. The existence of faith schools in England is a historical product of the powerful relationship between church and state. That the minority communities should have slotted into this divisive system to create more social, cultural and racial divisions is a product of an inherent contradiction in government policy. It is a symptom of the dominance of marketisation and diversity, a failure to depict the school as a model of the cohesive society and a retreat from a commitment to creating equality by eliminating racism.

Recommended reading

DfES (2005) *Ethnicity and Education: The Evidence on Minority Ethnic Pupils.* DfES. Online at: http://www.dfes.gov.uk/research/programmeofresearch/projectinformation.cfm?projectid= 14488&resultspage=1. A research report which brings together a range of data and explanations about the achievements of a range of minority ethnic groups.

Gillborn, D. (2008) *Racism and Education: Coincidence or Conspiracy.* London: Routledge. Gillborn gives an up-to date survey of the issues of racism in education.

Institute of Race Relations (1998) – see the IRR website: http://www.irr.org.uk for a weekly update on global events on race.

Kundnani, A. (2007) *The End of Tolerance: Racism in 21st Century Britain.* London: Pluto Press. Kundnani makes a strong critique of state policy on immigration and the war on terror as the new form of state racism.

Troyna, B. and Hatcher, R. (1992) *Racism in Children's Lives.* London: Routledge. Troyna and Hatcher's research provides telling examples of black children's experiences in Britain.

References

ALTARF (1984) *Combating Racism*. London: All London Teachers against Racism and Fascism.

Arora, R.K. and Duncan, C.G. (1986) *Multicultural Education: Towards Good Practice*. London: Routledge.

Barber, M. (2001) 'High expectations and standards for all, no matter what: creating a world-class education service in England', in M. Fielding (ed.), *Taking Education Really Seriously*. London: RoutledgeFalmer.

Cantle, T. (2001) *Community Coherence: A Report of the Independent Review Team Chaired by Ted Cantle*. London: Home Office.

Coard, B. (1979) *How the West Indian Child is Made Educationally Subnormal in the British School System: The Scandal of the Black Child in Schools in Britain*. London: New Beacon Books.

Cole, M. (2008) *Marxism and Educational Theory: Origins and Issues*. London: Routledge.

Cush, D. (2003) 'Should the state fund schools with a religious character?', *Religious Education (PCfRE)*, 25 (2): 10–15.

Dawar, A. (2008) 'Blears warns planners against creating "social apartheid"', *The Guardian*, 3 April. Online at: http://www.guardian.co.uk/politics/2008/apr/03/planning.local government (accessed 6 April 2008).

DfES (2001) *Schools: Building on Success*. London: TSO.

DfES (2005) *Education Act 2005*. London: TSO.

EHRC (2008) *Equality and Human Rights Commission*. London: EHRC.

Epstein, D. (1992) *Changing Classroom Cultures: Antiracism, Politics and Schools*. Stoke-on-Trent: Trentham.

Fryer, P. (1984) *Staying Power: The History of Black People in Britain*. London: Pluto.

Gaine, C. (1987) *No Problem Here*. London: Hutchinson.

Gaine, C. (1995) *Still No Problem Here*. London: Hutchinson.

Gamarnikov, E. and Green, A. (2005) 'Keeping faith with school capital: from Coleman to New Labour on social justice, religion and education', in R. Gardner, J. Cairns and D. Lawton (eds), *Faith Schools: Consensus or Conflict*. London: RoutledgeFalmer.

Gibbons, S. and Silva, O. (2006) *Faith Primary Schools: Better Schools or Better Pupils?* London: London School of Economics.

Gillborn, D. (2008) *Racism and Education: Coincidence or Conspiracy*. London: Routledge.

Gokulsing, K.M. (2006) 'Without prejudice: an exploration of religious diversity, secularism and citizenship in England (with particular reference to the state funding of Muslim faith schools and multiculturalism)', *Journal of Education Policy*, 21 (4): 459–70.

Gundara, J. (2000) *Interculturalism, Education and Inclusion*. London: Paul Chapman.

Houlton, D. (1985) *All Our Languages*. Leeds: E.J. Arnold.

Kundnani, A. (2007) *The End of Tolerance: Racism in 21st Century Britain*. London: Pluto Press.

Macpherson, Sir W. (1999) *The Stephen Lawrence Inquiry*, Cm 4264-1. London: TSO. Online at: http://www.archive.official-documents.co.uk/document/cm42/4262/4262.htm.

Madood, T., Beischon, S. and Virdec, S. (1994) *Changing Ethnic Identities*. London: Policy Studies Institute.

Mason, M. (2005) 'Religion and schools – a fresh way forward: a rights-based approach to diversity in schools', in R. Gardner, J. Cairns and D. Lawton (eds), *Faith Schools: Consensus or Conflict*. London: RoutledgeFalmer.

NUT (1980) *Combating Racism.* London: National Union of Teachers.

Office of Public Sector Information (OPSI) (2000) *Race Relations (Amendment) Act.* London: OPSI. Online at: http://www.opsi.gov.uk/acts/acts2000/ukpga_20000034_en_1.

Ouseley, Sir H. (2001) *Community Pride, Not Prejudice: Making Diversity Work in Bradford.* Bradford: Bradford County Council.

Parekh, B. (2000) *Re-thinking Multiculturalism.* London: Macmillan Press.

Phillips, T. (2005) *After 7/7: Sleepwalking to Segregation.* Speech to the Manchester Council for Community Relations, 22 September.

Rampton, Sir A. (1981) *West Indian Children in Our Schools: Interim Report of the Committee of Inquiry into the Education of Children from Ethnic Minority Groups.* London: HMSO.

Scarman, Lord (1982) *The Scarman Report: The Brixton Disorders 10–12 April 1981.* Harmondsworth: Penguin.

Schagen, I. and Schagen, B. (2005) 'The impact of faith schools on pupil performance', in R. Gardner, J. Cairns and D. Lawton (eds), *Faith Schools: Consensus or Conflict.* London: RoutledgeFalmer.

Sivanandan, A. (1982) *A Different Hunger: Writings on Black Resistance.* London: Institute of Race Relations.

Stewart, W. (2007) 'Creation row back on the boil', *Times Educational Supplement,* 1 June, p. 3.

Stone, M. (1981) *Educating the Black Child in Britain.* London: Fontana.

Swann, Lord (1985) *Education for All: Final Report of the Committee of Inquiry into the Education of Children from Ethnic Minority Groups,* Cmnd 9453. London: HMSO.

Taylor, M. (2007) 'Church of England plans to open 100 academy schools', *The Guardian,* 19 May, p. 7.

Thatcher, M. (1978) *Television interview for Granada 'World in Action', January 27, 1988.* Manchester: Granada Television.

Tomlinson, S. (1977) 'Race and education in Britain 1960–77: an overview of the literature', *Sage Race Relations Abstracts,* 2 (4): 3–33.

Toynbee, P. (2006) 'This is a clash of civilisations – between reason and superstition', *The Guardian,* 14 April. Online at: http://education.guardian.co.uk/schools/comment/story/0,,1753745,00.html.

Troyna, B. (1984) 'Multicultural education: emancipation or containment', in L. Barton and S. Walker (eds), *Social Crisis and Educational Research.* Buckingham: Croom-Helm, pp. 75–92.

Troyna, B. and Hatcher, R. (1992) *Racism in Children's Lives: A Study of Mainly White Primary Schools.* London: Routledge.

UK Border Agency (2004) *Citizenship Ceremonies.* London: UK Border Agency. Online at: http://www.ukba.homeoffice.gov.uk/britishcitizenship/applying/ceremony/.

United Church Schools Trust (2008) – see: http://www.ucstrust.org.uk/ (accessed 3 October 2008).

Walford, G. (2000) *Policy and Politics in Education: Sponsored Grant-Maintained Schools and Religious Diversity.* Aldershot: Ashgate.

Ward, S. (1998) 'Intercultural education and teacher education in the United Kingdom: a case of reversible decline', *European Journal of Intercultural Education Studies,* 9 (1): 41–52.

Watts, N. (2007) 'Revealed: UK schools dividing on race lines', *The Observer,* 27 May, p. 24.

Wrigley, T. (2006) *Another School Is Possible.* Stoke-on-Trent: Trentham.

10

Poverty and social class: *Every Child Matters*

Introduction

This chapter explores some of the most intractable issues of government education policy: social class, deprivation and poverty. Child poverty matters: children from poorer homes leave school earlier with fewer qualifications and fewer opportunities. The Joseph Rowntree Foundation (2007) in its *Education and Poverty* programme found that economic poverty prevents children from realising their full educational potential. The scale of the problem is illustrated by the following:

> 3.9 million children – one in three – are currently living in poverty in the UK, one of the highest rates in the industrialised world ... The *End Child Poverty* campaign argues that poverty can have a profound impact on the child, their family, and the rest of society. It often sets in motion a deepening spiral of social exclusion, creating problems in education, employment, mental and physical health and social interaction. Poverty shapes children's development. Before reaching his or her second birthday, a child from a poorer family is already more likely to show a lower level of attainment than a child from a better-off family. By the age of six a less able child from a rich family is likely to have overtaken an able child born into a poor family. (End Child Poverty, 2008: 1)

As we saw in Chapter 3, policy in the nineteenth and much of the twentieth centuries was to give workers basic literacy and numeracy and the values, attitudes and discipline needed in the workplace. The emphasis now is on educational achievement, social mobility, access to jobs and the ability to compete in the global market. Both Conservative and Labour governments agree that children should have opportunities to break cycles of poverty and deprivation, but there are differing views about how this should be done. Chapter 2 showed that policy in the last thirty years has seen the introduction of market forces into the education system in the belief that it would raise standards. But competition among schools increases inequalities: middle-class parents are better informed, more affluent and able to take advantage of market mechanisms. Pupils from poor economic backgrounds, particularly those considered to be more able, lose out in the process of raising standards. Dorling et al. (2007) show the significance of the geographical dimension: children raised in particular localities attend schools with other poor children. Education policies that separate pupils along class lines reinforce poverty and exclusion. This is in spite of the New Labour policy rhetoric about the need to challenge social class attainment gaps.

Education and Social Mobility

'Social class' is not easy to define. Government papers and data on attainment refer to 'deprivation' or 'socio-economic groupings'. 'Deprivation' includes material factors, particularly income. 'Socio-economic categories' refer to both material deprivation, social and cultural background and how people engage with the education system. Social class includes material factors, but also the values, life style, attitudes and motivation that help educational achievement known as 'cultural capital'.

Recent Labour and Conservative governments have both claimed that class is not a factor in educational inequality. The market ideology of Thatcher's Conservative government was to give people a sense of individual aspiration. The New Labour government of 1997 turned away from the traditional Marxist analysis of class conflict which it saw as irrelevant to modern society. In 1999, Tony Blair argued that the class war was over. New Labour accepted inequalities between people in a competitive society, something which was an anathema to traditional Labour Party values of equality.

One measure of society is 'inter-generational social mobility': the opportunity for everyone to move into an occupation that is of higher status and income than that of their parents. Education can be an *agent* of social mobility, giving young people the chance to climb the ladder of opportunity, or it can keep them reproducing their parents' lives. Social mobility is important for individuals because it helps them fulfil their potential, and for the economy because it contributes to productivity, employment, economic growth and social cohesion. The New Labour government has tried to find strategies to increase social mobility (DfES, 2006a). In his Beveridge Lecture, Tony Blair (1999) argued that the eradication of child poverty was the first step in breaking the cycle of poverty, saying 'the child born in the run-down estate, should have the same chance to be healthy and well educated as the child born in the leafy suburbs'. He committed the government to creating equality of opportunity and abolishing child poverty within twenty years. A later target was to reduce it to 50 per cent by 2010.

One of the difficulties about social class and attainment is that there is no consistent measure of social class across the different phases of education. One indicator is whether pupils are eligible for free school meals (FSM). This measures benefit dependency, and not all families eligible for FSM choose to receive them, but it does provide some useful comparative data over time. Another measure is the Income Deprivation Affecting Children Index (IDACI). Both show considerable social class gaps in educational attainment (DfES, 2006a: 14).

Discussion of social class implies a political critique of the way in which society is structured and organised. To talk of poverty encourages a focus on the experiences of individuals and families rather than the wider structural issues that generate social class divisions within society. Concerns about social class, poverty and educational achievement are associated with equity and social justice, but they are also rooted in views about a modern post-industrial society and its need for a highly skilled and qualified workforce. This two-pronged position in New Labour education policies reflected both the needs of the economy and an ideological commitment to social justice. Educational qualifications are a powerful determinant of the future opportunities of individuals and of their contribution to the economy of society.

〰 **Reader tasks**

- Do you agree that the New Labour government's policy of equipping 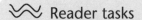 people for the global economy will help to solve poverty and bring social justice?
- Are you optimistic about the target to eliminate child poverty by 2020?

Government Policies to Reduce Poverty and Social Class Inequalities

New Labour's efforts to reduce social inequality through the education system are inherent in *Every Child Matters* (ECM) (DfES, 2003a, 2004) and *The Children's Plan* (DCSF, 2007a, 2007b). Between them the documents have only a single mention of 'social class', although child poverty and the targets to reduce poverty are mentioned. The concept of 'socio-economic groups' is used with references to material deprivation and low income and their impact on educational achievement (DfES, 2007, 2004). A commitment to individual achievement and the needs of the economy shine through the ECM Green Paper:

> Overall, this country is still one where life chances are unequal. This damages not only those children born into disadvantage, but our society as a whole. We all stand to share the benefits of an economy and society with less educational failure, higher skills, less crime, and better health. We all share a duty to do everything we can to ensure every child has the chance to fulfil their potential. (DfES, 2003a: para. 8)

Although the catalyst for ECM was the tragedy of Victoria Climbié's death, the Green Paper and legislation that followed were a continuation of the *Sure Start* approach for a wider age range. ECM was intended to prevent children at risk from finding themselves damaged, particularly from within their families, but it also aimed to tackle long-term deprivation by engaging with a variety of policy reforms, including education. *Every Child Matters*, from its inception, was presented as a long-term programme of change which would affect and spread into aspects of a child's life at school, but also in the family. ECM addressed a range of different services: childcare, nursery education, schools, family support, health, social care, employment advice and the criminal justice system. And services were to be properly coordinated.

ECM was a response to criticism that government initiatives to address educational inequalities have not taken account of wider social and economic conditions. The demands it makes on the education system are heavy, charging schools with achieving five outcomes:

- Being healthy
- Staying safe
- Enjoying and achieving
- Making a positive contribution
- Achieving economic well-being.

Its scope and detail recognise that it is difficult for education initiatives alone to deal with deprivation and social class gaps in attainment. ECM gave education a new role in the school and the family. The initial Green Paper outlines the scope:

> Our aim is to ensure that every child has the chance to fulfil their potential by reducing levels of educational failure, ill health, substance misuse, teenage pregnancy, abuse and neglect, crime and anti-social behaviour among children and young people. (DfES, 2003a: 8)

The Children Act (OPSI, 2004) and *Every Child Matters: Change for Children* (DfES, 2004) set the legislative framework for implementation of the aims of ECM with an emphasis on local communities:

> The transformation that we need can only be delivered through local leaders working together in strong partnership with local communities on a programme of change. That is why this document sets out what action needs to be taken locally and how Government will work with and support Local Authorities and their partners. (DfES, 2004: 2)

Further legislation and guidance came through the Children's Plan (DCSF, 2007a) and a series of documents which reflected the extension of educational responsibilities beyond the school. They stressed that children and families require integrated structures and services at a local community level. They have raised the profile and control of local authorities which had been relegated to a much reduced role in previous legislation (see Chapter 4). Children's centres are one-stop central 'hubs' for children under the age of five and their families. Centres serving the most deprived areas have access to family healthcare, advice and support for parents, including drop-in sessions, outreach services, integrated early education and childcare and links through to training and employment. In 2008 there were over 2,500 children's centres offering services to around 1.9 million children under five and their families; the Labour government promised a children's centre for every community by 2010.

The major features of the ECM agenda are as follows.

- It recognises that education policy does not engage sufficiently with social and economic factors and the needs of the wider community.
- The underlying assumption is that the state should set up systems and structures which intervene in parenting and the family on behalf of the child.
- It attempts to break down the insularity of professional groups and requires multi-agency working around the needs of the child.
- Authority and power are invested in the local authorities which are redefined as significant players in serving children's needs; directors of children's services have the responsibility for ensuring that the ECM agenda is realised in practice.
- The legislation and guidelines place the engagement of the local community and parents at the heart of the change.
- At the same time, there is a high level of state control, with expectations for schools and other professionals.
- Schools' delivery of the five outcomes of ECM is inspected by Ofsted, forming a layer of surveillance and accountability.

Every Child Matters reframes the relationship between education and the individual child's attainment. It assumes that the family unit as a whole needs to be supported and that extended schools enhance 'family learning'. Full-service extended schools provide breakfast clubs, after-school clubs and childcare, and have health and social care services on-site. This is a significant shift from the view that schools cannot compensate for society, the assumption inherent in most social and educational policy in the last thirty years. In the ECM guidance and legislation the 'heavy hand' of the state becomes the 'enabling hand': it attempts to engage communities in initiatives that will benefit those families who have been found wanting. While the ECM framework reflects significant state control, at the same time the claims made about the engagement of local communities allow the neo-liberal concept of choice and the market to still to operate (see Chapter 2).

Labour's commitment to equality by talking child poverty and socioeconomic educational gaps was strengthened in 2007 when the former Chancellor of the Exchequer Gordon Brown became Prime Minister. A paper published with the 2008 budget, *Ending Child Poverty: Everybody's Business* (HM Treasury, 2008) draws together policies on employment, welfare, health and childcare, as well as education. There is no mention of the entrepreneurial and market-driven initiatives that have sustained inequalities during Labour's period in office. Instead, the relationship between poverty and long-term educational achievement is emphasised:

> Early social experiences are important determinants of later life chances and children in low-income families can face a 'double disadvantage' as they may be less likely to receive the stimulation and resources they need at home and disadvantaged children tend to attend pre-school education for shorter periods of time than those from more advantaged groups. (HM Treasury, 2008: para. 3.6)

The report links child poverty directly to educational attainment from an early age, with the attainment gap continuing throughout a child's school career:

> Studies that assess children's ability over time show that those children who scored highly on tests aged 22 months, but were from low socio-economic groups, were overtaken by children from high socio-economic groups in tests when they reached primary school. These differences persist so that only 35.5 per cent of children eligible for Free School Meals achieve five good GCSEs compared to 62.8 per cent of other children. (HM Treasury, 2008: para. 3.7)

The paper makes claims for the wide-ranging government initiatives to tackle deprivation across social, educational and economic policy: children's centres and extended schools make affordable childcare for all families, bring together other services, make it easier for families to receive the help they need and for parents to access the support they need to be able to work. The paper spells out the advantages of extended schools and their support for families in parenting as well as access to specialist services. Schools are to provide the core extended services by 2010, with £680 m invested to achieve it and a further £1.3 bn over three years. The policies were helping to address educational achievement across social classes: 'As standards have risen, more pupils from all socio-economic groups are reaching higher thresholds of achievement. The performance gap between the most and least deprived schools has fallen on most indicators' (HM Treasury, 2008: para. 4.48). The document sets out ways of reducing inequalities with targets for educational achievement. It also addresses the problematic area of families and parental engagement with educational achievement. The education sector is charged with the responsibility for working with parents to boost the support for poor children, funding more outreach workers in children's centres (para. 5.50) and funding more school-based parent support advisers (para. 5.66). We now look at evidence to see whether such initiatives have had a genuine impact on poverty, social class and educational achievement.

〰️ Reader tasks

- Should the government try to use professional services to influence the way children are brought up in the home?
- Can government policy and social services provision change the ways in which people raise their children?

Child Poverty

Despite the optimism, it seems unlikely that the initial target of ending child poverty by 2020 will be achieved (Evans and Scarborough, 2006) and that the cost would be high, adding £28 billion to planned annual spending (Dorling et al., 2007). Whether income-based poverty has grown or diminished is disputed in different studies. In 2008 the Institute for Fiscal Studies argued that income inequality had risen for a second successive year, and from 1996 the very top incomes had grown faster. They also suggest that child poverty had risen slightly between 2000 and 2005:

> Our own indicator of relative material deprivation is unchanged since 2004–05, showing that the living standards of poor families with children have risen since 2004–05 but have not caught up with those of richer families with children. (Brewer et al., 2008: 2)

The same research recognised that the budgets of 2007 and 2008 would continue to cut child poverty, although 'the number of children in poverty in 2010–11 would exceed the government's target by 500,000' (Brewer et al., 2008: 54).

Social Class and Educational Achievement

We now look at the relationship between socio-economic background and educational attainment. Children from professional families gain basic skills, get better GCSEs, go to university and gain access to good, well-paid jobs. Palmer et al. (2007) found that 11-year-old pupils eligible for free school meals are twice as likely not to achieve basic standards in literacy and numeracy as other 11-year-olds, and that a third of white British boys eligible for free school meals do not obtain five or more GCSEs. Government policies have had some impact with year-on-year improvements in the proportion of 11-year-olds reaching Level 4 at Key Stage 2 in both English and Mathematics. Schools with high levels of pupils eligible for free school meals have seen an improvement greater than that for schools as a whole (Palmer et al., 2007).

Recent data confirm the strength of socio-economic factors in influencing qualification results. In 2007 at Key Stage 2:

- In English only 15 per cent of those eligible for free school meals (FSM) achieved level 5 compared to 36 per cent of the non-FSM pupils.
- In Mathematics 5 per cent of FSM pupils achieved Level 5, compared to 35 per cent of non-FSM pupils.
- While at GCSE, 49 per cent of non-FSM pupils achieved five A*–C GCSEs compared to only 21.1 per cent for FSM pupils.

(DCSF, 2008d: table 17)

When social class and ethnicity join together even starker gaps appear:

- 45 per cent of non FSM white British boys achieved five A*–C GCSEs, compared to 14.6 per cent for those eligible for FSM.
- Non-FSM black Caribbean boys achieved 29.2 per cent compared to the 17.4 per cent of FSM boys achieving these grades.

(DCSF, 2008e: table 17)

In March 2008 a government-backed study confirmed that white working-class teenagers performed less well than their black and Asian classmates. Living in poverty, in rented homes and deprived neighbourhoods had a worse effect on white working-class results than it did on minority ethnic groups (Strand, 2008). Mongon and Chapman (2008) also found that underachievement is endemic among white working-class pupils: 'white British' boys entitled to free school meals were the male group with the lowest attainment and 'white British' girls entitled to free school meals were the female group with the lowest attainment.

Reader task

Go to a recent DCFS website on key stage results and look at data that gives the FSM gap for recent years. Has this pattern changed?

The Joseph Rowntree Foundation has also found links between social class and educational achievement. They cover cognitive factors and language development: 'slow language development can impair later comprehension and learning, even the acquisition of numeracy' (Cassen and Kingdon, 2007: 8). Other reports show that class is associated with family processes and that cultural capital is reflected in aspirations and experience:

- Working-class parents may place different values on education, or have different expectations of it.
- While parents want the best for their children, working-class parents may not automatically expect certain outcomes in the same way as middle-class parents.

- Parents' expectations set the context within which young people develop, shape their own expectations and provide a framework within which decisions are taken.
- Differences in 'social capital': working class parents may have less personal knowledge and fewer skills and contacts to help their children effectively; children may not have role models within their immediate families who have succeeded in education.

(DfES, 2006a: para. 50)

There is some evidence that policy initiatives may be helping to close educational attainment gaps. The Foundation Stage Profile (FSP) results for 2007–8 show that the number of children achieving a good level of development increased to 49 per cent from 45 per cent in the previous year. At the same time the progress of the lowest achieving children has increased faster and, as a result, the gap between their achievement and other children's has narrowed from 37 per cent in 2007 to 36 per cent in 2008 (DCSF, 2008b).

Staying on at School Post-16

Since the 1980s the staying-on rate at age 16 in Britain has been low by international standards and fails to generate a workforce with the skills to compete in the international marketplace (Machin and Vignoles, 2006). The Longitudinal Youth Cohort Study (HM Treasury, 2008) shows continuous growth from 1989 to 2007 in pupils in full-time post-16 education. From 2000 to 2007 the figures show a continuing and greater increase in full-time education for those whose parents were in the 'routine' occupational group: a growth from 56 per cent to 62 per cent, while pupils whose parents were in the high professional category moved from 85 to 86 per cent (DCSF, 2008c: table 6.1.1).

Continuing in education after 16 is determined by GCSE attainment; five good GCSEs is a good indicator of the likelihood of staying on. This is linked to the social class of the pupil: 81 per cent of pupils with parents in the higher professional classification obtained five or more A*–C GCSEs, whereas only 42 per cent in the routine classification did so. Eighty-eight per cent of those who achieved these grades stayed on in full-time education, compared to 51 per cent who did not achieve these grades (DCSF, 2008c: table 6.1.1). The issue of social class and attitudes towards education is also reflected in the study: 93 per cent of parents in the higher professional classification wanted their children to stay on in full-time education compared to 70 per cent of those in the routine category (DCSF, 2008c: table 6.1.1).

All pupils have benefited from initiatives which have promoted staying on in schools, but those whose parents were in higher professional occupations were much more likely to be participating in full-time education than those whose parents had routine occupations, and were more than three times as likely to be in higher education: 44 per cent compared to 13 per cent (DfES, 2006b: tables A and B).

Social Class and Entry to University

In the last twenty years both Conservative and Labour governments have expanded higher education for two reasons: to offer equality of opportunity and to provide the skills for the expanding global knowledge economy. In compliance with European Union policy, the Labour government of 1997 set a target of getting 50 per cent of young people to attend university by 2010. But the expansion of higher education has not been equally to the benefit of all groups and the socio-economic gap in higher education participation has actually widened. Although poorer students are more likely to go on to higher education than they were in the past, the likelihood of them doing so, relative to their richer peers, is actually lower than was the case in earlier decades (Machin and Vignoles, 2006).

Political perspectives from the left emphasise that universities are dominated by the middle-class, particularly in the proportion of independent school pupils entering Oxford and Cambridge; from the right it is argued that attempting to influence access to universities is a form of social engineering which fails to acknowledge effort and ability. The dominance of the middle class is one of the ways in which power and advantage is transmitted from one generation to another. A study in 2005 found that young people from advantaged areas were up to six times more likely to go to university than those in the most disadvantaged areas, and that the pattern had changed little over five years (HEFCE, 2005). They found that 'in some English constituencies less than 1 in 10 young people enter higher education, whereas in others more than half do so' (p. 136).

The HEFCE's study of neighbourhood data found that areas with low participation rates were also disadvantaged on many other social and economic measures. What this means for children living in such areas is quoted in some length as it brings together a whole number of indicators of deprivation associated with socio-economic groupings and the way in which they can be compounded in certain neighbourhoods:

> Children in low participation areas are likely to be living in local authority rented homes in some of England's most deprived wards with, for example, less space and fewer household goods than their peers in high participation areas. The neighbourhood maps of participation show that often their nearest secondary school will have only a small proportion of its pupils gaining five GCSE A–C grades. In contrast, children in high participation areas are frequently near schools, often fee-paying, where very nearly all the pupils gain these grades. Adults in low participation areas are likely to work in a manual occupation, have a low income, receive means-tested benefits and not have, for example, a car or an overseas holiday. They are much less likely to have any experience of higher education than those in high participation areas, and the two groups differ sharply across a wide range of measures of political, cultural and consumption behaviour. (HEFCE, 2005: 138)

Given these figures it is not surprising that one of the commitments in the Labour government's White Paper, *The Future of Higher Education* (DfES, 2003b), was for 'widening participation', with the explicit intention of encouraging more people from lower socio-economic backgrounds to have some experience of higher education through initiatives such as Aim Higher. Strategies that encourage those from lower socio-economic groups to enter higher education are needed to meet the target of 50 per cent in higher education by 2010 (NAO, 2008: 1). John Denham, Secretary of State for Innovation and Skills, in 2007 said: 'Everyone who has the potential and qualifications to succeed in higher education, whatever their family background, should have the opportunity to participate. That is fair, and it is right for our economy' (DIUS, 2007).

There has been an assumption that it is at the point of entry to university that working-class children either make the choice to go or not, or find themselves not selected, and universities have come under attack for their admissions policies. The introduction of tuition fees in 1998 was thought to as exacerbate this, making students from poor socio-economic backgrounds reluctant to attend university. But a number of studies have concluded that, while there has been a widening of the social class gap in higher education, much of the impact from social class on university attendance actually occurs well before entry to higher education (Machin and Vignoles, 2006; Chowdry et al., 2008; NAO, 2008). The socio-economic gap in participation comes about because poorer pupils do not achieve as well in secondary school. In fact, the socio-economic gap that remains on entry into HE, after allowing for prior attainment, is very small indeed: just 1.0 percentage point for males and 2.1 percentage points for females (Chowdry et al., 2008). This highlights the importance of intervention before Key Stage 4 if the aim is to break down the socio economic pattern of higher education participation.

High-achieving young people from lower socio-economic groups are less likely to apply to the elite Russell Group universities, despite the fact that they are just as likely to be accepted as people from higher groups. There is an earnings premium for males of up to 6 per cent for attending a Russell Group university compared to a modern university (DfES, 2006b: 29). Drop-out rates are also linked to social class; among first-year students at English universities, the 20 per cent most deprived pupils in England are around three percentage points more likely to drop out than the most advantaged 20 per cent (Powdthavee and Vignoles, 2008).

Although there is evidence of a strong and negative social class gap in access to higher education, recent government data suggest that there have been small improvements:

- The proportion of young entrants (that is, aged 20 or younger) to full-time first-degree courses who are from state schools has risen from 86.9 per cent in 2005–6 to 87.2 per cent for 2006–7.
- The proportion of young entrants to full-time first-degree courses who are from low socio-economic backgrounds (NS-SEC groups 4 to 7) has increased from 29.1 per cent to 29.8 per cent.
- The proportion of young entrants who are from low-participation neighbourhoods has increased from 9.2 per cent to 9.6 per cent between 2005–6 and 2006–7.

(HESA, 2008: table T1a)

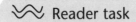 **Reader task**

Can you think of other ways of removing the social class gap in educational achievement?

Independent Schools

It is in the independent sector where children become most segregated by class, economic and social backgrounds. The Conservative politician Oliver Letwin claimed in October 2003 that he would rather beg than send his children to a local comprehensive (*The Guardian*, 2003). However much choice is created within the mainstream education sector, it is unlikely to offer the values and attitudes which the Letwins of the world want from the independent sector. The benefits that make parents buy independent education are both academic and cultural: a social environment and the future social status that their children will carry with them for the rest of their life. While overall 7 per cent of children attend private schools, this figure increases to nearly 20 per cent in the sixth form because far more fee-paying pupils stay on to the age of 18. Of pupils achieving the highest A level points score, 36 per cent come from the independent sector (ISC, 2008). These two statistics help to account for the way in which privately educated pupils are over-represented at elite universities (Sutton Trust, 2008a).

Government initiatives have tried to ensure that the independent sector collaborates with mainstream state education, for example through the sponsorship of academies. It assumes that the independent sector offers a better quality of education and that the culture and advantages will seep into the mainstream education system. What it fails to recognise is that the social privilege of private schooling is itself based on advantages for an elite few. The debates about achievement obscure the fact that independent schools are about social status and transmission of cultural values rather than just academic performance.

Independent schools give their students access to high-status universities. The Sutton Trust showed that independent schools dominate admissions to the 13 leading universities in the country, even where achievement levels are the same:

- The proportion of university entrants going to Oxbridge from the top performing 30 independent schools was nearly twice that of the 30 top-performing grammar schools despite students having similar average A level scores.
- The 100 schools with the highest admission rates to Oxbridge are composed of 78 independent schools, 21 grammar schools and one comprehensive.
- At the 30 top performing comprehensive schools, only half the expected number of pupils are admitted to the 13 Sutton Trust universities, given the overall relationship between schools' average A level results and university admissions.
- At the 30 top performing independent schools, a third more pupils are admitted to the 13 Sutton Trust universities than would be expected given the schools' average A level results.

(Sutton Trust, 2008a: 3–4)

Seven per cent of the population go to private schools, and yet Cambridge takes in 44 per cent of its students from the independent sector and Oxford 47 per cent. The advantage continues into the labour market, opening doors to high-status roles in the government and the establishment. In 2008, 59 per cent of Conservative MPs were privately educated; of the 27 members of David Cameron's Shadow Cabinet 17 went to private schools and just under a third of Labour ministers went to private schools (Harris, 2008).

The Sutton Trust (2008b) points out that in the past 18 years the proportion of privately educated High Court judges from independent school backgrounds has barely changed from 74 per cent in 1989 to 70 per cent in 2007. Their study of the educational backgrounds of 500 leading people in the UK found that over half of the top 500 were educated at independent schools (Sutton Trust, 2008c). Although politicians argue that social class has ceased to be significant in modern society, the evidence that it continues is overwhelming.

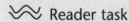 Reader task

Interview a group of fellow students about why pupils from independent schools (a) achieve better results; (b) get access to the high-ranking universities above those which their results would indicate.

Social Mobility

Data on social mobility gives a worrying picture for New Labour. In 2004 a review of two cohorts of individuals born in 1958 and 1970 explored the relationship between education and intergenerational mobility. It concluded:

> … the evidence presented here suggests that, at least in the earlier part of this period (the 1970s and 1980s), Britain actually regressed in terms of educational and economic and social mobility. Parental class and income became more important determinants of both ability and educational achievement. (Machin and Vignoles, 2004: 1)

Later research suggests that social mobility has not continued to fall but there has been no significant improvement (Blanden and Machin, 2007). A Cabinet Office (2008) report did claim changes in social mobility: '… many of the educational inequalities that prevent social mobility are being addressed. Indeed, recent academic research shows there have been positive changes since around 2000' (p. 3). This was some vindication of the massive injection of resources and initiatives poured into education by the Labour government since 1997. Not that it believed the job was done:

> … we still have a way to go to realise the Government's ambition of a society where social background does not determine future success in life, and where

everyone can reach their full potential. This paper illustrates the critical importance of four factors that have an impact on people's life chances: the care and
development of children in their early years, the quality of our schools, continued and high quality education and training post-16 and constantly improving
the skills of our workforce. This is why we are fully committed and focussed on
real action in these areas. (Cabinet Office, 2008: 4)

However, this was probably premature. There does seem to have been a weakening of the relationship between parental income and GCSE achievement at
age 16 for children born in 1990, as compared with those born in 1970. What
is less certain, and will only be revealed over time, is whether it will lead to
social mobility in terms of the income and assets of children compared to
those of their parents, given changes to the labour market and greatly
increased access to higher education. In a government paper on Social
Mobility prepared for the Secretary of State for Education and Skills (DfES,
2006a) it claims some closing of the social class attainment gap, while
acknowledging the challenge:

- In recent years there have been considerable improvements in attainment
  for all groups of pupils, regardless of family background. There has been
  some narrowing of the social class attainment gap at KS3 and KS4. The challenge is to continue to raise attainment for all, while also reducing the gap.
- Social factors and an individual's characteristics have the biggest influence
  on attainment, but we know less about how to effectively intervene in
  these areas. The potential pay-off warrants continued efforts in this area,
  but the effectiveness of any interventions must be closely monitored.
- The Government has a wide range of high-potential policies in place, or in
  train, but for many it is too early to know the impact they are having on
  social class attainment gaps.

(DfES, 2006a: 108)

Reader tasks

- Having reviewed the evidence about the effect of independent
  schools, what is your view of them?
- Can you imagine ways of reducing the social class gap in school
  achievement, university entrance and life chances?

Sure Start and *Every Child Matters*: The Evidence

In a review of social class inequalities in education Raffo et al. (2007) conclude:

At present educational policy is piecemeal and largely focuses on those issues …
that are easiest to examine, most susceptible to short-term interventions and least
socially and politically destabilising. This has resulted in a plethora of initiatives

at the school, family and, to a lesser extent, neighbourhood level. ... significantly less attention has been paid to the social and economic conditions created by aspects of globalisation and the associated class, gender and ethnicity issues within which these initiatives are set. (p. 9)

This damning judgement on the avalanche of state-sponsored educational initiatives of the last thirty years is supported by the evidence presented here. Many of the Conservative and New Labour policies have led to the fragmentation and stratification of school systems without closing attainment gaps. But the *Sure Start* and *Every Child Matters* policies take a wider perspective. Both assume that children's needs can only be met by an integrated approach, covering schooling, health, social care and the justice system. They assume that supporting children from deprived and difficult backgrounds requires professionals to work together in the interest of the child rather than in separate silos. They address the social and economic needs of the community in which children live and are intended to engage parents and empower local communities.

A critical initiative was the development of Sure Start Local Programmes (SSLP), area-based programmes with all children under four and their families being the targets for intervention. An aim of SSLPs was to improve the life chances of young children and their families by improving services in areas of high deprivation. SSLPs had a high degree of local autonomy to develop services according to local needs. The government commissioned a National Evaluation of Sure Start (NESS). Its 2005 evaluation did not show the improvements anticipated, but the 2008 impact evaluation suggests increased benefits. Comments are cautious, but suggest that positive changes have occurred:

> ... resulting from the increase in quality of service provision, greater attention to the hard to reach, the move to children's centres, as well as the greater exposure to the programme of children and families in the latest phase of the impact evaluation. These positive results are modest, but evidence that the impact of Sure Start programmes is improving. (NESS, 2008: vi)

SSLPs have begun directly to impact on both parents and children in areas of parenting and children's behaviour which extend beyond any educational outcome:

> Parents of three-year-old children now show less negative parenting and provide their children with a better home learning environment. Three-year-old children in SSLP areas displayed better social development with higher levels of positive social behaviour and independent self-regulation. (NESS, 2008: 7)

Another initiative in the ECM spirit has been 'full-service extended school' (FSES) partnerships in which schools work together to provide services and activities beyond the school day to meet the needs of pupils, their families and the wider community. The schools are the core of a wide range of services delivered in a coherent and coordinated way (Cummings et al., 2007). The evaluation of the first three years of FSES found the scheme overcame pupils' 'barriers to learning' and recognised that these were related to family and community problems:

- The FSES approach was impacting positively on pupils' attainments in case study schools ... These impacts were clearest in the case of pupils facing difficulties. FSESs were having a range of other impacts on outcomes for pupils, including engagement with learning, family stability and enhanced life chances.
- FSESs were also generating positive outcomes for families and local people, particularly where they were facing difficulties. Impacts were less strong in relation to local communities as a whole, but positive outcomes for some groups and individuals could nonetheless be identified.
- Though large-scale effects were not yet evident, they are not out of the question in the longer term if FSESs have a stable and supportive local context within which to work.

(Cummings et al., 2007: 7)

While this is a largely positive evaluation of the FSES schools, it recognises the long-term perspective that is needed to implement the ECM outcomes. It will take time for schools and other professionals to change their practices and structures, let alone their culture. It is not assumed that schools alone can succeed in effecting the ECM outcomes, but that they are key players. An attempt to identify the contribution of schools to *Every Child Matters* outcomes undertaken in 2007 commented that it was 'very difficult to quantify the impact that schools have on different outcomes' (DCSF, 2007c: 4).

An evaluation in 2008 focused on groups of children and young people for whom integrated children's services might make a difference. It found limited evidence on the impact of integrating children's services for service users (Lord et al., 2008), but it concluded that 'children, young people and parents ... report a range of improvements in outcomes as a result of the support they currently receive' (p. 4). The overall message from the evaluation is that the integration of children's services is at an early stage and further work is needed on the 'working together' elements, as well as workload, resources and communication.

Even though the ECM documents argue for participation and engagement by parents, the assumptions behind *Sure Start* and ECM are that parental upbringing alone is not sufficient to make them the active learners required of the education system and that they need input from professionals. Evaluations of *Sure Start* suggest that, for all the rhetoric about parental engagement, parents finish up with very little say in a system that is determined by professionals. Evaluations of the first three years of the Extended Full-Service Schools (EFSS) suggest that it has been difficult for schools to offer the full extended model where education, health and welfare come together on the school site (Cummings et al., 2007). It is not surprising that it is difficult to gain community involvement and participation by families who are normally outside educational and social services. It is also not surprising that professionals are finding the changes problematic.

This same issue of collaboration with local authorities and other professionals is identified in the NFER (2007) annual survey of trends in education. It notes that the main challenge in delivering the ECM agenda was to develop closer collaboration with other services/agencies: 'Schools described improvements or positive developments covering standard aspects of school life, but the main challenge for schools remained the need to develop closer collaborative working with the services involved in supporting children and young people's well-being' (NFER, 2007: 8).

An evaluation of the integration of social care professionals into schools sees positive outcomes:

> ... the extended school environment can provide an appropriate arena in which to strengthen multi-agency relationships and break down barriers to effective working. Besides resulting in significant benefits for children, young people and their families, linking social care professionals and extended schools has emerged as a successful way of integrating services, of providing a holistic and effective response to ECM, of shifting entrenched working practices, and of enhancing willingness for joint initiatives. (Wilkin et al., 2008: 10)

To facilitate the integration of education, health and social services, local authorities are required to develop children's trusts. The role of the trusts is likely to take some time to infiltrate the education system. In April 2008 Beverley Hughes, the Children's Minister, commented:

> It is fundamentally a deeper cultural change. It is about changing the bound-aries of professional behaviour and thinking in a completely different way. With the amount of change we are talking about here we will not see everyone having full implementation for another two or three years. (*TES*, 2008: 2)

In the same article the general secretary of the Association of School and College Leaders suggests that her timescale may be optimistic: 'Most of my members have yet to discover what a children's trust is, let alone what services it offers. Schools do not yet feel local authorities are giving them the services they require.'

This concern emerges even within a positive evaluation of the 35 children's trust pathfinders set up in 2004. They 'acted as a catalyst for a more integrated approach to the diagnosis and provision of services to children' (DfES, 2007: 1) and '25 sites reported specific examples of children's trust pathfinders arrangements improving outcomes for children and young people in the area' (DfES, 2007: 5). But the evaluation highlighted major issues such as legal structures associated with inter-agency governance and accountability. Children, young people, parents and carers who took part in the evaluation generally had 'limited awareness and understanding of the work of children's trust pathfinders' (DfES, 2007: 3). Overall they saw major issues about how integrated services could work in reality: 'At the level of service delivery there remain many practical, philosophical and resource related barriers to effective integration' (DfES, 2007: 4).

Some depict *Sure Start* and ECM as an invasion of the domestic unit of the family in order to bring 'the insufficient child or family' more closely under state surveillance and control. Barron et al. (2007) suggest that: 'Children and families who have recourse to agencies have generally been defined as deficient with respect to an idealised, if invisible, "normal" child or family, whose status and competence are never contested and who is not deemed to be in need of additional support' (p. 2). But the introduction of ECM and other child-protection policies have not prevented cases of child abuse, allowing the mass media to demand yet more surveillance.

In November 2008 Ofsted made its first report following its responsibility for inspecting child protection facilities and assessing procedures. Christine Gilbert, Ofsted's chief inspector, said: 'Too many vulnerable children are still being let down by the system and we are failing to learn from the worst cases of abuse.' She added:

> There is a strong link across every sector between deprivation and poor quality provision. This means that children and families already experiencing relative deprivation face further inequity in the quality of care and support for their welfare, learning and development. In short, if you are poor you are more likely to receive poor services: disadvantage compounds disadvantage. (Curtis and Lipsett, 2008)

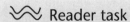 Reader task

- Review the evidence presented here. In your review, has the *Every Child Matters* policy been successful?
- Does ECM have a 'deficit' view of some families and pupils?

Conclusion

The chapter began by outlining the deluge of initiatives and legislation to deal with educational underachievement of children from deprived economic backgrounds. In spite of them, the evidence shows how strong the influence of social class and deprivation remains in determining pupil achievement. The education system remains split along class lines in attendance at types of schools, achievement at Foundation Stage or participation rates in higher education. We have also seen how the neighbourhoods where children live provide distinctly different chances of educational achievement and access to universities. The Labour government of 1997 was driven by a desire to challenge structural inequalities within society, but its policies of diversity and choice, which were largely developed to ensure middle-class parents did not abandon the state sector, have reinforced divisions and had negative consequences for children in certain neighbourhoods and low socio-economic groups.

There are glimmers of hope. Children eligible for free school meals are closing the gap; when pupils from lower socio-economic backgrounds do achieve good GCSEs and A levels, their chances of getting to university seem to be equal to pupils from affluent backgrounds; social mobility, which has stagnated in the UK for years, may be increasing. At the same time, the evidence on independent schools and the backgrounds of people in positions of power in the UK illustrates dramatically the continuing strength of social class.

The introduction of ECM demonstrated the Labour government's intention to change the patterns of achievement and social class. But the extent to which it changes underlying structural inequalities is questionable. The emphasis on young people developing skills to enable them to enter the labour force, on staying on at school to achieve better educational opportunities and addressing issues about women returning to work could all be seen to be part of an attempt to change the actual economic structure of deprivation and low achievement. However, initiatives such as *Sure Start*, the Educational Maintenance Grant, additional resources for children's centres and extended schools really only *compensate for* economic deprivation. The target groups for ECM are not 'all' children, only those deemed 'insufficient'. One interpretation of ECM is that such families and children will simply increase their capacity to deal with their disadvantage.

The other question is whether large-scale interventions like ECM can work within the structures that have been set up. An integrated children's service, bringing together a range of professionals, is appealing. Pilot studies show some effective developments, but there are major gaps in the extent to which teachers are really working with other professionals and seeing their role across the range of education and social care of children, including taking responsibility for child abuse. We know that policies are contested and interpreted, and how teachers respond to ECM is as yet unknown. It may be too ambitious to work effectively both from a multi-professional perspective and with the bureaucratic structures required. Such concerns could defeat what are undoubtedly intended to be laudable and positive outcomes. This would be a great shame. Evidence suggests that to promote higher aspirations and educational achievement for all pupils we need to recognise the way in which the different contexts of their lives interact and work with each other. It makes developing policy to support children much more complex. Duckworth (2008) has argued that 'there are unlikely to be one-size-fits-all quick fixes or a single policy silver bullet ... there is no one thing that is likely to radically transform young lives for the better' (p. 56). We are unlikely to know for a number of years whether the approach challenges entrenched inequalities. Its success may depend on how universal it becomes and whether the professionals on which it depends can develop the necessary working relationships to ensure that every child does matter.

Recommended reading

Ball, S. (2005) *Education Policy and Social Class.* Abingdon: Routledge. An extremely valuable book which covers both the debates and research relevant to social class as well as the political perspectives behind education policy.

Barron, I., Holmes, R., MacLure, M. and Runswick-Cole, K. (2007) *Primary Schools and Other Agencies,* Primary Review Research Survey 8/2. Cambridge: University of Cambridge Faculty of Education. Online at: http://www.primaryreview.org.uk/Downloads/Int_Reps/3.Children_lives_voices/Primar_Review_8-2_report_Primary_schools_other_agencies_071123.pdf. A discussion of the deficit model of families implicit in some government policies and ECM which also looks at issues associated with multi-agency working.

Cassen, R. and Kingdon, G. (2007) *Tackling Low Educational Achievement.* York: Joseph Rowntree Foundation. Online at: http://www.JosephRowntree Foundation.org.uk/bookshop/eBooks/2063-education-schools-achievement.pdf. (accessed 14 September 2008). A useful summary of evidence on poverty and its impact on achievement, information from the Joseph Rowntree Foundation which provides essential background data for any discussion on poverty.

Duckworth, K. (2008) *The Influence of Contexts on Attainment in Primary School: Interactions between Children, Family and School Contexts.* London: Centre for Research on the Wider Benefits of Learning, Institute of Education. Online at: http://www.learningbenefits.net/Publications/ResReps/ResRep28.pdf. A paper that explores the complexity of interrelationships between the different contexts of children's lives and their impact on attainment through research data.

References

Barron, I., Holmes, R., MacLure, M. and Runswick-Cole, K. (2007) *Primary Schools and Other Agencies,* Primary Review Research Survey 8/2. Cambridge: University of Cambridge Faculty of Education. Online at: http://www.primaryreview.org.uk/Downloads/Int_Reps/3.Children_lives_voices/Primary_Review_8-2_report_Primary_schools_other_agencies_071123.pdf (accessed 3 November 2008).

Blair, T. (1999) 'Beveridge revisited: a welfare state for the 21st century', in R. Walker (ed.), *Ending Child Poverty.* Bristol: Policy Press.

Blanden, J. and Machin, S. (2007) *Recent Changes in Intergenerational Mobility in Britain,* London: Sutton Trust. Online at: http://www.suttontrust.com/reports/mainreport.pdf (accessed 12 October 2008).

Brewer, M., Murie, A., Phillips, D. and Sibieta, L. (2008) *Poverty and Inequality in the UK: 2008.* London: Institute for Fiscal Studies. Online at: http://www.ifs.org.uk/comms/comm105.pdf (accessed 5 November 2008).

Cabinet Office (2008) *Getting On, Getting Ahead: A Discussion Paper: Analysing the Trends and Drivers of Social Mobility.* London: Cabinet Office. Online at: http://www.cabinetoffice.gov.uk/media/66447/gettingon.pdf (accessed 23 February 2009).

Cassen, R. and Kingdon, G. (2007) *Tackling Low Educational Achievement.* York: Joseph Rowntree Foundation. Online at: http://www.jrf.org.uk/sites/files/jrf/2063-education-schools-achievement.pdf (accessed 23 February 2009).

Chowdry, H., Crawford, C., Dearden, L. and Vignoles A. (2008) *Wasted Talent? Attrition Rates of High-Achieving Pupils Between School and University*. London: Sutton Trust. Online at: http://www.suttontrust.com/reports/wastedTalent.pdf (accessed 3 November 2008).

Cummings, C., Dyson, A., Muijs, D., Papps, I., Pearson, D., Raffo, C., Tiplady, C. and Todd, L. with Crowther, D. (2007) *Full Service Extended Schools Initiative Evaluation: Final Report*. London: DCSF. Online at: http://www.dcsf.gov.uk/research/programmeofresearch/ projectinformation.cfm?projectid=14494&resultspage=1 (accessed 23 November 2008).

Curtis, P. and Lipsett, A. (2008) 'Poor let down by education system, says Ofsted', *The Guardian*, 20 November, p. 4.

DCSF (2007a) *The Children's Plan: Building Brighter Futures*. London: DCSF. Online at: http://www.dcsf.gov.uk/publications/childrensplan/downloads/The_Childrens_Plan.pdf (accessed 4 November 2008).

DCSF (2007b) *Children and Young People Today: Evidence to Support the Development of the Children's Plan*. London: DCSF. Online at: http://publications.dcsf.gov.uk/eOrdering Download/Children&young_people_today.pdf (accessed 23 February 2009).

DCSF (2007c) *Contribution of Schools to Every Child Matters Outcomes: Evidence to Support Education Productivity Measures*. London: DCSF. Online at: http://www.dcsf.gov.uk/ rsgateway/DB/STA/t000745/Triangulation-30-08-07.pdf (accessed 3 November 2008).

DCSF (2007d) *National Statistics First Release (2007) National Curriculum Assessment, GCSE and Equivalent Attainment and Post-16 Attainment by Pupil Characteristics in England, 2006/07. November 2007*. London: DCSF. Online at: http://www.dcsf.gov.uk/rsgateway/ DB/SFR/s000739/SFR38_2007_Tables.xls (accessed 23 February 2009).

DCSF (2007e) 'Children who attend extended schools get better GCSE results', *News Centre*. London: DCSF. Online at: http://www.dcsf.gov.uk/pns/DisplayPN.cgi?pn_id=2007_0112 (accessed 4 November 2008).

DCSF (2008a) 'New figures show lowest achieving children starting to catch up', *News Centre*. London: DCSF. Online at: http://www.dcsf.gov.uk/pns/DisplayPN.cgi?pn_id=2008_0204 (accessed 3 November 2008).

DCSF (2008b) *Foundation Stage Profile Results in England, 2007/08*. London: DCSF. Online at: http://www.dcsf.gov.uk/rsgateway/DB/SFR/s000812/index.shtml (accessed 23 February 2009).

DCSF (2008c) *Attainment by Pupil Characteristics, in England 2007/08*. London: DCSF. Online at: http://www.dcsf.gov.uk/rsgateway/DB/SFR/s000822/index.shtml (accessed 23 February 2009).

DCSF (2008d) *Achievements at GCSE and Equivalents for pupils at the end of Key Stage 4, in maintained schools, by ethnicity, gender and free school meals Year: 2007 (Provisional)*. London: DCSF. Online at: http://www.dcsf.gov.uk/rsgateway/DB/SFR/s000759/Crosstabs forSFR.xls (Accessed 4 November 2008).

DCSF (2008e) *The Sure Start Journey: A Summary of Evidence*. London: DCSF. Online at: http://publications.teachernet.gov.uk/eOrderingDownload/FINAL%20The%20Sure%20 Start%20Journey.pdf (accessed 3 November 2008).

DCSF (2008f) *Youth Cohort Study and Longitudinal Study of Young People in England: The Activities and Experiences of 16 Year Olds: England 2007*. London: DCSF. Online at: http:// www.dcsf.gov.uk/rsgateway/DB/SBU/b000795/index.shtml (accessed 5 November 2008).

DfES (2003a) *Every Child Matters: A Green Paper.* London: DfES. Online at: http://publications.teachernet.gov.uk/eOrderingDownload/ECM-Summary.pdf (accessed 3 November 2008).

DfES (2003b) *The Future of Higher Education.* London: DfES. Online at: http://www.dcsf.gov.uk/hegateway/strategy/hestrategy/foreword.shtml (accessed 3 November 2008).

DfES (2004) *Every Child Matters: Change for Children.* London: DfES. Online at: http://www.everychildmatters.gov.uk/_files/F9E3F941DC8D4580539EE4C743E9371D.pdf (accessed 3 November 2008).

DfES (2006a) *Social Mobility: Narrowing Class Educational Attainment Gaps.* London: DfES. Online at: http://www.dcsf.gov.uk/rsgateway/DB/STA/t000657/SocialMobility26Apr06.pdf (accessed 3 November 2008).

DfES (2006b) *The Activities and Experiences of 18 Year Olds: England and Wales 2006.* London: DCSF. Online at: http://www.dcsf.gov.uk/rsgateway/DB/SFR/s000695/Addition1.xls (accessed 6 November 2008).

DfES (2007) *Children's Trust Pathfinders: Innovative Partnerships for Improving the Well-Being of Children and Young People: Findings from the National Evaluation of Children's Trust Pathfinders.* Norwich: University of East Anglia in association with the National Children's Bureau. Online at: http://www.everychildmatters.gov.uk/_files/B8FD7B0E555C71497035139DFCA270DF.pdf (accessed 3 November 2008).

DIUS (2007) *Increased Support for Students in Higher Education.* London: DIUS. Online at: http://www.dius.gov.uk/press/05-07-07.html (accessed 6 November 2008).

Dorling, D., Rigby, J., Wheeler, B., Ballas, D., Bethan, T., Eldin, A., David, G. and Lupton, R. (2007) *Poverty, Wealth and Place in Britain, 1968 to 2005.* York: Joseph Rowntree Foundation. Online at: http://www.jrf.org.uk/bookshop/eBooks/2019-poverty-wealth-place.pdf (accessed 3 November 2008).

Duckworth, K. (2008) *The Influence of Contexts on Attainment in Primary School: Interactions Between Children, Family and School Contexts.* London: Centre for Research on the Wider Benefits of Learning, Institute of Education. Online at: http://www.learningbenefits.net/Publications/ResReps/ResRep28.pdf (accessed 13 November 2008).

End Child Poverty (2008) *Why End Child Poverty: The Effects.* London: End Child Poverty. Online at: http://www.endchildpoverty.org.uk/why-end-child-poverty/the-effects (accessed 3 November 2008).

Evans, M. and Scarborough, J. (2006) *Can Current Policy End Child Poverty in Britain by 2020?* York: Joseph Rowntree Foundation.

Galindo-Rueda, F., Marcenaro-Gutierrez, O. and Vignoles, A. (2004) *The Widening Socio-economic Gap in UK Higher Education.* London: Centre for the Economics of Education, London School of Economics. Online at: http://cee.lse.ac.uk/cee%20dps/ceedp44.pdf (accessed 23 February 2009).

Guardian, The (2003) 'I'd rather beg than send children to state school, Letwin says', 10 October.

Guardian, The (2008) 'Oxbridge graduates in the cabinet', 9 May.

Harris, J. (2008) 'Networked from birth', *The Guardian,* 9 May, p. 7.

HEFCE (2005) *Young Participation in Higher Education.* Bristol: HEFCE. Online at: http://www.hefce.ac.uk/pubs/hefce/2005/05_03/05_03b.pdf (accessed 5 November 2008).

HESA (2008) *Widening Participation of Under-represented Groups.* Bristol: HESA. Online at: http://www.hesa.ac.uk/index.php/content/view/1174/141/ (accessed 3 November 2008).

HM Treasury (2008) *Ending Child Poverty: Everybody's Business.* London: HM Treasury. Online at: http://www.hm-treasury.gov.uk/d/bud08_childpoverty_1310.pdf (accessed 23 February 2009).

ISC (2008) *Pupil Numbers.* London: Independent Schools Council. Available at: http://www.isc.co.uk/FactsFigures_PupilNumbers.htm (accessed 31 July 2008).

Joseph Rowntree Foundation (2007) *The impact of poverty on young children's experience of school,* York: Joseph Rowntree Foundation. Online at: http://www.jrf.org.uk/knowledge/findings/socialpolicy/2146.asp (accessed 8 November 2008).

Lord, P., Kinder, K., Wilkin, A., Atkinson, M. and Haland, J. (2008) *Evaluating the Early Impact of Integrated Children's Services: Round 1 Final Report.* Slough: NFER

Machin, S. and Vignoles A. (2004) 'Educational inequality: the widening socio-economic gap', *Fiscal Studies,* 25 (2): 107–28.

Machin, S. and Vignoles A. (2006) *Education Policy in the UK.* London: Centre for the Economics of Education, London School of Economics. Online at: http://cee.lse.ac.uk/cee per cent20dps/ceedp57.pdf (accessed 3 November 2008).

Machin, S., McNally, S. and Meghir, C. (2007) *Resources and Standards in Urban Schools.* London: Centre for the Economics of Education, London School of Economics. Online at: http://cee.lse.ac.uk/cee per cent20dps/ceedp76.pdf (accessed 7 October 2008).

Mongon, D. and Chapman, C. (2008) *Successful Leadership for Promoting the Achievement of White Working Class Pupils – Summary.* Nottingham: National College for School Leadership. Online at: http://www.ncsl.org.uk/successful-leadership-for-promoting-full-report-4.pdf (accessed 3 November 2008).

NAO (2008) *Value for Money Report: Executive Summary Widening Participation in Higher Education.* London: National Audit Office. Online at: http://www.nao.org.uk/publications/0708/widening_participation_in_high.aspx (accessed 23 February 2009).

NESS (2008) *The Impact of Sure Start Local Programmes on Three Year Olds and Their Families.* London: National Evaluation of Sure Start.

NFER (2007) *How Is the Every Child Matters Agenda Affecting Schools? Annual Survey of Trends in Education 2007.* Slough: NFER.

OPSI (2004) *The Children Act 2004.* London: OPSI. Online at: http://www.opsi.gov.uk/acts/acts2004/ukpga_20040031_en_1 (accessed 3 November 2008).

Palmer, G., MacInnes, T. and Kenway, P. (2007) *Monitoring Poverty and Social Exclusion.* York: Joseph Rowntree Foundation. Online at: http://www.poverty.org.uk/reports/mpse per cent202007.pdf (accessed 26 September 2008).

Powdthavee, N. and Vignoles, A. (2008) *The Socio-Economic Gap in University Drop Out Rates.* York: University of York. Online at: http://www.york.ac.uk/depts/econ/documents/dp/0823.pdf (accessed 3 October 2008).

Raffo, C., Dyson, A., Gunter, H., Hall, D., Jones, L. and Kalambouka, A. (2007) *Education and Poverty: A Critical Review of Theory, Policy and Practice.* York: Rowntree Foundation. Online at: http://www.jrf.org.uk/sites/files/jrf/2028-education-poverty-theory.pdf (accessed 23 February 2009).

Strand, S. (2008) *Minority Ethnic Pupils in the Longitudinal Study of Young People in England.* London: DCSF. Online at: http://www.dcsf.gov.uk/research/data/uploadfiles/DCSF-RR029.pdf (accessed 3 November 2008).

Sutton Trust (2007) *Recent Changes in Intergenerational Ability in the UK: A Summary of the Findings*. London: Sutton Trust. Online at: http://www.suttontrust.com/reports/summary. pdf (accessed 3 November 2008).

Sutton Trust (2008a) *University Admissions by Individual Schools*. London: Sutton Trust. Online at: http://www.suttontrust.com/reports/UniversityAdmissions.pdf (accessed 3 November 2008).

Sutton Trust (2008b) *News and Features: Educational Backgrounds of 500 Leading People in the UK*. London: Sutton Trust. Online at: http://www.suttontrust.com/news.asp#a038 (accessed 3 November 2008).

Sutton Trust (2008c) *Research and Publications*. Online at: http://www.suttontrust.com/ annualreports.asp#vc.

TES (2008) 'Teachers with 2020 vision', *Times Educational Supplement*, 4 April, p. 2.

Wilkin, A., Murfield, J., Lamont, E., Kinder, K. and Dyson, P. (2008) *The Value of Social Care Professionals Working in Extended Schools*. Slough: NFER.

Index